NTC's Library of Classic Essays

Plato's Heirs

Classic Essays

James D. Lester
Austin Peay State University

NTC Publishing Group
Lincolnwood, Illinois USA

Executive Editor: John T. Nolan
Sponsoring Editor: Marisa L. L'Heureux
Cover and interior design: Ophelia M. Chambliss
Cover art: Celia Johnson/Gerald & Cullen Rapp, Inc.
Production Manager: Rosemary Dolinski

Acknowledgments for literary selections begin on page 293, which is to be considered an extension of this copyright page.

ISBN 0-8442-5878-4 (student text)
ISBN 0-8442-5879-2 (instructor's edition)

Published by NTC Publishing Group

Manufactured in the United States of America.

Library of Congress Cataloging-in-Publication Data

Plato's heirs : classic essays / [compiled by] James D. Lester.
p. cm.
Includes index.
ISBN 0-8442-5878-4 (pbk.)
1. Essays. I. Lester, James D., 1935–
PN6141.P53 1996
808.84—dc20 95-8290
CIP

5 6 7 8 9 VP 0 9 8 7 6 5 4 3 2 1

Contents

Preface

NTC's *Library of Classic Essays*

This is a four-volume collection of some of the finest essays ever written, providing a broad yet in-depth overview of the development and scope of the genre. In essence, an essay is a short prose composition, usually exploring one subject and often presenting the personal view of the author. An essay may take a variety of forms (from narration to description to autobiography) and may reflect any number of moods (from critical to reflective to whimsical).

Although we recognize a few early works by Plato, Aristotle, and others as essays, it was really Michel de Montaigne, a French philosopher and writer, who substantially defined the form when he published two volumes of his own essays under the title *Essais* in 1580. Montaigne considered himself to be representative of humankind in general; thus, his essays, though they are to be read as general treatises on the human condition, are largely reflective of Montaigne's own attitudes and experiences.

The essay proved to be a most adaptable form. In the eighteenth century, both journalists and philosophers in England and pamphleteers and patriots in the American colonies quickly discovered the power of a well-crafted and provocative essay. By the middle of the nineteenth century, the essay was the form of choice for such brilliant writers as the American Ralph Waldo Emerson and the British George Eliot. In the twentieth century, the essay has become the most widely read genre—from personal essays in periodicals to scholarly essays in scientific journals to argumentative essays on the editorial pages of newspapers worldwide.

Plato's Heirs: Classic Essays

This volume contains thirty-two classic essays that illustrate the full flowering of the essay form. Organized chronologically, these essays explore an amazing diversity of topics. If, however, one of your favorites is not included here, it may well be in one of the other volumes: *Daughters of the Revolution: Classic Essays by Women; Diverse Identities: Classic Multicultural Essays;* or *Of Bunsen Burners, Bones, and Belles Lettres: Classic Essays across the Curriculum.*

This volume brings you those special essays that have established and standardized the form. It is our hope that this collection will allow you to examine who you are and better enable you to explore your place—and the place of others—in the universe.

CLASSIC ESSAYS

The Origins of the Form

The Allegory of the Cave

PLATO

Plato (ca. 427–347 B.C.) was born in Greece with the name Aristocles; the name Plato was a nickname that means "broad shouldered." When young, he wanted to become a politician in the tradition of Pericles, the great statesman who ruled Athens with brilliance in the mid–400s B.C. However, several events discouraged him in this endeavor. His cousin Critias and his Uncle Charmides installed themselves as dictators of Athens, and Plato was dismayed by their cruelty and graft. In 402 B.C., the citizens of Athens unseated the dictators, established a democracy, and encouraged Plato to participate. However, when the Athenians sentenced his friend Socrates to death in 399, Plato left both Athens and an active political life to travel widely in the ancient world. In 387, Plato returned to Athens and founded the Academy, a school of science and philosophy that endured for about one thousand years. His most distinguished student was Aristotle (see page 11).

It is an injustice to try to reduce Plato's teachings to a few sentences, but, in short, he found the physical senses to be unreliable for understanding the ideal eternity that abides in the spiritual kingdom. Perceived by all humans before birth, the ideal realm can be perceived in life only faintly. The vague memory of the ideal realm keeps alive our search for renewal.

Plato's favorite literary form was the dialogue, which is an interchange of ideas by two characters who argue the opposing sides of philosophical questions. A few of his best-known dialogues are *The Apology, Crito, Phaedrus, The Republic,* and *Theaetetus.*

"The Allegory of the Cave," from *The Republic*, is primarily a political statement about who is qualified to lead the state. True leaders must ascend out of the shadows of the cave to gain enlightenment but be willing to reenter the cave to guide the people. Plato's wisdom is appropriate still today, especially his belief that "the truth is that the State in which the rulers are most reluctant to govern is always the best and most quietly governed, and the State in which they are most eager, the worst."

1 And now, I said, let me show in a figure how far our nature is enlightened or unenlightened;—Behold! human beings living in an underground den, which has a mouth open towards the light and reaching all along the den; here they have been from their childhood, and have their legs and necks chained so that they cannot move, and can only see before them, being prevented by the chains from turning round their heads. Above and behind them a fire is blazing at a distance, and between the fire and the prisoners there is a raised way; and you will see, if you look, a low wall built along the way, like the screen which marionette players have in front of them, over which they show the puppets.

2 I see.

3 And do you see, I said, men passing along the wall carrying all sorts of vessels, and statues and figures of animals made of wood and stone and various materials, which appear over the wall? Some of them are talking, others silent.

4 You have shown me a strange image, and they are strange prisoners.

5 Like ourselves, I replied; and they see only their own shadows, or the shadows of one another, which the fire throws on the opposite wall of the cave?

6 True, he said; how could they see anything but the shadows if they were never allowed to move their heads?

7 And of the objects which are being carried in like manner they would only see the shadows?

8 Yes, he said.

9 And if they were able to converse with one another, would they not suppose that they were naming what was actually before them?

10 Very true.

11 And suppose further that the prison had an echo which came from the other side, would they not be sure to fancy when one of the passers-by spoke that the voice which they heard came from the passing shadow?

12 No question, he replied.

13 To them, I said, the truth would be literally nothing but the shadows of the images.

14 That is certain.

15 And now look again, and see what will naturally follow if the prisoners are released and disabused of their error. At first, when any of them is liberated and compelled suddenly to stand up and turn his neck round and walk and look towards the light, he will suffer sharp pains; the glare will distress him, and he will be unable to see the realities of which in his former state he had seen the shadows; and then conceive some one saying to him, that what he saw before was an illusion, but that now, when he is approaching nearer to being and his eye is turned towards more real existence, he has a clearer vision—what will be his reply? And you may further imagine that his instructor is pointing to the objects as they pass and requiring him to name them,—will he not be perplexed? Will he not fancy that the shadows which he formerly saw are truer than the objects which are now shown to him?

16 Far truer.

17 And if he is compelled to look straight at the light, will he not have a pain in his eyes which will make him turn away to take refuge in the objects of vision which he can see, and which he will conceive to be in reality clearer than the things which are now being shown to him?

18 True, he said.

19 And suppose once more, that he is reluctantly dragged up a steep and rugged ascent, and held fast until he is forced into the presence of the sun himself, is he not likely to be pained and irritated? When he approaches the light his eyes will be dazzled, and he will not be able to see anything at all of what are now called realities.

20 Not all in a moment, he said.

21 He will require to grow accustomed to the sight of the upper world. And first he will see the shadows best, next the reflections of men and other objects in the water, and then the objects themselves;

then he will gaze upon the light of the moon and the stars and the spangled heaven; and he will see the sky and the stars by night better than the sun or the light of the sun by day?

22 Certainly.

23 Last of all he will be able to see the sun, and not mere reflections of him in the water, but he will see him in his own proper place, and not in another; and he will contemplate him as he is.

24 Certainly.

25 He will then proceed to argue that this is he who gives the season and the years, and is the guardian of all that is in the visible world, and in a certain way the cause of all things which he and his fellows have been accustomed to behold?

26 Clearly, he said, he would first see the sun and then reason about him.

27 And when he remembered his old habitation, and the wisdom of the den and his fellow prisoners, do you not suppose that he would felicitate himself on the change, and pity them?

28 Certainly, he would.

29 And if they were in the habit of conferring honors among themselves on those who were quickest to observe the passing shadows and to remark which of them went before, and which followed after, and which were together; and who were therefore best able to draw conclusions as to the future, do you think that he would care for such honors and glories, or envy the possessors of them? Would he not say with Homer,

> Better to be the poor servant of a poor master,

and to endure anything, rather than think as they do and live after their manner?

30 Yes, he said, I think that he would rather suffer anything than entertain these false notions and live in this miserable manner.

31 Imagine once more, I said, such an one coming suddenly out of the sun to be replaced in his old situation; would he not be certain to have his eyes full of darkness?

32 To be sure, he said.

33 And if there were a contest, and he had to compete in measuring the shadows with the prisoners who had never moved out of the den, while his sight was still weak, and before his eyes had become steady (and the time which would be needed to acquire this new habit of sight might be very considerable), would he not be ridiculous? Men

would say of him that up he went and down he came without his eyes; and that it was better not even to think of ascending; and if any one tried to loose another and lead him up to the light, let them only catch the offender, and they would put him to death.

34 No question, he said.

35 This entire allegory, I said, you may now append, dear Glaucon, to the previous argument; the prison house is the world of sight, the light of the fire is the sun, and you will not misapprehend me if you interpret the journey upwards to be the ascent of the soul into the intellectual world according to my poor belief, which, at your desire, I have expressed—whether rightly or wrongly God knows. But, whether true or false, my opinion is that in the world of knowledge the idea of good appears last of all, and is seen only with an effort; and, when seen, is also inferred to be the universal author of all things beautiful and right, parent of light and of the lord of light in this visible world, and the immediate source of reason and truth in the intellectual; and that this is the power upon which he who would act rationally either in public or private life must have his eye fixed.

36 I agree, he said, as far as I am able to understand you.

37 Moreover, I said, you must not wonder that those who attain to this beatific vision are unwilling to descend to human affairs; for their souls are ever hastening into the upper world where they desire to dwell; which desire of theirs is very natural, if our allegory may be trusted.

38 Yes, very natural.

39 And is there anything surprising in one who passes from divine contemplations to the evil state of man, misbehaving himself in a ridiculous manner; if, while his eyes are blinking and before he has become accustomed to the surrounding darkness, he is compelled to fight in courts of law, or in other places, about the images or the shadows of images of justice, and is endeavoring to meet the conceptions of those who have never yet seen absolute justice?

40 Anything but surprising, he replied.

41 Anyone who has common sense will remember that the bewilderments of the eyes are of two kinds, and arise from two causes, either from coming out of the light or from going into the light, which is true of the mind's eye, quite as much as of the bodily eye; and he who remembers this when he sees anyone whose vision is perplexed and weak, will not be too ready to laugh; he will first ask whether

that soul of man has come out of the brighter life, and is unable to see because unaccustomed to the dark, or having turned from darkness to the day is dazzled by excess of light. And he will count the one happy in his condition and state of being, and he will pity the other; or, if he have a mind to laugh at the soul which comes from below into the light, there will be more reason in this than in the laugh which greets him who returns from above out of the light into the den.

42 That, he said, is a very just distinction.

43 But then, if I am right, certain professors of education must be wrong when they say that they can put a knowledge into the soul which was not there before, like sight into blind eyes.

44 They undoubtedly say this, he replied.

45 Whereas, our argument shows that the power and capacity of learning exists in the soul already; and that just as the eye was unable to turn from darkness to light without the whole body, so too the instrument of knowledge can only by the movement of the whole soul be turned from the world of becoming into that of being, and learn by degrees to endure the sight of being, and of the brightest and best of being, or in other words, of the good.

46 Very true.

47 And must there not be some art which will effect conversion in the easiest and quickest manner; not implanting the faculty of sight, for that exists already, but has been turned in the wrong direction, and is looking away from the truth?

48 Yes, he said, such an art may be presumed.

49 And whereas the other so-called virtues of the soul seem to be akin to bodily qualities, for even when they are not originally innate they can be implanted later by habit and exercise, the virtue of wisdom more than anything else contains a divine element which always remains, and by this conversion is rendered useful and profitable; or, on the other hand, hurtful and useless. Did you never observe the narrow intelligence flashing from the keen eye of a clever rogue—how eager he is, how clearly his paltry soul sees the way to his end; he is the reverse of blind, but his keen eyesight is forced into the service of evil, and he is mischievous in proportion to his cleverness?

50 Very true, he said.

51 But what if there had been a circumcision of such natures in the days of their youth; and they had been severed from those sensual pleasures, such as eating and drinking, which, like leaden weights, were attached to them at their birth, and which drag them down

and turn the vision of their souls upon the things that are below—if, I say, they had been released from these impediments and turned in the opposite direction, the very same faculty in them would have seen the truth as keenly as they see what their eyes are turned to now.

52 Very likely.

53 Yes, I said; and there is another thing which is likely, or rather a necessary inference from what has preceded, that neither the uneducated and uninformed of the truth, nor yet those who never make an end of their education, will be able ministers of State; not the former, because they have no single aim of duty which is the rule of all their actions, private as well as public; nor the latter, because they will not act at all except upon compulsion, fancying that they are already dwelling apart in the islands of the blessed.

54 Very true, he replied.

55 Then, I said, the business of us who are the founders of the State will be to compel the best minds to attain that knowledge which we have already shown to be the greatest of all—they must continue to ascend until they arrive at the good; but when they have ascended and seen enough we must not allow them to do as they do now.

56 What do you mean?

57 I mean that they remain in the upper world: but this must not be allowed; they must be made to descend again among the prisoners in the den, and partake of their labors and honors, whether they are worth having or not.

58 But is not this unjust? he said; ought we to give them a worse life, when they might have a better?

59 You have again forgotten, my friend, I said, the intention of the legislator, who did not aim at making any one class in the State happy above the rest; the happiness was to be in the whole State, and he held the citizens together by persuasion and necessity, making them benefactors of the State, and therefore benefactors of one another; to this end he created them, not to please themselves, but to be his instruments in binding up the State.

60 True, he said, I had forgotten.

61 Observe, Glaucon, that there will be no injustice in compelling our philosophers to have a care and providence of others; we shall explain to them that in other States, men of their class are not obliged to share in the toils of politics: and this is reasonable, for they grow up at their own sweet will, and the government would rather not

have them. Being self-taught, they cannot be expected to show any gratitude for a culture which they have never received. But we have brought you into the world to be rulers of the hive, kings of yourselves and of the other citizens, and have educated you far better and more perfectly than they have been educated, and you are better able to share in the double duty. Wherefore each of you, when his turn comes, must go down to the general underground abode, and get the habit of seeing in the dark. When you have acquired the habit, you will see ten thousand times better than the inhabitants of the den, and you will know what the several images are, and what they represent, because you have seen the beautiful and just and good in their truth. And thus our State, which is also yours, will be a reality, and not a dream only, and will be administered in a spirit unlike that of other States, in which men fight with one another about shadows only and are distracted in the struggle for power, which in their eyes is a great good. Whereas the truth is that the State in which the rulers are most reluctant to govern is always the best and most quietly governed, and the State in which they are most eager, the worst.

62 Quite true, he replied.

63 And will our pupils, when they hear this, refuse to take their turn at the toils of State, when they are allowed to spend the greater part of their time with one another in the heavenly light?

64 Impossible, he answered; for they are just men, and the commands which we impose upon them are just; there can be no doubt that every one of them will take office as a stern necessity, and not after the fashion of our present rulers of State.

65 Yes, my friend, I said; and there lies the point. You must contrive for your future rulers another and a better life than that of a ruler, and then you may have a well-ordered State; for only in the State which offers this, will they rule who are truly rich, not in silver and gold, but in virtue and wisdom, which are the true blessings of life. Whereas if they go to the administration of public affairs, poor and hungering after their own private advantage, thinking that hence they are to snatch the chief good, order there can never be; for they will be fighting about office, and the civil and domestic broils which thus arise will be the ruin of the rulers themselves and of the whole State.

66 Most true, he replied.

67 And the only life which looks down upon the life of political ambition is that of true philosophy. Do you know of any other?

68 Indeed, I do not, he said.

The Aim of Man

ARISTOTLE

Aristotle (384–322 B.C.) was born in Stagira, a town in northern Greece. He and his teacher Plato are recognized as two of the most distinguished philosophers of Western culture. After studying under Plato for about twenty years, Aristotle came into his own renown. He educated Alexander of Macedon, who later conquered all of Greece, overthrew the Persian Empire, and became known as Alexander the Great.

In about 334 B.C., Aristotle founded the Lyceum, a school in Athens that espoused the Peripatetic philosophy (*peripatetic* means "walking around," which describes Aristotle's habit of teaching while walking with his students). He fled Athens after the death of Alexander in 323 and died in Chalcis a year later.

Most of Aristotle's popular writings and scholarly memoranda have not survived. His treatises form most of his surviving material. The *Organon* (instrument) investigates thought, which is the instrument of knowledge. In *Physics,* he examined the nature of physical changes in the natural world. In *On the Soul,* he explored the relationship of the soul to the body. In *Metaphysics,* he explored the science of matter that does not change. His interest in practical knowledge led to *The Nicomachean Ethics* and *Politics,* which search out moral virtue in human beings who avoid extremes in behavior. Finally, his *Poetics* examines the nature of tragedy and, by examining Sophocles' *Oedipus Rex,* establishes his theory of *catharsis* (which attempts to explain why spectators experience pity and fear, which cleanses them of deep emotions).

"The Aim of Man" comes from *The Nichomachean Ethics,* which he wrote in part for his son, Nichomachus. Aristotle gives primacy to the role of government, *statecraft,* because "it prescribes which of the sciences are to have a place in the state, and which of them are to be studied by the different classes of citizens." Even today, we ask "the government" to provide for our needs, so Aristotle's arguments are still well-founded.

Definition of the Good

1 Every art and every "scientific investigation," as well as every action and "purposive choice," appears to aim at some good; hence the good has rightly been declared to be that at which all things aim. A difference is observable, to be sure, among the several ends: some of them are activities, while others are products over and above the activities that produce them. Wherever there are certain ends over and above the actions themselves, it is the nature of such products to be better than the activities.

2 As actions and arts and sciences are of many kinds, there must be a corresponding diversity of ends: health, for example, is the aim of medicine, ships of shipbuilding, victory of military strategy, and wealth of domestic economics. Where several such arts fall under some one faculty—as bridle-making and the other arts concerned with horses' equipment fall under horsemanship, while this in turn along with all other military matters falls under the head of strategy, and similarly in the case of other arts—the aim of the master art is always more choiceworthy than the aims of its subordinate arts, inasmuch as these are pursued for its sake. And this holds equally good whether the end in view is just the activity itself or something distinct from the activity, as in the case of the sciences above mentioned.

Primacy of Statecraft

3 If in all our conduct, then, there is some end that we wish on its own account, choosing everything else as a means to it; if, that is to say, we do not choose everything as a means to something else (for at that rate we should go on *ad infinitum,* and our desire would be left empty and vain); then clearly this one end must be the good—even, indeed, the highest good. Will not a knowledge of it, then, have an important influence on our lives? Will it not better enable us to hit the right mark, like archers who have a definite target to aim at? If so, we must try to comprehend, in outline at least, what that highest end is, and to which of the sciences or arts it belongs.

4 Evidently the art or science in question must be the most absolute and most authoritative of all. Statecraft answers best to this description; for it prescribes which of the sciences are to have a place in the state, and which of them are to be studied by the different classes of citizens, and up to what point; and we find that even the most highly esteemed of the arts are subordinated to it, e.g., military strategy, domestic economics, and oratory. So then, since statecraft employs all the other sciences, prescribing also what the citizens are to do and what they are to refrain from doing, its aim must embrace the aims of all the others; whence it follows that the aim of statecraft is man's proper good. Even supposing the chief good to be eventually the same for the individual as for the state, that of the state is evidently of greater and more fundamental importance both to attain and to preserve. The securing of even one individual's good is cause for rejoicing, but to secure the good of a nation or of a city-state is nobler and more divine. This, then, is the aim of our present inquiry, which is in a sense the study of statecraft.

Two Observations on the Study of Ethics

5 Our discussion will be adequate if we are content with as much precision as is appropriate to the subject matter; for the same degree

of exactitude ought no more to be expected in all kinds of reasoning than in all kinds of handicraft. Excellence and justice, the things with which statecraft deals, involve so much disagreement and uncertainty that they come to be looked on as mere conventions, having no natural foundation. The good involves a similar uncertainty, inasmuch as good things often prove detrimental: there are examples of people destroyed by wealth, of others destroyed by courage. In such matters, then, and starting from such premises as we do, we must be content with a rough approximation to the truth; for when we are dealing with and starting out from what holds good only "as a general rule," the conclusions that we reach will have the same character. Let each of the views put forward be accepted in this spirit, for it is the mark of an educated mind to seek only so much exactness in each type of inquiry as may be allowed by the nature of the subject matter. It is equally wrong to accept probable reasoning from a mathematician and to demand strict demonstrations from an orator.

6 A man judges well and is called a good judge of the things about which he knows. If he has been educated in a particular subject he is a good judge of that subject; if his education has been well-rounded he is a good judge in general. Hence no very young man is qualified to attend lectures on statecraft; for he is inexperienced in the affairs of life, and these form the data and subject matter of statecraft. Moreover, so long as he tends to be swayed by his feelings he will listen vainly and without profit, for the purport of these [lectures] is not purely theoretical but practical. Nor does it make any difference whether his immaturity is a matter of years or of character: the defect is not a matter of time, but consists in the fact that his life and all his pursuits are under the control of his passions. Men of this sort, as is evident from the case of those we call incontinent, do not turn their knowledge to any account in practice; but those whose desires and actions are controlled by reason will derive much profit from a knowledge of these matters.

7 So much, then, for our prefatory remarks about the student, the manner of inquiry, and the aim.

The Good as Happiness

8 To resume, then: since all knowledge and all purpose aims at some good, what is it that we declare to be the aim of statecraft; or, in

other words, what is the highest of all realizable goods? As to its name there is pretty general agreement: the majority of men, as well as the cultured few, speak of it as happiness; and they would maintain that to live well and to do well are the same thing as to be happy. They differ, however, as to what happiness is, and the mass of mankind give a different account of it from philosophers. The former take it to be something palpable and obvious, like pleasure or wealth or fame; they differ, too, among themselves, nor is the same man always of one mind about it: when ill he identifies it with health, when poor with wealth; then growing aware of his ignorance about the whole matter he feels admiration for anyone who proclaims some grand ideal above his comprehension. And to add to the confusion, there have been some philosophers who held that besides the various particular good things there is an absolute good which is the cause of all particular goods. As it would hardly be worthwhile to examine all the opinions that have been entertained, we shall confine our attention to those that are most popular or that appear to have some rational foundation.

9 One point not to be overlooked is the difference between arguments that start from first principles and arguments that lead up to first principles. Plato very wisely used to raise this question, and to ask whether the right way is from or toward first principles—as in the racecourse there is a difference between running from the judges to the boundary line and running back again. Granted that we must start with what is known, this may be interpreted in a double sense: as what is familiar to us or as what is intelligible in itself. Our own method, at any rate, must be to start with what is familiar to us. That is why a sound moral training is required before a man can listen intelligently to discussions about excellence and justice, and generally speaking, about statecraft. For in this field we must take as our "first principles" plain facts; if these are sufficiently evident we shall not insist upon the whys and wherefores. Such principles are in the possession of, or at any rate readily accessible to, the man with a sound moral training. As for the man who neither possesses nor can acquire them, let him hear the words of Hesiod:

> Best is he who makes his own discoveries;
> Good is he who listens to the wise;
> But he who, knowing not, rejects another's wisdom
> Is a plain fool.

Conflicting Views of Happiness

10 Let us now resume our discussion from the point at which we digressed. What is happiness, or the chief good? If it is permissible to judge from men's actual lives, we may say that the mass of them, being vulgarians, identify it with pleasure, which is the reason why they aim at nothing higher than a life of enjoyment. For there are three outstanding types of life: the one just mentioned, the political, and, thirdly, the contemplative. "The mass of men" reveal their utter slavishness by preferring a life fit only for cattle; yet their views have a certain plausibility from the fact that many of those in high places share the tastes of Sardanapalus. Men of superior refinement and active disposition, on the other hand, identify happiness with honor, this being more or less the aim of a statesman's life. It is evidently too superficial, however, to be the good that we are seeking; for it appears to depend rather on him who bestows than on him who receives it, while we may suspect the chief good to be something peculiarly a man's own, which he is not easily deprived of. Besides, men seem to pursue honor primarily in order to assure themselves of their own merit; at any rate, apart from personal acquaintances, it is by those of sound judgment that they seek to be appreciated, and on the score of virtue. Clearly, then, they imply that virtue is superior to honor: and so, perhaps, we should regard this rather than honor as the end and aim of the statesman's life. Yet even about virtue there is a certain incompleteness; for it is supposed that a man may possess it while asleep or during lifelong inactivity, or even while suffering the greatest disasters and misfortunes; and surely no one would call such a man happy, unless for the sake of a paradox. But we need not further pursue this subject, which has been sufficiently treated of in current discussions. Thirdly, there is the contemplative life, which we shall examine at a later point.

11 As for the life of money-making, it is something unnatural. Wealth is clearly not the good that we are seeking, for it is merely useful as a means to something else. Even the objects above mentioned come closer to possessing intrinsic goodness than wealth does, for they at least are cherished on their own account. But not even they, it seems, can be the chief good, although much labor has been lost in

attempting to prove them so. With this observation we may close the present subject. . . .

Functional Definition of Man's Highest Good

12 Returning now to the good that we are seeking, let us inquire into its nature. Evidently it is different in different actions and arts: it is not the same thing in medicine as in strategy, and so on. What definition of good will apply to all the arts? Let us say it is that for the sake of which all else is done. In medicine this is health, in the art of war victory, in building it is a house, and in each of the arts something different, although in every case, wherever there is action and choice involved, it is a certain end; because it is always for the sake of a certain end that all else is done. If, then, there is one end and aim of all our actions, this will be the realizable good; if there are several such ends, these jointly will be our realizable goods. Thus in a roundabout way the discussion has been brought back to the same point as before; which we must now try to explain more clearly.

13 As there is evidently a plurality of ends, and as some of these are chosen only as means to ulterior ends (e.g., wealth, flutes, and instruments in general), it is clear that not all ends are final. But the supreme good must of course be something final. Accordingly, if there is only one final end, this will be the good that we are seeking; and if there is more than one such end, the most complete and final of them will be this good. Now we call what is pursued as an end in itself more final than what is pursued as a means to something else; and what is never chosen as a means we call more final than what is chosen both as an end in itself and as a means; in fact, when a thing is chosen always as an end in itself and never as a means we call it absolutely final. Happiness seems, more than anything else, to answer to this description: for it is something we choose always for its own sake and never for the sake of something else; while honor, pleasure, reason, and all the virtues, though chosen partly for themselves (for we might choose any one of them without heeding the result), are chosen also for the sake of the happiness which we suppose they will bring us. Happiness, on the other hand, is never chosen for the sake of any of these, nor indeed as a means to anything else at all.

14 We seem to arrive at the same conclusion if we start from the

notion of self-sufficiency; for the final good is admittedly self-sufficient. To be self-sufficient we do not mean that an individual must live in isolation. Parents, children, wife, as well as friends and fellow citizens generally, are all permissible; for man is by nature political. To be sure, some limit has to be set to such relationships, for if they are extended to embrace ancestors, descendants, and friends of friends, we should go on *ad infinitum.* But this point will be considered later on; provisionally we may attribute self-sufficiency to that which taken by itself makes life choiceworthy and lacking in nothing. Such a thing we conceive happiness to be. Moreover, we regard happiness as the most choiceworthy of all things; nor does this mean that it is merely one good thing among others, for if that were the case it is plain that the addition of even the least of those other goods would increase its desirability; since the addition would create a larger amount of good, and of two goods the greater is always to be preferred. Evidently, then, happiness is something final and self-sufficient, and is the end and aim of all that we do.

But perhaps it will be objected that to call happiness the supreme good is a mere truism, and that a clearer account of it is still needed. We can give this best, probably, if we ascertain the proper function of man. Just as the excellence and good performance of a flute player, a sculptor, or any kind of artist, and generally speaking of anyone who has a function or business to perform, lies always in that function, so man's good would seem to lie in the function of man, if he has one. But can we suppose that while a carpenter and a cobbler each has a function and mode of activity of his own, man qua man has none, but has been left by nature functionless? Surely it is more likely that as his several members, eye and hand and foot, can be shown to have each its own function, so man too must have a function over and above the special functions of his various members. What will such a function be? Not merely to live, of course: he shares that even with plants, whereas we are seeking something peculiar to himself. We must exclude, therefore, the life of nutrition and growth. Next comes sentient life, but this again is had in common with the horse, the ox, and in fact all animals whatever. There remains only the "practical" life of his rational nature; and this has two aspects, one of which is rational in the sense that it obeys a "rational principle," the other in the sense that it possesses and exercises reason. To avoid ambiguity let us specify that by "rational" we mean the "exercise or activity," not the mere possession, of reason; for it is the former that would seem more properly entitled to the name. Thus we conclude that man's function is an activity of the soul in conformity with, or at any rate involving the use of, "rational principle."

16 An individual and a superior individual who belong to the same class we regard as sharing the same function: a harpist and a good harpist, for instance, are essentially the same. This holds true of any class of individuals whatever; for superior excellence with respect to a function is nothing but an amplification of that selfsame function: e.g., the function of a harpist is to play the harp, while that of a good harpist is to play it well. This being so, if we take man's proper function to be a certain kind of life, viz. an activity and conduct of the soul that involves reason, and if it is the part of a good man to perform such activities well and nobly, and if a function is well performed when it is performed in accordance with its own proper excellence; we may conclude that the good of man is an activity of the soul in accordance with virtue, or, if there be more than one virtue, in accordance with the best and most perfect of them. And we must add, in a complete life. For one swallow does not make a spring, nor does one fine day; and similarly one day or brief period of happiness does not make a man happy and blessed.

17 So much, then, for a rough outline of the good: the proper procedure being, we may suppose, to sketch an outline first and afterwards to fill in the details. When a good outline has been made, almost anyone presumably can expand it and fill it out; and time is a good inventor and collaborator in this work. It is in just such a way that progress has been made in the various "human techniques," for filling in the gaps is something anybody can do.

18 But in all this we must bear constantly in mind our previous warning: not to expect the same degree of precision in all fields, but only so much as belongs to a given subject matter and is appropriate to a particular "type of inquiry." Both the carpenter and the geometer investigate the right angle, but in different ways: the one wants only such an approximation to it as will serve his work; the other, being concerned with truth, seeks to determine its essence or essential attributes. And so in other subjects we must follow a like procedure, lest we be so much taken up with side issues that we pass over the matter in hand. Similarly we ought not in all cases to demand the "reason why"; sometimes it is enough to point out the bare fact. This is true, for instance, in the case of "first principles"; for a bare

fact must always be the ultimate starting point of any inquiry. First principles may be arrived at in a variety of ways: some by induction, some by direct perception, some by a kind of habituation, and others in other ways. In each case we should try to apprehend them in whatever way is proper to them, and we should take care to define them clearly, because they will have a considerable influence upon the subsequent course of our inquiry. A good beginning is more than half of the whole inquiry, and once established clears up many of its difficulties.

Confirmation by Popular Beliefs

19 It is important to consider our ethical "first principle" not merely as a conclusion drawn from certain premises, but also in its relation to popular opinion; for all data harmonize with a true principle, but with a false one they are soon found to be discordant. Now it has been customary to divide good things into three classes: external goods on the one hand, and on the other goods of the soul and goods of the body; and those of the soul we call good in the highest sense, and in the fullest degree. "Conscious actions," i.e., "active expressions of our nature," we take, of course, as belonging to the soul; and thus our account is confirmed by the doctrine referred to, which is of long standing and has been generally accepted by students of philosophy. . . .

20 We are in agreement also with those who identify happiness with virtue or with some particular virtue; for our phrase "activity in accordance with virtue" is the same as what they call virtue. It makes quite a difference, however, whether we conceive the supreme good as the mere possession of virtue or as its employment—i.e., as a state of character or as its active expression in conduct. For a state of character may be present without yielding any good result, as in a man who is asleep or in some other way inactive; but this is not true of its active expression, which must show itself in action, indeed in good action. As at the Olympic games it is not merely the fairest and strongest that receive the victory wreath, but those who compete (since the victors will of course be found among the competitors), so in life too those who carry off the finest prizes are those who manifest their excellence in their deeds.

21 Moreover, the life of those active in virtue is intrinsically pleasant. For besides the fact that pleasure is something belonging to the soul, each man takes pleasure in what he is said to love—the horse lover in horses, the lover of sights in public spectacles, and similarly the lover of justice in just acts, and more generally, the lover of virtue in virtuous acts. And while most men take pleasure in things which, as they are not truly pleasant by nature, create warring factions in the soul, the lovers of what is noble take pleasure in things that are truly pleasant in themselves. Virtuous actions are things of this kind; hence they are pleasant for such men, as well as pleasant intrinsically. The life of such men, therefore, requires no adventitious pleasures, but finds its own pleasure within itself. This is further shown by the fact that a man who does not enjoy doing noble actions is not a good man at all: surely no one would call a man just who did not enjoy performing just actions, nor generous who did not enjoy performing generous actions, and so on. On this ground too, then, actions in conformity with virtue must be intrinsically pleasant. And certainly they are good as well as noble, and both in the highest degree, if the judgment of the good man is any criterion; for he will judge them as we have said. It follows, therefore, that happiness is at once the best and noblest and pleasantest of things, and that these attributes are not separable as the inscription at Delos pretends:

> Perfect justice is noblest, health is best,
> But to gain one's heart's desire is pleasantest.

For our best activities possess all of these attributes; and it is in our best activities, or in the best one of them, that we say happiness consists.

22 Nevertheless, happiness plainly requires external goods as well; for it is impossible, or at least not easy, to act nobly without the proper equipment. There are many actions that can only be performed through such instruments as friends, wealth, or political influence; and there are some things, again, the lack of which must mar felicity, such as good birth, fine children, and personal comeliness: for the man who is repulsive in appearance, or ill-born, or solitary and childless does not meet the requirements of a happy man, and still less does one who has worthless children and friends, or who has lost good ones by death. As we have said, then, happiness seems to require the addition of external prosperity, and this has led some

to identify it with "good fortune," just as others have made the opposite mistake of identifying it with virtue.

Sources of Happiness

23 For the same reason there are many who wonder whether happiness is attained by learning, or by habituation or some other kind of training, or whether it comes by some divine dispensation, or even by chance. Well, certainly if the gods do give any gifts to men we may reasonably suppose that happiness is god-given; indeed, of all human blessings it is the most likely to be so, inasmuch as it is the best of them all. While this question no doubt belongs more properly to another branch of inquiry, we remark here that even if happiness is not god-sent but comes as a result of virtue or some kind of learning or training, still it is evidently one of the most divine things in the world, because that which is the reward as well as the end and aim of virtuous conduct must evidently be of supreme excellence, something divine and most blessed. If this is the case, happiness must further be something that can be generally shared; for with the exception of those whose capacity for virtue has been stunted or maimed, everyone will have the ability, by study and diligence, to acquire it. And if it is better that happiness should be acquired in this way than by chance, we may reasonably suppose that it happens so; because everything in nature is arranged in the best way possible—just as in the case of man-made products, and of every kind of causation, especially the highest. It would be altogether wrong that what is greatest and noblest in the world should be left to the dispensation of chance.

24 Our present difficulty is cleared up by our previous definition of happiness, as a certain activity of the soul in accordance with virtue; whereas all other sorts of good are either necessary conditions of, or cooperative with and naturally useful instruments of this. Such a conclusion, moreover, agrees with the proposition we laid down at the outset: that the end of statecraft is the best of all ends, and that the principal concern of statecraft is to make the citizens of a certain character—namely, good and disposed to perform noble actions.

25 Naturally, therefore, we do not call an ox or a horse or any other brute happy, since none of them is able to participate in conduct of

this kind. For the same reason a child is not happy, since at his age he too is incapable of such conduct. Or if we do call a child happy, it is in the sense of predicting for him a happy future. Happiness, as we have said, involves not only a completeness of virtue but also a complete lifetime for its fulfillment. Life brings many vicissitudes and chance happenings, and it may be that one who is now prosperous will suffer great misfortunes in his old age, as is told of Priam in the Trojan legends; and a man who is thus buffeted by fortune and comes to a miserable end can scarcely be called happy.

Happiness and the Vicissitudes of Fortune

26 Are we, then, to call no one happy while he lives? Must we, as Solon advises, wait to see his end? And if we accept this verdict, are we to interpret it as meaning that a man actually becomes happy only after he is dead? Would not this be downright absurd, especially for us who define happiness as a kind of vital activity? Or if we reject this interpretation, and suppose Solon to mean rather that it is only after death, when beyond the reach of further evil and calamity that a man can safely be said to have been happy during his life, there is still a possible objection that may be offered. For many hold that both good and evil may in a certain sense befall a dead man (just as they may befall a living man even when he is unconscious of them)—e.g., honors and disgraces, and the prosperity or misfortune of his children and the rest of his descendants. And this presents a further problem: suppose a man to have lived to a happy old age, and to have ended as he lived, there are still plenty of reverses that may befall his descendants—some of them will perhaps lead a good life and be dealt with by fortune as they deserve, others not. (It is clear, too, that a man's relationship to his descendants admits of various degrees.) It would be odd, then, if the dead man were to change along with the fortunes of his descendants, becoming happy and miserable by turns; although, to be sure, it would be equally odd if the fortunes of his descendants did not affect him at all, even for a brief time.

27 But let us go back to our earlier question, which may perhaps clear up the one we are raising at present. Suppose we agree that we must look to the end of a man's life, and only then call him happy,

not because he then *is* happy but because we can only then know him to have been so: is it not paradoxical to have refused to call him happy during just the period when happiness was present to him? On the other hand, we are naturally loath to apply the term to living men, considering the vicissitudes to which they are liable. Happiness, we argue, must be something that endures without any essential change, whereas a living individual may experience many turns of fortune's wheel. Obviously if we judge by his changing fortunes we shall have to call the same man now happy now wretched, thereby regarding the happy man as a kind of chameleon and his happiness as built on no secure foundation; yet it surely cannot be right to regard a man's happiness as wholly dependent on his fortunes. True good and evil are not of this character; rather, as we have said, although good fortune is a necessary adjunct to a complete human life, it is virtuous activities that constitute happiness, and the opposite sort of activities that constitute its opposite.

28 The foregoing difficulty [that happiness can be judged of only in retrospect] confirms, as a matter of fact, our theory. For none of man's functions is so permanent as his virtuous activities—indeed, many believe them to be more abiding even than a knowledge of the sciences; and of his virtuous activities those are the most abiding which are of highest worth, for it is with them that anyone blessed with supreme happiness is most fully and most continuously occupied, and hence never oblivious of. The happy man, then, will possess this attribute of permanence or stability about which we have been inquiring, and will keep it all his life; because at all times and in preference to everything else he will be engaged in virtuous action and contemplation, and he will bear the changes of fortune as nobly and in every respect as decorously as possible, inasmuch as he is truly good and "four-square beyond reproach."

29 But the dispensations of fortune are many, some great, others small. Small ones do not appreciably turn the scales of life, but a multitude of great ones, if they are of the nature of blessings, will make life happier; for they add to life a grace of their own, provided that a man makes noble and good use of them. If, however, they are of an evil kind, they will crush and maim happiness, in that they bring pain and thereby hinder many of our natural activities. Yet true nobility shines out even here, if a multitude of great misfortunes be borne with calmness—not, to be sure, with the calmness of insensibility, but of nobility and greatness of soul.

30 If, as we have declared, it is our activities that give life its character, then no happy man can become miserable, inasmuch as he will never do what is hateful or base. For we hold that the truly good and wise man will bear with dignity whatever fortune sends, and will always make the best of his circumstances, as a good general makes the most effective use of the forces at his command, and a good shoemaker makes the best shoes out of the leather that is available, and so in the case of the other crafts. On this interpretation, the happy man can never become miserable—although of course he will not be blessed with happiness in the full sense of the word if he meets with such a fate as Priam's. At all events, he is not variable and always changing; for no ordinary misfortunes but only a multitude of great ones will dislodge him from his happy state, and should this occur he will not readily recover his happiness in a short time, but only, if at all, after a long period has run its course, during which he has achieved distinctions of a high order.

31 Is there any objection, then, to our defining a happy man as one whose activities are an expression of complete virtue, and who at the same time enjoys a sufficiency of worldly goods, not just for some limited period, but for his entire lifetime? Or perhaps we had better add the proviso that he shall be destined to go on living in this manner, and die as he has lived; for, whereas the future is obscure to us, we conceive happiness to be an end, something altogether and in every respect final and complete. Granting all this, we may declare those living men to be "blessed with supreme happiness" in whom these conditions have been and are continuing to be fulfilled. Their blessedness, however, is of a human order.

32 So much for our discussion of this question.

Derivation of the Two Kinds of Human Excellence

33 Since happiness is a certain activity of the soul in accordance with perfect virtue, we must next examine the nature of virtue. Not only will such an inquiry perhaps clarify the problem of happiness; it will also be of vital concern to the true student of statecraft, whose aim is to make his fellow citizens good and law-abiding. The Cretan and

Spartan lawgivers, as well as such others as may have resembled them, exemplify this aim. And clearly, if such an inquiry has to do with statecraft, it will be in keeping with our original purpose to pursue it.

34 It goes without saying that the virtue we are to study is human virtue, just as the good that we have been inquiring about is a human good, and the happiness a human happiness. By human virtue we mean virtue not of the body but of the soul, and by happiness too we mean an activity of the soul. This being the case, it is no less evident that the student of statecraft must have some knowledge of the soul, than that a physician who is to heal the eye or the whole body must have some knowledge of these organs; more so, indeed, in proportion as statecraft is superior to and more honorable than medicine. Now all physicians who are educated take much pains to know about the body. Hence as students of statecraft, too, we must inquire into the nature of the soul; but we must do so with reference to our own distinctive aim and only to the extent that it requires, for to go into minuter detail would be more laborious than is warranted by our subject matter.

35 We may adopt here certain doctrines about the soul that have been adequately stated in our public discourses: as that the soul may be distinguished into two parts, one of which is irrational while the other possesses reason. Whether these two parts are actually distinct like the parts of the body or any other divisible thing, or are distinct only in a logical sense, like convex and concave in the circumference of a circle, is immaterial to our present inquiry.

36 Of the irrational part, again, one division is apparently of a vegetative nature and common to all living things: I mean that which is the cause of nutrition and growth. It is more reasonable to postulate a vital faculty of this sort, present in all things that take nourishment, even when in an embryo stage, and retained by the full-grown organism, than to assume a special nutritive faculty in the latter. Hence we may say that the excellence belonging to this part of the soul is common to all species, and not specifically human: a point that is further confirmed by the popular view that this part of the soul is most active during sleep. For it is during sleep that the distinction between good men and bad is least apparent; whence the saying that for half their lives the happy are no better off than the wretched. This, indeed, is natural enough, for sleep is an inactivity of the soul in those respects in which the soul is called good or bad. (It is true,

however, that to a slight degree certain bodily movements penetrate to the soul; which is the reason why good men's dreams are superior to those of the average person.) But enough of this subject: let us dismiss the nutritive principle, since it has by nature no share in human excellence.

37 There seems to be a second part of the soul, which though irrational yet in some way partakes of reason. For while we praise the rational principle and the part of the soul that manifests it in the case of the continent and incontinent man alike, on the ground that it exhorts them rightly and urges them to do what is best; yet we find within these men another element different in nature from the rational element, and struggling against and resisting it. Just as ataxic limbs, when we choose to move them to the right, turn on the contrary to the left, so it is with the soul: the impulses of the incontinent man run counter to his ruling part. The only difference is that in the case of the body we see what it is that goes astray, while in the soul we do not. Nevertheless the comparison will doubtless suffice to show that there is in the soul something besides the rational element, opposing and running counter to it. (In what sense the two elements are distinct is immaterial.) But this other element, as we have said, seems also to have some share in a rational principle: at any rate, in the continent man it submits to reason, while in the man who is at once temperate and courageous it is presumably all the more obedient; for in him it speaks on all matters harmoniously with the voice of reason.

38 Evidently, then, the irrational part of the soul is twofold. There is the vegetative element, which has no share in reason, and there is the concupiscent, or rather the appetitive element, which does in a sense partake of reason, in that it is amenable and obedient to it: i.e., it is rational in the sense that we speak of "having *logos* of" [paying heed to] father and friends, not in the sense of "having *logos* of" [having a rational understanding of] mathematical truths. That this irrational element is in some way amenable to reason is shown by our practice of giving admonishment, and by rebuke and exhortation generally. If on this account it is deemed more correct to regard this element as also possessing reason, then the rational part of the soul, in turn, will have two subdivisions: the one being rational in the strict sense as actually possessing reason, the other merely in the sense that a child obeys its father.

39 Virtue, too, is differentiated in accordance with this division of

the soul: for we call some of the virtues intellectual and others moral: wisdom, understanding, and sagacity being among the former, liberality and temperance among the latter. In speaking of a man's character we do not say that he is wise or intelligent, but that he is gentle or temperate; yet we praise the wise man too for the disposition he has developed within himself, and praiseworthy dispositions we call virtues.

The Qualities of the Prince

NICCOLÒ MACHIAVELLI

Niccolò Machiavelli (1469–1527) has come to represent all that is dark and treacherous about politics and statesmanship. He was an Italian nobleman who both practiced and studied politics on the local and national level. For fourteen years, he functioned as first secretary of the council that ruled the Republic of Florence.

The Prince is his best-known work, written in 1513 and published in 1532, five years after his death. In *The Prince,* Machiavelli argues that rulers must employ any method, no matter how contemptible, to defeat their enemies and control their own people.

In "The Qualities of the Prince," Machiavelli offers several pieces of practical advice. For example, he tells princes to be misers with their own wealth and that of their subjects, although princes can give liberally of goods plundered from their enemies. He says that princes should quell disorder, even if they are thought to be cruel, for "it is far safer to be feared than loved." Princes can escape hatred if they do "not meddle with the property or with the women" of their citizens and subjects. He also says that "a prudent Prince neither can nor ought to keep his word when to keep it is hurtful to him and the causes which led him to pledge it are removed." Thus, the prince should appear to be "merciful, faithful, humane, religious, and upright" but at the same time must use any means to maintain authority.

A Prince's Duty Concerning Military Matters

1 A prince, therefore, must not have any other object nor any other thought, nor must he take anything as his profession but war, its institutions, and its discipline; because that is the only profession which befits one who commands; and it is of such importance that not only does it maintain those who were born princes, but many times it enables men of private station to rise to that position; and, on the other hand, it is evident that when princes have given more thought to personal luxuries than to arms, they have lost their state. And the first way to lose it is to neglect this art; and the way to acquire it is to be well versed in this art.

2 Francesco Sforza became Duke of Milan from being a private citizen because he was armed; his sons, since they avoided the inconveniences of arms, became private citizens after having been dukes. For, among the other bad effects it causes, being disarmed makes you despised; this is one of those infamies a prince should guard himself against, as will be treated below: for between an armed and an unarmed man there is no comparison whatsoever, and it is not reasonable for an armed man to obey an unarmed man willingly, nor that an unarmed man should be safe among armed servants; since, when the former is suspicious and the latter are contemptuous, it is impossible for them to work well together. And therefore, a prince who does not understand military matters, besides the other misfortunes already noted, cannot be esteemed by his own soldiers, nor can he trust them.

3 He must, therefore, never raise his thought from this exercise of war, and in peacetime he must train himself more than in time of war; this can be done in two ways: one by action, the other by the mind. And as far as actions are concerned, besides keeping his soldiers well disciplined and trained, he must always be out hunting, and must accustom his body to hardships in this manner; and he must also learn the nature of the terrain, and know how mountains slope, how valleys open, how plains lie, and understand the nature of rivers and swamps; and he should devote much attention to such activities. Such knowledge is useful in two ways: first, one learns to know one's own country and can better understand how to defend it; second,

with the knowledge and experience of the terrain, one can easily comprehend the characteristics of any other terrain that it is necessary to explore for the first time; for the hills, valleys, plains, rivers, and swamps of Tuscany, for instance, have certain similarities to those of other provinces; so that by knowing the lay of the land in one province one can easily understand it in others. And a prince who lacks this ability lacks the most important quality in a leader; because this skill teaches you to find the enemy, choose a campsite, lead troops, organize them for battle, and besiege towns to your own advantage.

4 Philopoemon, Prince of the Achaeans, among the other praises given to him by writers, is praised because in peacetime he thought of nothing except the means of waging war; and when he was out in the country with his friends, he often stopped and reasoned with them: "If the enemy were on that hilltop and we were here with our army, which of the two of us would have the advantage? How could we attack them without breaking formation? If we wanted to retreat, how could we do this? If they were to retreat, how could we pursue them?" And he proposed to them, as they rode along, all the contingencies that can occur in an army; he heard their opinions, expressed his own, and backed it up with arguments; so that, because of these continuous deliberations, when leading his troops no unforeseen incident could arise for which he did not have the remedy.

5 But as for the exercise of the mind, the prince must read histories and in them study the deeds of great men; he must see how they conducted themselves in wars; he must examine the reasons for their victories and for their defeats in order to avoid the latter and to imitate the former; and above all else he must do as some distinguished man before him has done, who elected to imitate someone who had been praised and honored before him, and always keep in mind his deeds and actions; just as it is reported that Alexander the Great imitated Achilles; Caesar, Alexander; Scipio, Cyrus. And anyone who reads the life of Cyrus written by Xenophon then realizes how important in the life of Scipio that imitation was to his glory and how much, in purity, goodness, humanity, and generosity, Scipio conformed to those characteristics of Cyrus that Xenophon had written about.

6 Such methods as these a wise prince must follow, and never in peaceful times must he be idle; but he must turn them diligently to his advantage in order to be able to profit from them in times of adversity, so that, when Fortune changes, she will find him prepared to withstand such times.

On Those Things for Which Men, and Particularly Princes, Are Praised or Blamed

7 Now there remains to be examined what should be the methods and procedures of a prince in dealing with his subjects and friends. And because I know that many have written about this, I am afraid that by writing about it again I shall be thought of as presumptuous, since in discussing this material I depart radically from the procedures of others. But since my intention is to write something useful for anyone who understands it, it seemed more suitable to me to search after the effectual truth of the matter rather than its imagined one. And many writers have imagined for themselves republics and principalities that have never been seen nor known to exist in reality; for there is such a gap between how one lives and how one ought to live that anyone who abandons what is done for what ought to be done learns his ruin rather than his preservation: for a man who wishes to make a vocation of being good at all times will come to ruin among so many who are not good. Hence it is necessary for a prince who wishes to maintain his position to learn how not to be good, and to use this knowledge or not to use it according to necessity.

8 Leaving aside, therefore, the imagined things concerning a prince, and taking into account those that are true, I say that all men, when they are spoken of, and particularly princes, since they are placed on a higher level, are judged by some of these qualities which bring them either blame or praise. And this is why one is considered generous, another miserly (to use a Tuscan word, since "avaricious" in our language is still used to mean one who wishes to acquire by means of theft; we call "miserly" one who excessively avoids using what he has); one is considered a giver, the other rapacious; one cruel, another merciful; one treacherous, another faithful; one effeminate and cowardly, another bold and courageous; one humane, another haughty; one lascivious, another chaste; one trustworthy, another cunning; one harsh, another lenient; one serious, another frivolous; one religious, another unbelieving; and the like. And I know that everyone will admit that it would be a very praiseworthy

thing to find in a prince, of the qualities mentioned above, those that are held to be good; but since it is neither possible to have them nor to observe them all completely, because human nature does not permit it, a prince must be prudent enough to know how to escape the bad reputation of those vices that would lose the state for him, and must protect himself from those that will not lose it for him, if this is possible; but if he cannot, he need not concern himself unduly if he ignores these less serious vices. And, moreover, he need not worry about incurring the bad reputation of those vices without which it would be difficult to hold his state; since, carefully taking everything into account, one will discover that something which appears to be a virtue, if pursued, will end in his destruction; while some other thing which seems to be a vice, if pursued, will result in his safety and his well-being.

On Generosity and Miserliness

9 Beginning, therefore, with the first of the above-mentioned qualities, I say that it would be good to be considered generous; nevertheless, generosity used in such a manner as to give you a reputation for it will harm you; because if it is employed virtuously and as one should employ it, it will not be recognized and you will not avoid the reproach of its opposite. And so, if a prince wants to maintain his reputation for generosity among men, it is necessary for him not to neglect any possible means of lavish display; in so doing such a prince will always use up all his resources and he will be obliged, eventually, if he wishes to maintain his reputation for generosity, to burden the people with excessive taxes and to do everything possible to raise funds. This will begin to make him hateful to his subjects, and, becoming impoverished, he will not be much esteemed by anyone; so that, as a consequence of his generosity, having offended many and rewarded few, he will feel the effects of any slight unrest and will be ruined at the first sign of danger; recognizing this and wishing to alter his policies, he immediately runs the risk of being reproached as a miser.

10 A prince, therefore, unable to use this virtue of generosity in a manner which will not harm himself if he is known for it, should, if he is wise, not worry about being called a miser; for with time he

will come to be considered more generous once it is evident that, as a result of his parsimony, his income is sufficient, he can defend himself from anyone who makes war against him, and he can undertake enterprises without overburdening his people, so that he comes to be generous with all those from whom he takes nothing, who are countless, and miserly with all those to whom he gives nothing, who are few. In our times we have not seen great deeds accomplished except by those who were considered miserly; all others were done away with. Pope Julius II, although he made use of his reputation for generosity in order to gain the papacy, then decided not to maintain it in order to be able to wage war; the present King of France has waged many wars without imposing extra taxes on his subjects, only because his habitual parsimony has provided for the additional expenditures; the present King of Spain, if he had been considered generous, would not have engaged in nor won so many campaigns.

11 Therefore, in order not to have to rob his subjects, to be able to defend himself, not to become poor and contemptible, and not to be forced to become rapacious, a prince must consider it of little importance if he incurs the name of miser, for this is one of those vices that permits him to rule. And if someone were to say: Caesar with his generosity came to rule the empire, and many others, because they were generous and known to be so, achieved very high positions; I reply: you are either already a prince or you are on the way to becoming one; in the first instance such generosity is damaging; in the second it is very necessary to be thought generous. And Caesar was one of those who wanted to gain the principality of Rome; but if, after obtaining this, he had lived and had not moderated his expenditures, he would have destroyed that empire. And if someone were to reply: there have existed many princes who have accomplished great deeds with their armies who have been reputed to be generous; I answer you: a prince either spends his own money and that of his subjects or that of others; in the first case he must be economical; in the second he must not restrain any part of his generosity. And for that prince who goes out with his soldiers and lives by looting, sacking, and ransoms, who controls the property of others, such generosity is necessary; otherwise he would not be followed by his troops. And with what does not belong to you or to your subjects you can be a more liberal giver, as were Cyrus, Caesar, and Alexander; for spending the wealth of others does not lessen your reputation

but adds to it; only the spending of your own is what harms you. And there is nothing that uses itself up faster than generosity, for as you employ it you lose the means of employing it, and you become either poor or despised or, in order to escape poverty, rapacious and hated. And above all other things a prince must guard himself against being despised and hated; and generosity leads you to both one and the other. So it is wiser to live with the reputation of a miser, which produces reproach without hatred, than to be forced to incur the reputation of rapacity, which produces reproach along with hatred, because you want to be considered as generous.

On Cruelty and Mercy and Whether It Is Better to be Loved Than to be Feared or the Contrary

12 Proceeding to the other qualities mentioned above, I say that every prince must desire to be considered merciful and not cruel; nevertheless, he must take care not to misuse this mercy. Cesare Borgia was considered cruel; nonetheless, his cruelty had brought order to Romagna, united it, restored it to peace and obedience. If we examine this carefully, we shall see that he was more merciful than the Florentine people, who, in order to avoid being considered cruel, allowed the destruction of Pistoia. Therefore, a prince must not worry about the reproach of cruelty when it is a matter of keeping his subjects united and loyal; for with a very few examples of cruelty he will be more compassionate than those who, out of excessive mercy, permit disorders to continue, from which arise murders and plundering; for these usually harm the community at large, while the executions that come from the prince harm one individual in particular. And the new prince, above all other princes, cannot escape the reputation of being called cruel, since new states are full of dangers. And Virgil, through Dido, states: "My difficult condition and the newness of my rule make me act in such a manner, and to set guards over my land on all sides."

13 Nevertheless, a prince must be cautious in believing and in acting,

nor should he be afraid of his own shadow; and he should proceed in such a manner, tempered by prudence and humanity, so that too much trust may not render him imprudent nor too much distrust render him intolerable.

14 From this arises an argument: whether it is better to be loved than to be feared, or the contrary. I reply that one should like to be both one and the other; but since it is difficult to join them together, it is much safer to be feared than to be loved when one of the two must be lacking. For one can generally say this about men: that they are ungrateful, fickle, simulators and deceivers, avoiders of danger, greedy for gain; and while you work for their good they are completely yours, offering you their blood, their property, their lives, and their sons, as I said earlier, when danger is far away; but when it comes nearer to you they turn away. And that prince who bases his power entirely on their words, finding himself stripped of other preparations, comes to ruin; for friendships that are acquired by a price and not by greatness and nobility of character are purchased but are not owned, and at the proper moment they cannot be spent. And men are less hesitant about harming someone who makes himself loved than one who makes himself feared because love is held together by a chain of obligation which, since men are a sorry lot, is broken on every occasion in which their own self-interest is concerned; but fear is held together by a dread of punishment which will never abandon you.

15 A prince must nevertheless make himself feared in such a manner that he will avoid hatred, even if he does not acquire love; since to be feared and not to be hated can very well be combined; and this will always be so when he keeps his hands off the property and the women of his citizens and his subjects. And if he must take someone's life, he should do so when there is proper justification and manifest cause; but, above all, he should avoid the property of others; for men forget more quickly the death of their father than the loss of their patrimony. Moreover, the reasons for seizing their property are never lacking; and he who begins to live by stealing always finds a reason for taking what belongs to others; on the contrary, reasons for taking a life are rarer and disappear sooner.

16 But when the prince is with his armies and has under his command a multitude of troops, then it is absolutely necessary that he not worry about being considered cruel; for without that reputation he will never keep an army united or prepared for any combat. Among

the praiseworthy deeds of Hannibal is counted this: that, having a very large army, made up of all kinds of men, which he commanded in foreign lands, there never arose the slightest dissention, neither among themselves nor against their prince, both during his good and his bad fortune. This could not have arisen from anything other than his inhuman cruelty, which, along with his many other abilities, made him always respected and terrifying in the eyes of his soldiers; and without that, to attain the same effect, his other abilities would not have sufficed. And the writers of history, having considered this matter very little, on the one hand admire these deeds of his and on the other condemn the main cause of them.

17 And that it be true that his other abilities would not have been sufficient can be seen from the example of Scipio, a most extraordinary man not only in his time but in all recorded history, whose armies in Spain rebelled against him; this came about from nothing other than his excessive compassion, which gave to his soldiers more liberty than military discipline allowed. For this he was censured in the senate by Fabius Maximus, who called him the corruptor of the Roman militia. The Locrians, having been ruined by one of Scipio's officers, were not avenged by him, nor was the arrogance of that officer corrected, all because of his tolerant nature; so that someone in the senate who tried to apologize for him said that there were many men who knew how not to err better than they knew to correct errors. Such a nature would have, in time, damaged Scipio's fame and glory if he had maintained it during the empire; but, living under the control of the senate, this harmful characteristic of his not only concealed itself but brought him fame.

18 I conclude, therefore, returning to the problem of being feared and loved, that since men love at their own pleasure and fear at the pleasure of the prince, a wise prince should build his foundation upon that which belongs to him, not upon that which belongs to others: he must strive only to avoid hatred, as has been said.

How a Prince Should Keep His Word

19 How praiseworthy it is for a prince to keep his word and to live by integrity and not by deceit everyone knows; nevertheless, one sees from the experience of our times that the princes who have

accomplished great deeds are those who have cared little for keeping their promises and who have known how to manipulate the minds of men by shrewdness; and in the end they have surpassed those who laid their foundations upon honesty.

20 You must, therefore, know that there are two means of fighting: one according to the laws, the other with force; the first way is proper to man, the second to beasts; but because the first, in many cases, is not sufficient, it becomes necessary to have recourse to the second. Therefore, a prince must know how to use wisely the natures of the beast and the man. This policy was taught to princes allegorically by the ancient writers, who described how Achilles and many other ancient princes were given to Chiron the Centaur to be raised and taught under his discipline. This can only mean that, having a half-beast and half-man as a teacher, a prince must know how to employ the nature of the one and the other; and the one without the other cannot endure.

21 Since, then, a prince must know how to make good use of the nature of the beast, he should choose from among the beasts the fox and the lion; for the lion cannot defend itself from traps and the fox cannot protect itself from wolves. It is therefore necessary to be a fox in order to recognize the traps and a lion in order to frighten the wolves. Those who play only the part of the lion do not understand matters. A wise ruler, therefore, cannot and should not keep his word when such an observance of faith would be to his disadvantage and when the reasons which made him promise are removed. And if men were all good, this rule would not be good; but since men are a sorry lot and will not keep their promises to you, you likewise need not keep yours to them. A prince never lacks legitimate reasons to break his promises. Of this one could cite an endless number of modern examples to show how many pacts, how many promises have been made null and void because of the infidelity of princes; and he who has known best how to use the fox has come to a better end. But it is necessary to know how to disguise this nature well and to be a great hypocrite and a liar: and men are so simpleminded and so controlled by their present necessities that one who deceives will always find another who will allow himself to be deceived.

22 I do not wish to remain silent about one of these recent instances. Alexander VI did nothing else, he thought about nothing else, except to deceive men, and he always found the occasion to do this. And

there never was a man who had more forcefulness in his oaths, who affirmed a thing with more promises, and who honored his word less; nevertheless, his tricks always succeeded perfectly since he was well acquainted with this aspect of the world.

23 Therefore, it is not necessary for a prince to have all of the above-mentioned qualities, but it is very necessary for him to appear to have them. Furthermore, I shall be so bold as to assert this: that having them and practicing them at all times is harmful; and appearing to have them is useful; for instance, to seem merciful, faithful, humane, forthright, religious, and to be so; but his mind should be disposed in such a way that should it become necessary not to be so, he will be able and know how to change to the contrary. And it is essential to understand this: that a prince, and especially a new prince, cannot observe all those things by which men are considered good, for in order to maintain the state he is often obliged to act against his promise, against charity, against humanity, and against religion. And therefore, it is necessary that he have a mind ready to turn itself according to the way the winds of Fortune and the changeability of affairs require him; and, as I said above, as long as it is possible, he should not stray from the good, but he should know how to enter into evil when necessity commands.

24 A prince, therefore, must be very careful never to let anything slip from his lips which is not full of the five qualities mentioned above: he should appear, upon seeing and hearing him, to be all mercy, all faithfulness, all integrity, all kindness, all religion. And there is nothing more necessary than to seem to possess this last quality. And men in general judge more by their eyes than their hands; for everyone can see but few can feel. Everyone sees what you seem to be, few perceive what you are, and those few do not dare to contradict the opinion of the many who have the majesty of the state to defend them; and in the actions of all men, and especially of princes, where there is no impartial arbiter, one must consider the final result. Let a prince therefore act to seize and to maintain the state; his methods will always be judged honorable and will be praised by all; for ordinary people are always deceived by appearances and by the outcome of a thing; and in the world there is nothing but ordinary people; and there is no room for the few, while the many have a place to lean on. A certain prince of the present day, whom I shall refrain from naming, preaches nothing but peace and faith, and to both one and the other he is entirely opposed; and both, if he had put them into

practice, would have cost him many times over either his reputation or his state.

On Avoiding Being Despised and Hated

25 But since, concerning the qualities mentioned above, I have spoken about the most important, I should like to discuss the others briefly in this general manner: that the prince, as was noted above, should think about avoiding those things which make him hated and despised; and when he has avoided this, he will have carried out his duties and will find no danger whatsoever in other vices. As I have said, what makes him hated above all else is being rapacious and a usurper of the property and the women of his subjects; he must refrain from this; and in most cases, so long as you do not deprive them of either their property or their honor, the majority of men live happily; and you have only to deal with the ambition of a few, who can be restrained without difficulty and by many means. What makes him despised is being considered changeable, frivolous, effeminate, cowardly, irresolute; from these qualities a prince must guard himself as if from a reef, and he must strive to make everyone recognize in his actions greatness, spirit, dignity, and strength; and concerning the private affairs of his subjects, he must insist that his decision be irrevocable; and he should maintain himself in such a way that no man could imagine that he can deceive or cheat him.

26 That prince who projects such an opinion of himself is greatly esteemed; and it is difficult to conspire against a man with such a reputation and difficult to attack him, provided that he is understood to be of great merit and revered by his subjects. For a prince must have two fears: one, internal, concerning his subjects; the other, external, concerning foreign powers. From the latter he can defend himself by his good troops and friends; and he will always have good friends if he has good troops; and internal affairs will always be stable when external affairs are stable, provided that they are not already disturbed by a conspiracy; and even if external conditions change, if he is properly organized and lives as I have said and does not lose control of himself, he will always be able to withstand every attack, just as I said that Nabis the Spartan did. But concerning his subjects, when external affairs do not change, he has to fear that they may

conspire secretly: the prince secures himself from this by avoiding being hated or despised and by keeping the people satisfied with him; this is a necessary matter, as was treated above at length. And one of the most powerful remedies a prince has against conspiracies is not to be hated by the masses; for a man who plans a conspiracy always believes that he will satisfy the people by killing the prince; but when he thinks he might anger them, he cannot work up the courage to undertake such a deed; for the problems on the side of the conspirators are countless. And experience demonstrates that conspiracies have been many but few have been concluded successfully; for anyone who conspires cannot be alone, nor can he find companions except from amongst those whom he believes to be dissatisfied; and as soon as you have uncovered your intent to one dissatisfied man, you give him the means to make himself happy, since he can have everything he desires by uncovering the plot; so much is this so that, seeing a sure gain on the one hand and one doubtful and full of danger on the other, if he is to maintain faith with you he has to be either an unusually good friend or a completely determined enemy of the prince. And to treat the matter briefly, I say that on the part of the conspirator there is nothing but fear, jealousy, and the thought of punishment that terrifies him; but on the part of the prince there is the majesty of the principality, the laws, the defenses of friends and the state to protect him; so that, with the good will of the people added to all these things, it is impossible for anyone to be so rash as to plot against him. For, where usually a conspirator has to be afraid before he executes his evil deed, in this case he must be afraid, having the people as an enemy, even after the crime is performed, nor can he hope to find any refuge because of this.

27 One could cite countless examples on this subject; but I want to satisfy myself with only one which occurred during the time of our fathers. Messer Annibale Bentivogli, prince of Bologna and grandfather of the present Messer Annibale, was murdered by the Canneschi family, who conspired against him; he left behind no heir except Messer Giovanni, then only a baby. As soon as this murder occurred, the people rose up and killed all the Canneschi. This came about because of the good will that the house of the Bentivogli enjoyed in those days; this good will was so great that with Annibale dead, and there being no one of that family left in the city who could rule Bologna, the Bolognese people, having heard that in Florence

there was one of the Bentivogli blood who was believed until that time to be the son of a blacksmith, went to Florence to find him, and they gave him the control of that city; it was ruled by him until Messer Giovanni became of age to rule.

28 I conclude, therefore, that a prince must be little concerned with conspiracies when the people are well disposed toward him; but when the populace is hostile and regards him with hatred, he must fear everything and everyone. And well-organized states and wise princes have, with great diligence, taken care not to anger the nobles and to satisfy the common people and keep them contented; for this is one of the most important concerns that a prince has.

Of Drunkenness

MICHEL DE MONTAIGNE

Michel Eyquem de Montaigne (1533–1592) is considered the creator of the personal essay, which features an informal, conversational style. Montaigne was born in his wealthy family's castle near Bordeaux. He studied law, practiced briefly, and worked as a civil servant, but he devoted most of his life to writing. He did serve as mayor of Bordeaux from 1581 to 1585.

The style of his writing is primarily the self-portrait of personal opinion, but his ideas are so universal that readers find themselves nodding in agreement with his sentiments. He decorates his essays with concrete and elaborate imagery to bring alive his observations and convictions.

In "Of the Inconsistency of Our Actions," he surmises, "Our ordinary practice is to follow the inclinations of our appetite, to the left, to the right, uphill and down, as the wind of circumstance carries us. We think of what we want only the moment we want it, and we change like that animal which takes the color of the place you set it on." Like all humans, he admits to being both chaste and lascivious, talkative and taciturn, tough and delicate, clever and stupid. He argues ultimately that "we must probe inside" each person to "discover what springs set men in motion." He closes, however, with this humorous line: "But since this is an arduous and hazardous undertaking, I wish fewer people would meddle with it."

In "Of Drunkenness," he complains "the worst condition of man is when he loses knowledge and control of himself," a result of wine and strong drink. Yet he argues the benefits of strong drink in moderation. He says, "I cannot understand . . . how people come to prolong the pleasure of drinking beyond their thirst, and forge themselves in their imagination an artificial and unnatural appetite."

1 The world is nothing but variety and dissimilarity. Vices are all alike in that they are all vices, and perhaps this is the way the Stoics understand it. But although they are equally vices, they are not equal vices. And it is not credible that the man who has transgressed the limits by a hundred paces,

> Short of which or beyond which there is no right path,
>
> HORACE

is in as good condition as the one who is only ten paces beyond; nor is it credible that sacrilege is no worse than the theft of a cabbage from our garden:

> Nor will reason convince me that the sin's the same
> To trample someone's cabbages, as without shame
> To rob by night the sacred temples of the gods.
>
> HORACE

There is as much diversity in this as in anything else.

2 Confusion about the order and measurement of sins is dangerous. Murderers, traitors, tyrants, gain too much by it. It is not right that their conscience should be relieved because some other man is indolent, or lascivious, or less assiduous in his devotions. Each man lays weight on his neighbor's sin and lightens his own. Even our teachers often rank sins badly, in my opinion.

3 As Socrates used to say that the principal function of wisdom was to distinguish good things from bad, so we lesser men, who even at our best are always tainted with vice, should say the same thing about the science of distinguishing among the vices; if we do not make this distinction very nicely, the virtuous man and the wicked man will remain confused and unrecognized.

4 Now drunkenness, among the others, seems to me a gross and brutish vice. The mind has more of a part in the others; and there are vices that have about them something indefinably noble, if we must call it that. There are some that involve knowledge, diligence, valor, prudence, skill, and subtlety; this one is all bodily and earthy. Thus the grossest nation in existence today is the only one that holds it in esteem. The other vices affect the understanding; this one overturns it, and stuns the body:

> When we are conquered by the strength of wine,
> Our limbs grow heavy, our legs intertwine;
> With sodden mind, slow tongue, and swimming
> eyes,
> We reel amid the hiccups, brawls and cries.
>
> LUCRETIUS

The worst condition of man is when he loses knowledge and control of himself.

5 And they say among other things that just as must, fermenting in a vessel, pushes to the top all these is on the bottom, so wine, in those who have taken it in excess, uncorks the most intimate secrets:

> In Bacchic revel
> The sage to you his cares
> And secret counsel bares.
>
> HORACE

6 Josephus tells how he wormed the secrets out of a certain ambassador that the enemy had sent to him by having him drink his fill. However, Augustus confided his most private affairs to Lucius Piso, who conquered Thrace, and never found himself mistaken about him; nor was Tiberius mistaken about Cossus, to whom he unburdened himself of all his plans; though we know both to have been so subject to wine that they often had to be carried drunk out of the Senate,

> His veins, as always, swol'n with wine of yesterday.
>
> VIRGIL

And they confided the plan to kill Caesar as trustingly to Cimber, although he often got drunk, as to Cassius, a water drinker. Wherefore he retorted wittily: "I should bear up under a tyrant, I who cannot bear up under my wine!" We see our Germans, drowned in wine, remember their quarters, the watchword, and their rank:

Steeped though they are in wine, drunk, staggering,
Beating them down is still no easy thing.
JUVENAL

7 I should not have believed in a drunkenness so deep, so dead and buried, if I had not read of this instance of it in the histories. Attalus, having invited Pausanias to supper in order to do him some notable indignity—that same Pausanias who for this same reason later killed Philip, king of Macedon, a king who by his fine qualities bore witness to the education he had received in the house and company of Epaminondas—made him drink so much that he could abandon his body insensibly, like the body of some whore under a hedge, to the muleteers and a number of vile slaves of Attalus' household. And I learned from a lady whom I hold in singular honor and esteem that near Bordeaux (toward Castres, where her house is) a village woman, a widow of chaste reputation, feeling the first inklings of pregnancy, told her neighbors that she would think she was with child if she had a husband. But as the occasion of this suspicion grew from day to day and finally became evident, she brought herself to have it announced at the service in her church that if anyone would admit the deed, she promised to pardon him and, if he saw fit, to marry him. A young farmhand of hers, emboldened by this proclamation, declared that he had found her, one holiday when she had taken her wine very freely, so fast asleep by her fireplace, and in so indecent a posture, that he had been able to enjoy her without waking her. They are still alive and married to each other.

8 It is certain that antiquity did not strongly decry this vice. Indeed, the writings of several philosophers speak of it very mildly, and even among the Stoics there are some who recommend that we allow ourselves sometimes to drink our fill, and get drunk in order to relax the soul:

In this contest like others, so they say,
The great Socrates bore the prize away.
MAXIMIANUS

9 That censor and corrector of others, Cato, was reproached for drinking well:

Old Cato's virtue drew from wine,
So we are told, a glow more fine.
HORACE

10 Cyrus, such a renowned king, to put himself ahead of his brother Artaxerxes, alleged among other things in his own praise that he could drink much better. And in the best-regulated and best-governed nations this test of drinking one's fill was much in use. I have heard Silvius, an excellent doctor from Paris, say that to keep the digestive powers from getting lazy, it is good to rouse them once a month by this excess, and stimulate them to keep them from getting sluggish. And they say that the Persians used to consult about their principal affairs after wine.

11 My taste and constitution are more inimical to this vice than my reason. For, quite aside from the fact that I easily submit my beliefs to the authority of ancient opinions, I find it indeed a loose and stupid vice, but less malicious and harmful than the others, which almost all clash more directly with society in general. And if we cannot give ourselves pleasure without its costing us something, as they maintain, I find that this vice costs our conscience less than the others. Moreover, it is not hard to prepare for and find: a consideration not to be despised.

12 A man advanced in dignity and age counted drink among the three principal comforts that he used to say he had left in life. But he took it in the wrong way. Fastidiousness is to be avoided in it, and careful selection of wines. If you make your pleasure depend on drinking good wine, you condemn yourself to the pain of sometimes drinking bad wine. We must have a less exacting and freer taste. To be a good drinker, one must not have so delicate a palate. The Germans drink almost all wines with equal pleasure. Their aim is to swallow rather than to taste. They have much the better of the bargain. Their pleasure is much more plentiful and ready at hand.

13 Second, to drink French style, at two meals and moderately, for fear of your health, is to restrain the god's favor too much. You need more time and persistence. The ancients spent whole nights at this exercise, and often added the days. And so we should make our daily drinking habits more expansive and vigorous. I have seen a great lord in my time, a personage of high enterprises and famous successes, who, without effort and in the course of his ordinary meals, used to drink scarcely fewer than ten quarts of wine, and showed himself on leaving only too wise and circumspect, at the expense of our affairs.

14 The pleasure we want to reckon on for the course of our life should occupy more space in it. Like shop apprentices and workmen, we should refuse no chance to drink, and have this desire always in our

head. It seems that every day we cut down on our eating and drinking, and that in our houses, as I remember from my childhood, lunches, suppers, and collations used to be much more frequent and usual than they are now. Could it be that in some respects we are moving toward improvement? Surely not. The fact is that we are much more addicted to lechery than were our fathers. These two occupations interfere with each other in their vigor. Lechery has weakened our stomach on the one hand; and on the other hand, sobriety serves to make us more lively and lusty for the exercise of love.

It is marvelous what stories I have heard my father tell of the chastity of his day. He was the man to tell them, being very well suited to the service of the ladies, both by nature and by art. He spoke little and well, and sprinkled his language with ornamental expressions from books in the modern vernaculars, especially Spanish; and among the Spanish his usual reading was the book they call Marcus Aurelius. His bearing was one of gentle, humble, and very modest gravity. A singular care for neatness and propriety of person and dress, whether afoot or on horseback. A prodigious fidelity in keeping his word, and a general conscientiousness and scrupulousness leaning rather toward than away from superstition. For a small man, full of vigor, and straight and well-proportioned in stature. An attractive face, inclining to brown. Adroit and distinguished in all gentlemanly exercises. I have even seen some canes filled with lead, with which they say he exercised his arms to prepare for throwing the bar or the stone, or for fencing, and some shoes with leaded soles to train him to be lighter in running and jumping. Of his vaulting, he has left some small miracles in people's memory. I have seen him, past sixty, put our agility to shame: leap into the saddle in his furred gown, do a turn over the table on his thumb, hardly ever go up to his room without taking three or four steps at a time. On this subject of mine, he used to say that in a whole province there was scarcely one woman of quality who had a bad reputation; and he would tell of remarkable intimacies, especially of his own, with respectable women, free from any suspicion. And of himself he solemnly swore that he had come to his marriage a virgin. And yet he had taken a very long part in the Italian wars, of which he has left a diary in his own hand, following what happened point by point, in both public and his own private matters. Consequently he married well along in age, in the year 1528, which was his thirty-third, on his return from Italy. Let's get back to our bottles.

16 The discomforts of old age, which need some support and refreshment, might reasonably make me wish to be a better drinker; for drinking is almost the last pleasure that the years steal from us. Natural liveliness, good fellows say, first starts in the feet: this is true of children. From there it rises to the middle region, where it plants itself for a long time, and produces there, in my opinion, the only true pleasures of bodily life; the other pleasures are asleep by comparison. Toward the end, like a vapor that rises upward and is exhaled, it arrives at the gullet, where it makes its last stop.

17 I cannot understand, for all that, how people come to prolong the pleasure of drinking beyond their thirst, and forge themselves in their imagination an artificial and unnatural appetite. My stomach would not go that far; it has enough trouble taking care of what it takes for its need. My disposition is not to set store by drinking except after eating; and for that reason my last drink is almost always the biggest. Anacharsis was amazed that the Greeks drank in bigger glasses at the end of the meal than at the beginning. That was, I suppose, for the same reason that the Germans do it, who then begin their drinking bouts.

18 Plato forbids children to drink wine before eighteen, and to get drunk before forty; but those who have passed forty he orders to enjoy drinking, and to mix freely in their banquets the influence of Dionysus, that good god who restores gaiety to all men and youth to the old, who softens and mollifies the passions of the soul as iron is softened by fire. And in his *Laws* he finds such drinking parties useful, provided there is a leader of the group to control and regulate them. For drunkenness to Plato is a good and certain test of each and every man's nature, and at the same time suited to give older people the courage to make merry in dances and music, useful pastimes that they shy away from in a sober mood. He adds that wine is capable of giving temperance to the soul and health to the body. However, he likes these restrictions, borrowed partly from the Carthaginians: that it be used sparingly on a military expedition; that every magistrate and every judge abstain from it when he is on the point of carrying out his duties and consulting on public affairs; that the day, a time due to other occupations, should not be spent in drinking, or a night when we intend to beget children.

19 They say that the philosopher Stilpo, weighed down with old age, deliberately hastened his end by drinking undiluted wine. The same

cause, but not by his own design, also stifled the worn-out vital forces of the philosopher Arcesilaus.

20 But it is an old and amusing question whether the soul of the sage is such that it would yield to the power of wine,

> If wine can storm the very fort of wisdom.
> HORACE

To how much vanity are we driven by the high opinion we have of ourselves! The best-regulated soul in the world has only too much to do to stay on its feet and keep itself from collapsing to the ground through its own weakness. Out of a thousand souls, there is not one that is straight and composed for a single moment in a lifetime; and it may be questioned, given the soul's natural condition, whether it can ever be so. But when straightness and composure are combined with constancy, then the soul attains its ultimate perfection; I mean even if nothing should jar it, which a thousand accidents can do.

21 Look at Lucretius, that great poet; all his philosophizing and self-discipline cannot prevent him from being driven insane by an aphrodisiac. Is there anybody who believes that an apoplexy will not stun Socrates as well as a porter? Some have been driven by an illness to forget their very name, and a slight wound has overturned the judgment of others.

22 For all his wisdom, the sage is still a man: what is there more vulnerable, more wretched, and more null? Wisdom does not overcome our natural limitations:

> Over the whole body therefore we see arise
> Pallor and sweat; the tongue is tied, and the voice dies,
> The eyes grow dim, ears ring, the limbs give way; the whole
> At last collapses from the terror of the soul.
> LUCRETIUS

The sage must blink his eyes at the blow that threatens him; if you set him on the edge of a precipice, he must shudder like a child. Nature has willed to reserve to herself these slight marks of her authority, invincible to our reason and to Stoic virtue, in order to teach man his mortality and frailty. He pales with fear, he reddens with shame; he complains at a sharp attack of the colic, if not in a desperate and clamorous voice, at least with a voice broken and hoarse:

> Let him think nothing human foreign to him.
> ADAPTED FROM TERENCE

The poets, who invent everything as they please, do not dare to exempt their heroes even from tears:

> Thus weeping does he speak, and bids his fleet depart.
> VIRGIL

Enough for the sage to curb and moderate his inclinations; for to do away with them is not in him.

23 Even that Plutarch of ours, so perfect and excellent a judge of human actions, on seeing Brutus and Torquatus kill their children, came to doubt whether virtue could go that far, and to wonder whether those personages had not rather been motivated by some other passion. All actions outside the ordinary limits are subject to sinister interpretation, inasmuch as our taste responds no more to what is above it than to what is below.

24 Let us leave aside that other sect that makes an express profession of pride. But even in the sect that is considered the softest, we hear these boasts of Metrodorus: *Fortune, I have anticipated you and seized you; I have cut off all your access, so that you cannot come near me* [Cicero]. Anaxarchus, who had been laid in a stone trough by the orders of Nicocreon, tyrant of Cyprus, and fatally beaten with an iron mallet, does not stop saying: "Strike, break; it is not Anaxarchus but his shell that you are pounding." Our martyrs were heard crying out to the tyrant in the midst of the flame: "It's roasted enough on that side, chop it up, eat it, it's cooked, start on the other side!" And that boy in Josephus, all torn by biting pincers and pierced by the awls of Antiochus, still defied him, crying out with a firm and steady voice: "Tyrant, you're wasting your time, here I am still at ease; where is that pain, where are those torments, with which you were threatening me? Is this all you know how to do? My constancy gives you more pain than I feel from your cruelty. O cowardly wretch, you are giving up, and I am growing stronger; make me complain, make me bend, make me yield, if you can; give your satellites and your executioners courage; see, they have lost heart, they can do no more; arm them, goad them!" When we hear such defiance, surely

we must confess that in these souls there is some alteration, some frenzy, however holy it be.

25 When we come to such Stoic sallies as *I would rather be insane than voluptuous,* a saying of Antisthenes; when Sextius tells us that he would rather be pierced through by pain than by sensual pleasure; when Epicurus undertakes to be caressed by the gout, refuses rest and health, cheerfully defies ills, and, scorning the less severe pains and disdaining to struggle with them, invokes and wishes for pains strong, biting, and worthy of him—

> Among his harmless flocks, it is his prayer to meet
> A foaming boar, or tawny lion from the hills
> VIRGIL

—who does not judge that these are the sallies of a runaway courage? Our soul from its abode could not reach so high. It must leave its dwelling place and rise, and, taking the bit in its teeth, abduct its man and carry him off so far that afterward he is himself astonished at his deeds; as, in exploits of war, the heat of combat often impels high-souled soldiers to go through such dangers that when they have come back to themselves they are the first to be struck with amazement; as also poets are often rapt in wonder at their own works and no longer recognize the track over which they ran so fine a race. That is what is called poetic frenzy and madness. And as Plato says that a sedate man knocks in vain on the door of poetry, so Aristotle says that no excellent soul is free from an admixture of madness. And he is right to call madness any transport, however laudable, that transcends our own judgment and reason; inasmuch as wisdom is an orderly management of our soul, which she conducts with measure and proportion and is responsible for.

26 Plato argues thus: that the faculty of prophecy is above us; that we must be outside of ourselves when we exercise it; that our wisdom must be obscured either by sleep or by some illness, or lifted from its place by some celestial rapture.

The Four Idols

FRANCIS BACON

Francis Bacon (1561–1626) lived in a great age; his contemporaries were William Shakespeare, Sir Francis Drake, Queen Elizabeth I, and other notable figures. He served for a time as Lord High Chancellor of England. Writing was a by-product of his Renaissance spirit. His *Essays* (1597) expressed his position on many aspects of life, from love and marriage to envy and human failure. His *Novum Organum* (1620) was his effort to update Aristotle's treatises on philosophy and political statehood. Bacon felt that the new age needed less abstract logic and more scientific inquiry.

In "The Four Idols," which appeared in *Novum Organum,* Bacon examines four prejudices that human beings bring to scientific inquiry: (1) that our perceptions are true and can be trusted; (2) that our experience makes us wise; (3) that language provides us with superior knowledge; and (4) that we tend always to believe previous scientific theories and philosophical assertions. To replace these prejudices, he argues that we must constantly challenge existing theories by careful scientific examination. His theories set in motion the use of *empirical* methods for solving problems. That is, instead of assuming that we know the truth, we must advance a generalization and then try to prove it by collecting evidence. The collected data will enable us, inductively, to arrive at the truth.

1 The idols and false notions which are now in possession of the human understanding, and have taken deep root therein, not only so beset men's minds that truth can hardly find entrance, but even after entrance obtained, they will again in the very instauration of the sciences meet and trouble us, unless men being forewarned of the danger fortify themselves as far as may be against their assaults.

2 There are four classes of idols which beset men's minds. To these for distinction's sake I have assigned names—calling the first class *Idols of the Tribe;* the second, *Idols of the Cave;* the third, *Idols of the Marketplace;* the fourth, *Idols of the Theater.*

3 The formation of ideas and axioms by true induction is no doubt the proper remedy to be applied for the keeping off and clearing away of idols. To point them out, however, is of great use; for the doctrine of idols is to the interpretation of nature what the doctrine of the refutation of sophisms is to common logic.

4 The *Idols of the Tribe* have their foundation in human nature itself, and in the tribe or race of men. For it is a false assertion that the sense of man is the measure of things. On the contrary, all perceptions as well of the sense as of the mind are according to the measure of the individual and not according to the measure of the universe. And the human understanding is like a false mirror, which, receiving rays irregularly, distorts and discolors the nature of things by mingling its own nature with it.

5 The *Idols of the Cave* are the idols of the individual man. For everyone (besides the errors common to human nature in general) has a cave or den of his own, which refracts and discolors the light of nature; owing either to his own proper and peculiar nature; or to his education and conversation with others; or to the reading of books, and the authority of those whom he esteems and admires; or to the differences of impressions, accordingly as they take place in a mind preoccupied and predisposed or in a mind indifferent and settled; or the like. So that the spirit of man (according as it is meted out to different individuals) is in fact a thing variable and full of perturbation, and governed as it were by chance. Whence it was well observed by Heraclitus that men look for sciences in their own lesser worlds, and not in the greater or common world.

6 There are also idols formed by the intercourse and association of men with each other, which I call *Idols of the Marketplace,* on account of the commerce and consort of men there. For it is by discourse that men associate; and words are imposed according to the apprehension

of the vulgar. And therefore the ill and unfit choice of words wonderfully obstructs the understanding. Nor do the definitions or explanations wherewith in some things learned men are wont to guard and defend themselves, by any means set the matter right. But words plainly force and overrule the understanding, and throw all into confusion and lead men away into numberless empty controversies and idle fancies.

7 Lastly, there are idols which have immigrated into men's minds from the various dogmas of philosophies, and also from wrong laws of demonstration. These I call *Idols of the Theater;* because in my judgment all the received systems are but so many stage-plays, representing worlds of their own creation after an unreal and scenic fashion. Nor is it only of the systems now in vogue, or only of the ancient sects and philosophies, that I speak; for many more plays of the same kind may yet be composed and in like artificial manner set forth; seeing that errors the most widely different have nevertheless causes for the most part alike. Neither again do I mean this only of entire systems, but also of many principles and axioms in science, which by tradition, credulity, and negligence, have come to be received.

8 But of these several kinds of idols I must speak more largely and exactly, that the understanding may be duly cautioned.

9 The human understanding is of its own nature prone to suppose the existence of more order and regularity in the world than it finds. And though there be many things in nature which are singular and unmatched, yet it devises for them parallels and conjugates and relatives which do not exist. Hence the fiction that all celestial bodies move in perfect circles; spirals and dragons being (except in name) utterly rejected. Hence too the element of fire with its orb is brought in, to make up the square with the other three which the sense perceives. Hence also the ratio of density of the so-called elements is arbitrarily fixed at ten to one. And so on of other dreams. And these fancies affect not dogmas only, but simple notions also.

10 The human understanding when it has once adopted an opinion (either as being the received opinion or as being agreeable to itself) draws all things else to support and agree with it. And though there be a greater number and weight of instances to be found on the other side, yet these it either neglects and despises, or else by some distinction sets aside and rejects; in order that by this great and pernicious predetermination the authority of its former conclusions may remain inviolate. And therefore it was a good answer that was made by one who when they showed him hanging in a temple a

picture of those who had paid their vows as having escaped shipwreck, and would have him say whether he did not now acknowledge the power of the gods—"Ay," asked he again,"but where are they painted that were drowned after their vows?" And such is the way of all superstition, whether in astrology, dreams, omens, divine judgments, or the like; wherein men having a delight in such vanities, mark the events where they are fulfilled, but where they fail, though this happen much oftener, neglect and pass them by. But with far more subtlety does this mischief insinuate itself into philosophy and the sciences; in which the first conclusion colors and brings into conformity with itself all that come after, though far sounder and better. Besides, independently of that delight and vanity which I have described, it is the peculiar and perpetual error of the human intellect to be more moved and excited by affirmatives than by negatives; whereas it ought properly to hold itself indifferently disposed towards both alike. Indeed, in the establishment of any true axiom, the negative instance is the more forcible of the two.

11 The human understanding is moved by those things most which strike and enter the mind simultaneously and suddenly, and so fill the imagination; and then it feigns and supposes all other things to be somehow, though it cannot see how, similar to those few things by which it is surrounded. But for that going to and fro to remote and heterogeneous instances, by which axioms are tried as in the fire, the intellect is altogether slow and unfit, unless it be forced thereto by severe laws and overruling authority.

12 The human understanding is unquiet; it cannot stop or rest, and still presses onward, but in vain. Therefore it is that we cannot conceive of any end or limit to the world, but always as of necessity it occurs to us that there is something beyond. Neither again can it be conceived how eternity has flowed down to the present day; for that distinction which is commonly received of infinity in time past and in time to come can by no means hold; for it would thence follow that one infinity is greater than another, and that infinity is wasting away and tending to become finite. The like subtlety arises touching the infinite divisibility of lines, from the same inability of thought to stop. But this inability interferes more mischievously in the discovery of causes: for although the most general principles in nature ought to be held merely positive, as they are discovered, and cannot with truth be referred to a cause; nevertheless, the human understanding being unable to rest still seeks something prior in the

order of nature. And then it is that in struggling towards that which is further off, it falls back upon that which is more nigh at hand; namely, on final causes: which have relation clearly to the nature of man rather than to the nature of the universe, and from this source have strangely defiled philosophy. But he is no less an unskilled and shallow philosopher who seeks causes of that which is most general, than he who in things subordinate and subaltern omits to do so.

13 The human understanding is no dry light, but receives an infusion from the will and affections; whence proceed sciences which may be called "sciences as one would." For what a man had rather were true he more readily believes. Therefore he rejects difficult things from impatience of research; sober things, because they narrow hope; the deeper things of nature, from superstition; the light of experience, from arrogance and pride, lest his mind should seem to be occupied with things mean and transitory; things not commonly believed, out of deference to the opinion of the vulgar. Numberless in short are the ways, and sometimes imperceptible, in which the affections color and infect the understanding.

14 But by far the greatest hindrance and aberration of the human understanding proceeds from the dullness, incompetency, and deceptions of the senses; in that things which strike the sense outweigh things which do not immediately strike it, though they be more important. Hence it is that speculation commonly ceases where sight ceases; insomuch that of things invisible there is little or no observation. Hence all the working of the spirits enclosed in tangible bodies lies hid and unobserved of men. So also all the more subtle changes of form in the parts of coarser substances (which they commonly call alteration, though it is in truth local motion through exceedingly small spaces) is in like manner unobserved. And yet unless these two things just mentioned be searched out and brought to light, nothing great can be achieved in nature, as far as the production of works is concerned. So again the essential nature of our common air, and of all bodies less dense than air (which are very many) is almost unknown. For the sense by itself is a thing infirm and erring; neither can instruments for enlarging or sharpening the senses do much; but all the truer kind of interpretation of nature is effected by instances and experiments fit and apposite; wherein the sense decides touching the experiment only, and the experiment touching the point in nature and the thing itself.

15 The human understanding is of its own nature prone to abstrac-

tions and gives a substance and reality to things which are fleeting. But to resolve nature into abstractions is less to our purpose than to dissect her into parts; as did the school of Democritus, which went further into nature than the rest. Matter rather than forms should be the object of our attention, its configurations and changes of configuration, and simple action, and law of action or motion; for forms are figments of the human mind, unless you will call those laws of action forms.

16 Such then are the idols which I call *Idols of the Tribe;* and which take their rise either from the homogeneity of the substance of the human spirit, or from its preoccupation, or from its narrowness, or from its restless motion, or from an infusion of the affections, or from the incompetency of the senses, or from the mode of impression.

17 The *Idols of the Cave* take their rise in the peculiar constitution, mental or bodily, of each individual; and also in education, habit, and accident. Of this kind there is a great number and variety; but I will instance those the pointing out of which contains the most important caution, and which have most effect in disturbing the clearness of the understanding.

18 Men become attached to certain particular sciences and speculations, either because they fancy themselves the authors and inventors thereof, or because they have bestowed the greatest pains upon them and become most habituated to them. But men of this kind, if they betake themselves to philosophy and contemplations of a general character, distort and color them in obedience to their former fancies; a thing especially to be noticed in Aristotle, who made his natural philosophy a mere bondservant to his logic, thereby rendering it contentious and well nigh useless. The race of chemists again out of a few experiments of the furnace have built up a fantastic philosophy, framed with reference to a few things; and Gilbert also, after he had employed himself most laboriously in the study and observation of the loadstone, proceeded at once to construct an entire system in accordance with his favorite subject.

19 There is one principal and, as it were, radical distinction between different minds, in respect of philosophy and the sciences, which is this: that some minds are stronger and apter to mark the differences of things, others to mark their resemblances. The steady and acute mind can fix its contemplations and dwell and fasten on the subtlest distinctions: the lofty and discursive mind recognizes and puts together the finest and most general resemblances. Both kinds how-

ever easily err in excess, by catching the one at gradations, the other at shadows.

20 There are found some minds given to an extreme admiration of antiquity, others to an extreme love and appetite for novelty; but few so duly tempered that they can hold the mean, neither carping at what has been well laid down by the ancients, nor despising what is well introduced by the moderns. This however turns to the great injury of the sciences and philosophy; since these affectations of antiquity and novelty are the humors of partisans rather than judgments; and truth is to be sought for not in the felicity of any age, which is an unstable thing, but in the light of nature and experience, which is eternal. These factions therefore must be abjured, and care must be taken that the intellect be not hurried by them into assent.

21 Contemplations of nature and of bodies in their simple form break up and distract the understanding, while contemplations of nature and bodies in their composition and configuration overpower and dissolve the understanding: a distinction well seen in the school of Leucippus and Democritus as compared with the other philosophies. For that school is so busied with the particles that it hardly attends to the structure; while the others are so lost in admiration of the structure that they do not penetrate to the simplicity of nature. These kinds of contemplation should therefore be alternated and taken by turns; that so the understanding may be rendered at once penetrating and comprehensive, and the inconveniences above mentioned, with the idols which proceed from them, may be avoided.

22 Let such then be our provision and contemplative prudence for keeping off and dislodging the *Idols of the Cave,* which grow for the most part either out of the predominance of a favorite subject, or out of an excessive tendency to compare or to distinguish, or out of partiality for particular ages, or out of the largeness or minuteness of the objects contemplated. And generally let every student of nature take this as a rule—that whatever his mind seizes and dwells upon with peculiar satisfaction is to be held in suspicion, and that so much the more care is to be taken in dealing with such questions to keep the understanding even and clear.

23 But the *Idols of the Marketplace* are the most troublesome of all: idols which have crept into the understanding through the alliances of words and names. For men believe that their reason governs words; but it is also true that words react on the understanding; and this it is that has rendered philosophy and the sciences sophistical and

inactive. Now words, being commonly framed and applied according to the capacity of the vulgar, follow those lines of division which are most obvious to the vulgar understanding. And whenever an understanding of greater acuteness or a more diligent observation would alter those lines to suit the true divisions of nature, words stand in the way and resist the change. Whence it comes to pass that the high and formal discussions of learned men end oftentimes in disputes about words and names; with which (according to the use and wisdom of the mathematicians) it would be more prudent to begin, and so by means of definitions reduce them to order. Yet even definitions cannot cure this evil in dealing with natural and material things; since the definitions themselves consist of words, and those words beget others: so that it is necessary to recur to individual instances, and those in due series and order; as I shall say presently when I come to the method and scheme for the formation of notions and axioms.

24 The idols imposed by words on the understanding are of two kinds. They are either names of things which do not exist (for as there are things left unnamed through lack of observation, so likewise are there names which result from fantastic suppositions and to which nothing in reality responds), or they are names of things which exist, but yet confused and ill-defined, and hastily and irregularly derived from realities. Of the former kind are Fortune, the Prime Mover, Planetary Orbits, Element of Fire, and like fictions which owe their origin to false and idle theories. And this class of idols is more easily expelled, because to get rid of them it is only necessary that all theories should be steadily rejected and dismissed as obsolete.

25 But the other class, which springs out of a faulty and unskillful abstraction, is intricate and deeply rooted. Let us take for example such a word as *humid;* and see how far the several things which the word is used to signify agree with each other; and we shall find the word *humid* to be nothing else than a mark loosely and confusedly applied to denote a variety of actions which will not bear to be reduced to any constant meaning. For it both signifies that which easily spreads itself round any other body; and that which in itself is indeterminate and cannot solidize; and that which readily yields in every direction; and that which easily divides and scatters itself; and that which easily unites and collects itself; and that which readily flows and is put in motion; and that which readily clings to another body and wets it; and that which is easily reduced to a liquid, or

being solid easily melts. Accordingly when you come to apply the word—if you take it in one sense, flame is humid; if in another, air is not humid; if in another, fine dust is humid; if in another, glass is humid. So that it is easy to see that the notion is taken by abstraction only from water and common and ordinary liquids, without any due verification.

26 There are however in words certain degrees of distortion and error. One of the least faulty kinds is that of names of substances, especially of lowest species and well-deduced (for the notion of *chalk* and of *mud* is good, of *earth* bad); a more faulty kind is that of actions, as *to generate, to corrupt, to alter;* the most faulty is of qualities (except such as are the immediate objects of the sense), as *heavy, light, rare, dense,* and the like. Yet in all these cases some notions are of necessity a little better than others, in proportion to the greater variety of subjects that fall within the range of the human sense.

27 But the *Idols of the Theater* are not innate, nor do they steal into the understanding secretly, but are plainly impressed and received into the mind from the play-books of philosophical systems and the perverted rules of demonstration. To attempt refutations in this case would be merely inconsistent with what I have already said: for since we agree neither upon principles nor upon demonstrations, there is no place for argument. And this is so far well, inasmuch as it leaves the honor of the ancients untouched. For they are no wise disparaged—the question between them and me being only as to the way. For as the saying is, the lame man who keeps the right road outstrips the runner who takes a wrong one. Nay, it is obvious that when a man runs the wrong way, the more active and swift he is the further he will go astray.

28 But the course I propose for the discovery of sciences is such as leaves but little to the acuteness and strength of wits, but places all wits and understandings nearly on a level. For as in the drawing of a straight line or perfect circle, much depends on the steadiness and practice of the hand, if it be done by aim of hand only, but if with the aid of rule or compass, little or nothing; so is it exactly with my plan. But though particular confutations would be of no avail, yet touching the sects and general divisions of such systems I must say something; something also touching the external signs which show that they are unsound; and finally something touching the causes of such great infelicity and of such lasting and general agreement in error; that so the access to truth may be made less difficult, and the

human understanding may the more willingly submit to its purgation and dismiss its idols.

29 *Idols of the Theater*, or of systems, are many, and there can be and perhaps will be yet many more. For were it not that now for many ages men's minds have been busied with religion and theology; and were it not that civil governments, especially monarchies, have been averse to such novelties, even in matters speculative; so that men labor therein to the peril and harming of their fortunes—not only unrewarded, but exposed also to contempt and envy; doubtless there would have arisen many other philosophical sects like to those which in great variety flourished once among the Greeks. For as on the phenomena of the heavens many hypotheses may be constructed, so likewise (and more also) many various dogmas may be set up and established on the phenomena of philosophy. And in the plays of this philosophical theater you may observe the same thing which is found in the theater of the poets, that stories invented for the stage are more compact and elegant, and more as one would wish them to be, than true stories out of history.

30 In general, however, there is taken for the material of philosophy either a great deal out of a few things, or a very little out of many things; so that on both sides philosophy is based on too narrow a foundation of experiment and natural history, and decides on the authority of too few cases. For the rational school of philosophers snatches from experience a variety of common instances, neither duly ascertained nor diligently examined and weighed, and leaves all the rest to meditation and agitation of wit.

31 There is also another class of philosophers, who having bestowed much diligent and careful labor on a few experiments, have thence made bold to educe and construct systems; wresting all other facts in a strange fashion to conformity therewith.

32 And there is yet a third class, consisting of those who out of faith and veneration mix their philosophy with theology and traditions; among whom the vanity of some has gone so far aside as to seek the origin of sciences among spirits and genii. So that this parent stock of errors—this false philosophy—is of three kinds; the sophistical, the empirical, and the superstitious. . . .

33 But the corruption of philosophy by superstition and an admixture of theology is far more widely spread, and does the greatest harm, whether to entire systems or to their parts. For the human understanding is obnoxious to the influence of the imagination no less

than to the influence of common notions. For the contentious and sophistical kind of philosophy ensnares the understanding; but this kind, being fanciful and tumid and half poetical, misleads it more by flattery. For there is in man an ambition of the understanding, no less than of the will, especially in high and lofty spirits.

34 Of this kind we have among the Greeks a striking example in Pythagoras, though he united with it a coarser and more cumbrous superstition; another in Plato and his school, more dangerous and subtle. It shows itself likewise in parts of other philosophies, in the introduction of abstract forms and final causes and first causes, with the omission in most cases of causes intermediate, and the like. Upon this point the greatest caution should be used. For nothing is so mischievous as the apotheosis of error; and it is a very plague of the understanding for vanity to become the object of veneration. Yet in this vanity some of the moderns have with extreme levity indulged so far as to attempt to found a system of natural philosophy on the first chapter of Genesis, on the book of Job, and other parts of the sacred writings; seeking for the dead among the living: which also makes the inhibition and repression of it the more important, because from this unwholesome mixture of things human and divine there arises not only a fantastic philosophy but also an heretical religion. Very meet it is therefore that we be sober-minded, and give to faith that only which is faith's. . . .

35 So much concerning the several classes of Idols, and their equipage: all of which must be renounced and put away with a fixed and solemn determination, and the understanding thoroughly freed and cleansed; the entrance into the kingdom of man, founded on the sciences, being not much other than the entrance into the kingdom of heaven, whereinto none may enter except as a little child.

CLASSIC ESSAYS
OF THE 18*th* AND 19*th*
CENTURIES

The Form Refined

A Modest Proposal

JONATHAN SWIFT

Jonathan Swift (1667–1745) was born in Dublin, Ireland, to English parents. After his education in Dublin, he moved to England and took a position as secretary to Sir William Temple. Feeling confined in that position, he returned to Ireland, where he was ordained and served as a clergyman at Kilroot. Again, he grew restless for the active life in England, so he returned to Temple's service, but he soon returned to Dublin as clergyman at St. Patrick's Cathedral. Thereafter, he made frequent visits to London and became heavily involved in the writing and publishing of political pamphlets, working at times with Addison and Steele (see page 77). He performed several missions in Ireland for Queen Anne, who rewarded him in 1713 by naming him dean of St. Patrick's Cathedral in Dublin. Thereafter, he defended the Irish against encroachments by English politicians.

Among his many works, the most famous remains *Gulliver's Travels*, the story of Lemuel Gulliver, who relates his shipwrecks and adventures in Lilliput, a land of tiny, petty, and miserable people; in Brobdingnag, a land of huge, gross, and disgusting people; in Laputa, a land of highly intellectual people who are utter fools in practical matters; and in Houyhnhnm, a land of intellectual horses and filthy Yahoos (who, in truth, are human beings).

"A Modest Proposal" serves as Swift's wake-up call to the Irish people who, in his eyes, submitted too willingly to abuse from absentee British landlords and to their own pride, vanity, idleness, and lust. By 1729, a long period of drought and economic depression had afflicted Ireland, and beggars by the thousands roamed the city streets and village pathways. Tenant farmers were ignored by large landowners, who lived abroad to avoid taxes and the faces of the starving people. Entire displaced families roamed the countryside. Swift, with biting satire, suggests a radical plan, one that outraged the public into a new awareness of the problem. For a view of Swift's serious answer to Ireland's condition, look closely at paragraph 29.

For Preventing the Children of Poor People in Ireland from Being a Burden to Their Parents or Country, and for Making Them Beneficial to the Public

1 It is a melancholy object to those who walk through this great town or travel in the country, when they see the streets, the roads, and cabin doors, crowded with beggars of the female sex, followed by three, four, or six children, all in rags and importuning every passenger for an alms. These mothers, instead of being able to work for their honest livelihood, are forced to employ all their time in strolling to beg sustenance for their helpless infants, who, as they grow up, either turn thieves for want of work, or leave their dear native country to fight for the Pretender in Spain, or sell themselves to the Barbados.

2 I think it is agreed by all parties that this prodigious number of children in the arms, or on the backs, or at the heels of their mothers, and frequently of their fathers, is in the present deplorable state of the kingdom a very great additional grievance; and therefore whoever could find out a fair, cheap, and easy method of making these children sound, useful members of the commonwealth would deserve so well of the public as to have his statue set up for a preserver of the nation.

3 But my intention is very far from being confined to provide only for the children of professed beggars; it is of a much greater extent, and shall take in the whole number of infants at a certain age who are born of parents in effect as little able to support them as those who demand our charity in the streets.

4 As to my own part, having turned my thoughts for many years upon this important subject, and maturely weighed the several schemes of other projectors, I have always found them grossly mistaken in their computation. It is true, a child just dropped from its dam may be supported by her milk for a solar year, with little other nourishment; at most not above the value of two shillings, which the mother may certainly get, or the value in scraps, by her lawful occupation of begging; and it is exactly at one year that I propose to provide for them in such a manner as instead of being a charge upon their parents or the parish, or wanting food and raiment for the rest of their lives, they shall on the contrary contribute to the feeding, and partly to the clothing, of many thousands.

5 There is likewise another great advantage in my scheme, that it will prevent those voluntary abortions, and that horrid practice of women murdering their bastard children, alas, too frequent among us, sacrificing the poor innocent babes, I doubt, more to avoid the expense than the shame, which would move tears and pity in the most savage and inhuman breast.

6 The number of souls in this kingdom being usually reckoned one million and a half, of these I calculate there may be about two hundred thousand couples whose wives are breeders; from which number I subtract thirty thousand couples who are able to maintain their own children, although I apprehend there cannot be so many under the present distress of the kingdom; but this being granted, there will remain an hundred and seventy thousand breeders. I again subtract fifty thousand for those women who miscarry, or whose children die by accident or disease within the year. There only remain an hundred and twenty thousand children of poor parents annually born. The question therefore is, how this number shall be reared and provided for, which, as I have already said, under the present situation of affairs, is utterly impossible by all the methods hitherto proposed. For we can neither employ them in handicraft or agriculture; we neither build houses (I mean in the country) nor cultivate land. They can very seldom pick up a livelihood stealing till they arrive at six years old, except where they are of towardly parts; although I

confess they learn the rudiments much earlier, during which time they can however be looked upon only as probationers, as I have been informed by a principal gentleman in the country of Cavan, who protested to me that he never knew above one or two instances under the age of six, even in a part of the kingdom so renowned for the quickest proficiency in that art.

7 I am assured by our merchants that a boy or a girl before twelve years old is no salable commodity; and even when they come to this age they will not yield above three pounds, or three pounds and half a crown at most on the Exchange; which cannot turn to account either to the parents or the kingdom, the charge of nutriment and rags having been at least four times that value.

8 I shall now therefore humbly propose my own thoughts, which I hope will not be liable to the least objection.

9 I have been assured by a very knowing American of my acquaintance in London, that a young healthy child well nursed is at a year old a most delicious, nourishing, and wholesome food, whether stewed, roasted, baked, or boiled; and I make no doubt that it will equally serve in a fricassee or a ragout.

10 I do therefore humbly offer it to public consideration that of the hundred and twenty thousand children, already computed, twenty thousand may be reserved for breed, whereof only one fourth part to be males, which is more that we allow to sheep, black cattle, or swine; and my reason is that these children are seldom the fruits of marriage, a circumstance not much regarded by our savages, therefore one male will be sufficient to serve four females. That the remaining hundred thousand may at a year old be offered in sale to the persons of quality and fortune through the kingdom, always advising the mother to let them suck plentifully in the last month, so as to render them plump and fat for a good table. A child will make two dishes at an entertainment for friends; and when the family dines alone, the fore or hind quarter will make a reasonable dish, and seasoned with a little pepper or salt will be very good boiled on the fourth day, especially in winter.

11 I have reckoned upon a medium that a child just born will weigh twelve pounds, and in a solar year if tolerably nursed increaseth to twenty-eight pounds.

12 I grant this food will be somewhat dear, and therefore very proper for landlords, who, as they have already devoured most of the parents, seem to have the best title to the children.

13 Infant's flesh will be in season throughout the year, but more plentiful in March, and a little before and after. For we are told by a grave author, an eminent French physician, that fish being a prolific diet, there are more children born in Roman Catholic countries about nine months after Lent than at any other season; therefore, reckoning a year after Lent, the markets will be more glutted than usual, because the number of popish infants is at least three to one in this kingdom; and therefore it will have one other collateral advantage, by lessening the number of Papists among us.

14 I have already computed the charge of nursing a beggar's child (in which list I reckon all cottagers, laborers, and four-fifths of the farmers) to be about two shillings per annum, rags included; and I believe no gentleman would repine to give ten shillings for the carcass of a good fat child, which, as I have said, will make four dishes of excellent nutritive meat, when he hath only some particular friend or his own family to dine with him. Thus the squire will learn to be a good landlord, and grow popular among the tenants; the mother will have eight shillings net profit, and be fit for work till she produces another child.

15 Those who are more thrifty (as I must confess the times require) may flay the carcass; the skin of which artificially dressed will make admirable gloves for ladies, and summer boots for fine gentlemen.

16 As to our city of Dublin, shambles may be appointed for this purpose in the most convenient parts of it, and butchers we may be assured will not be wanting; although I rather recommend buying the children alive, and dressing them hot from the knife as we do roasting pigs.

17 A very worthy person, a true lover of his country, and whose virtues I highly esteem, was lately pleased in discoursing on this matter to offer a refinement upon my scheme. He said that many gentlemen of his kingdom, having of late destroyed their deer, he conceived that the want of venison might be well supplied by the bodies of young lads and maidens, not exceeding fourteen years of age nor under twelve, so great a number of both sexes in every country being now ready to starve for want of work and service; and these to be disposed of by their parents, if alive, or otherwise by their nearest relations. But with due deference to so excellent a friend and so deserving a patriot, I cannot be altogether in his sentiments; for as to the males, my American acquaintance assured me from frequent experience that their flesh was generally tough and lean,

like that of our schoolboys, by continual exercise, and their taste disagreeable; and to fatten them would not answer the charge. Then as to the females, it would, I think with humble submission, be a loss to the public, because they soon would become breeders themselves; and besides, it is not improbable that some scrupulous people might be apt to censure such a practice (although indeed very unjustly) as a little bordering upon cruelty; which, I confess, hath always been with me the strongest objection against any project, how well soever intended.

18 But in order to justify my friend, he confessed that this expedient was put into his head by the famous Psalmanazar, a native of the island Formosa, who came from thence to London above twenty years ago, and in conversation told my friend that in his country when any young person happened to be put to death, the executioner sold the carcass to persons of quality as a prime dainty; and that in his time the body of a plump girl of fifteen, who was crucified for an attempt to poison the emperor, was sold to his Imperial Majesty's prime minister of state, and other great mandarins of the court, in joints from the gibbet, at four hundred crowns. Neither indeed can I deny that if the same use were made of several plump young girls in this town, who without one single groat to their fortunes cannot stir abroad without a chair, and appear at the playhouse and assemblies in foreign fineries which they never will pay for, the kingdom would not be the worse.

19 Some persons of a desponding spirit are in great concern about that vast number of poor people who are aged, diseased, or maimed, and I have been desired to employ my thoughts what course may be taken to ease the nation of so grievous an encumbrance. But I am not in the least pain upon that matter, because it is very well known that they are every day dying and rotting by cold and famine, and filth and vermin, as fast as can be reasonably expected. And as to the younger laborers, they are now in almost as hopeful a condition. They cannot get work, and consequently pine away for want of nourishment to a degree that if any time they are accidentally hired to common labor, they have not strength to perform it; and thus the country and themselves are happily delivered from the evils to come.

20 I have too long digressed, and therefore shall return to my subject. I think the advantages by the proposal which I have made are obvious and many, as well as of the highest importance.

21 For first, as I have already observed, it would greatly lessen the number of Papists, with whom we are yearly overrun, being the principal breeders of the nation as well as our most dangerous enemies; and who stay at home on purpose to deliver the kingdom to the Pretender, hoping to take their advantage by the absence of so many good Protestants, who have chosen rather to leave their country than to stay at home and pay tithes against their conscience to an Episcopal curate.

22 Secondly, the poorer tenants will have something valuable of their own, which by law may be made liable to distress, and help to pay their landlord's rent, their corn and cattle being already seized and money a thing unknown.

23 Thirdly, whereas the maintenance of an hundred thousand children, from two years old and upwards, cannot be computed at less than ten shillings a piece per annum, the nation's stock will be thereby increased fifty thousand pounds per annum, besides the profit of a new dish introduced to the tables of all gentlemen of fortune in the kingdom who have any refinement in taste. And the money will circulate among ourselves, the goods being entirely of our own growth and manufacture.

24 Fourthly, the constant breeders, besides the gain of eight shillings sterling per annum by the sale of their children, will be rid of the charge of maintaining them after the first year.

25 Fifthly, this food would likewise bring great custom to taverns, where the vintners will certainly be so prudent as to procure the best receipts for dressing it to perfection, and consequently have their houses frequented by all the fine gentlemen, who justly value themselves upon their knowledge in good eating; and a skillful cook, who understands how to oblige his guests, will contrive to make it as expensive as they please.

26 Sixthly, this would be a great inducement to marriage, which all wise nations have either encouraged by rewards or enforced by laws and penalties. It would increase the care and tenderness of mothers toward their children, when they were sure of a settlement for life to the poor babes, provided in some sort by the public, to their annual profit instead of expense. We should see an honest emulation among the married women, which of them could bring the fattest child to the market. Men would become as fond of their wives during the time of their pregnancy as they are now of their mares in foal, their cows in calf, or sows when they are ready to farrow; nor offer

to beat or kick them (as is too frequent a practice) for fear of a miscarriage.

27 Many other advantages might be enumerated. For instance, the addition of some thousand carcasses in our exportation of barreled beef, the propagation of swine's flesh, and improvements in the art of making good bacon, so much wanted among us by the great destruction of pigs, too frequent at our tables, which are no way comparable in taste or magnificence to a well-grown, fat, yearling child, which roasted whole will make a considerable figure at a lord mayor's feast or any other public entertainment. But this and many others I omit, being studious of brevity.

28 Supposing that one thousand families in this city would be constant customers for infants' flesh, besides others who might have it at merry meetings, particularly weddings and christenings, I compute that Dublin would take off annually about twenty thousand carcasses, and the rest of the kingdom (where probably they will be sold somewhat cheaper) the remaining eighty thousand.

29 I can think of no one objection that will possibly be raised against this proposal, unless it should be urged that the number of people will be thereby much lessened in the kingdom. This I freely own, and it was indeed one principal design in offering it to the world. I desire the reader will observe, that I calculate my remedy for this one individual kingdom of Ireland and for no other that ever was, is, or I think ever can be upon earth. Therefore let no man talk to me of other expedients: of taxing our absentees at five shillings a pound: of using neither clothes nor household furniture except what is of our own growth and manufacture: of utterly rejecting the materials and instruments that promote foreign luxury: of curing the expensiveness of pride, vanity, idleness, and gaming in our women: of introducing a vein of parsimony, prudence, and temperance: of learning to love our country, in the want of which we differ even from Laplanders and the inhabitants of Topinamboo: of quitting our animosities and factions, nor acting any longer like the Jews, who were murdering one another at the very moment their city was taken: of being a little cautious not to sell our country and conscience for nothing: of teaching landlords to have at least one degree of mercy toward their tenants: lastly, of putting a spirit of honesty, industry, and skill into our shopkeepers; who, if a resolution could now be taken to buy only our native goods, would immediately unite to cheat and exact upon us in the price, the measure, and the goodness,

nor could ever yet be brought to make one fair proposal of just dealing, though often and earnestly invited to it.

30 Therefore I repeat, let no man talk to me of these and the like expedients, till he hath at least some glimpse of hope that there will ever be some hearty and sincere attempt to put them in practice.

31 But as to myself, having been wearied out for many years with offering vain, idle, visionary thoughts, and at length utterly despairing of success, I fortunately fell upon this proposal, which, as it is wholly new, so it hath something solid and real, of no expense and little trouble, full in our own power, and whereby we can incur no danger in disobliging England. For this kind of commodity will not bear exportation, the flesh being of too tender a consistence to admit a long continuance in salt, although perhaps I could name a country which would be glad to eat up our whole nation without it.

32 After all, I am not so violently bent upon my own opinion as to reject any offer proposed by wise men, which shall be found equally innocent, cheap, easy, and effectual. But before something of that kind shall be advanced in contradiction to my scheme, and offering a better, I desire the author or authors will be pleased maturely to consider two points. First, as things now stand, how they will be able to find food and raiment for an hundred thousand useless mouths and backs. And secondly, there being a round million of creatures in human figure throughout this kingdom, whose sole subsistence put into a common stock would leave them in debt two millions of pounds sterling, adding those who are beggars by profession to the bulk of farmers, cottagers, and laborers, with their wives and children who are beggars in effect; I desire those politicians who dislike my overture, and may perhaps be so bold to attempt an answer, that they will first ask the parents of these mortals whether they would not at this day think it a great happiness to have been sold for food at a year old in this manner I prescribe, and thereby have avoided such a perpetual scene of misfortunes as they have since gone through by the oppression of landlords, the impossibility of paying rent without money or trade, the want of common sustenance, with neither house nor clothes to cover them from the inclemencies of the weather, and the most inevitable prospect of entailing the like or greater miseries upon their breed forever.

33 I profess, in the sincerity of my heart, that I have not the least personal interest in endeavoring to promote this necessary work,

having no other motive than the public good of my country, by advancing our trade, providing for infants, relieving the poor, and giving some pleasure to the rich. I have no children by which I can propose to get a single penny; the youngest being nine years old, and my wife past childbearing.

Humour

JOSEPH ADDISON AND RICHARD STEELE

The Englishman Joseph Addison (1672–1719) and the Irishman Richard Steele (1672–1729) collaborated in writing *The Spectator*, a collection of 555 popular essays published during 1711 and 1712. The two wanted to improve the cultural level of their middle-class readers by presenting common-sense advice on social behavior and by articulating theories of science and philosophy.

Addison was a scholar, author, and politician. He served as a fellow at Magdalen College. He wrote "The Campaign," a hugely popular political poem, the opera *Rosamond*, and the comedy *The Drummer*. He served in the Parliament from 1708 until his death. He also served one year as secretary of state.

Steele was born in Dublin. In 1684, he enrolled in the Charterhouse School in London; it was there that he began his enduring friendship with fellow student Joseph Addison. He attended Oxford University but, unlike Addison, did not earn his degree. He chose, instead, a brief stint in the military with the Coldstream Guards. Later, while holding minor political appointments, he wrote several plays, such as *The Funeral* (1701), *The Tender Husband* (1705), and *The Conscious Lovers* (1722). He is remembered primarily for his essay writing. He published *The Tatler*, a series of essays, from April 1709 to January 1711. Two months later, he began collaborating with Addison on *The Spectator*.

In this essay on humor, the authors argue that writers of humor must be people of good sense while seeming capricious and absurd. The truly humorous person looks serious while those around him or her laugh, but the person with false humor will be laughing while the listeners remain silent. Being "entirely devoid of reason," the writer of false humor "pursues no point either of morality or instruction, but is ludicrous only for the sake of being so."

35 Tuesday April 10, 1711

Risu inepto res ineptior nulla est. * Mart.

1 Among all kinds of writing, there is none in which authors are more apt to miscarry than in works of humour, as there is none in which they are more ambitious to excel. It is not an imagination that teems with monsters, an head that is filled with extravagant conceptions, which is capable of furnishing the world with diversions of this nature; and yet if we look into the productions of several writers, who set up for men of humour, what wild irregular fancies, what unnatural distortions of thought, do we meet with? If they speak nonsense, they believe they are talking humour; and when they have drawn together a scheme of absurd, inconsistent ideas, they are not able to read it over to themselves without laughing. These poor gentlemen endeavour to gain themselves the reputation of wits and humorists, by such monstrous conceits as almost quality them for Bedlam; not considering that humour should always lie under the check of reason, and that it requires the direction of the nicest judgment, by so much the more as it indulges itself in the most boundless freedoms. There is a kind of nature that is to be observed in this sort of compositions, as well as in all other, and a certain regularity of thought which must discover the writer to be a man of sense, at the same time that he appears altogether given up to caprice: for my part, when I read the delirious mirth of an unskillful author, I cannot be so barbarous as to divert myself with it, but am rather apt to pity the man, than to laugh at anything he writes.

* There is nothing more tactless than a tactless laugh.

2 The deceased Mr. Shadwell, who had himself a great deal of the talent, which I am treating of, represents an empty rake, in one of his plays, as very much surprised to hear one say that breaking of windows was not humour; and I question not but several English readers will be as much startled to hear me affirm, that many of those raving incoherent pieces, which are often spread among us, under odd chimerical titles, are rather the offsprings of a distempered brain, than works of humour.

3 It is indeed much easier to describe what is not humour, than what is; and very difficult to define it otherwise than as Cowley has done wit, by negatives. Were I to give my own notions of it, I would deliver them after Plato's manner, in a kind of allegory, and by supposing humour to be a person, deduce to him all his qualifications, according to the following genealogy. Truth was the founder of the family, and the father of Good Sense. Good Sense was the father of Wit, who married a lady of a collateral line called Mirth, by whom he had issue Humour. Humour therefore being the youngest of this illustrious family, and descended from parents of such different dispositions, is very various and unequal in his temper; sometimes you see him putting on grave looks and a solemn habit, sometimes airy in his behaviour and fantastic in his dress: insomuch that at different times he appears as serious as a judge, and as jocular as a Merry-Andrew. But as he has a great deal of the mother in his constitution, whatever mood he is in, he never fails to make his company laugh.

4 But since there is an impostor abroad, who takes upon him the name of this young gentleman, and would willingly pass for him in the world; to the end that well-meaning persons may not be imposed upon by cheats, I would desire my readers, when they meet with this pretender, to look into his parentage, and to examine him strictly, whether or no he be remotely allied to Truth, and lineally descended from Good Sense? if not, they may conclude him a counterfeit. They may likewise distinguish him by a loud and excessive laughter, in which he seldom gets his company to join with him. For as True Humour generally looks serious, whilst everybody laughs about him; False Humour is always laughing, whilst everybody about him looks serious. I shall only add, if he has not in him a mixture of both parents, that is, if he would pass for the offspring of Wit without Mirth, or Mirth without Wit, you may conclude him to be altogether spurious, and a cheat.

5 The impostor of whom I am speaking, descends originally from Falsehood, who was the mother of Nonsense, who was brought to bed of a son called Frenzy, who married one of the daughters of Folly, commonly known by the name of Laughter, on whom he begot that monstrous infant of which I have been here speaking. I shall set down at length the genealogical table of False Humour, and, at the same time, place under it the genealogy of True Humour, that the reader may at one view behold their different pedigrees and relations.

Falsehood
Nonsense
Frenzy—Laughter
False Humour

Truth
Good Sense
Wit—Mirth
Humour

6 I might extend the allegory, by mentioning several of the children of False Humour, who are more in number than the sands of the sea, and might in particular enumerate the many sons and daughters which he has begot in this island. But as this would be a very invidious task, I shall only observe in general, that False Humour differs from the True, as a monkey does from a man.

7 First of all, he is exceedingly given to little apish tricks and buffooneries.

8 Secondly, he so much delights in mimicry, that it is all one to him whether he exposes by it vice and folly, luxury and avarice; or, on the contrary, virtue and wisdom, pain and poverty.

9 Thirdly, he is wonderfully unlucky, insomuch that he will bite the hand that feeds him, and endeavour to ridicule both friends and foes indifferently. For having but small talents, he must be merry where he *can*, not where he *should*.

10 Fourthly, being entirely void of reason, he pursues no point either of morality or instruction, but is ludicrous only for the sake of being so.

11 Fifthly, being incapable of anything but mock-representations, his ridicule is always personal, and aimed at the vicious man, or the writer; not at the vice, or at the writing.

12 I have here only pointed at the whole species of false humorists,

but as one of my principal designs in this paper is to beat down that malignant spirit, which discovers itself in the writings of the present age, I shall not scruple, for the future, to single out any of the small wits, that infest the world with such compositions as are ill-natured, immoral and absurd. This is the only exception which I shall make to the general rule I have prescribed myself, of *attacking multitudes.* Since every honest man ought to look upon himself as in a natural state of war with the libeller and lampooner, and to annoy them wherever they fall in his way, this is but retaliating upon them and treating them as they treat others.

The Crisis

THOMAS PAINE

Thomas Paine (1737–1809) was born in Thetford, England, to a poor family, and he did not have a good education. He entered the workforce at thirteen, spent time on the high seas, and worked as a customs collector, but he was discharged from that work. In 1774, he met Benjamin Franklin in London. Franklin encouraged Paine to venture to America. Soon, in Philadelphia, he began working for America's independence, writing articles for the *Pennsylvania Magazine* and, in 1776, publishing his popular pamphlet *Common Sense*. Later that year, he began publishing a series of pamphlets entitled *The Crisis*. He served for a short time in the army, then as secretary to the Congressional Committee of Foreign Affairs, and as clerk of the Pennsylvania Assembly.

In 1787, Paine traveled to France and embraced the revolutionary fervor of that country. Back in his home country, England, in the early 1790s, he aroused the fury of the government with his famous "Rights of Man," an essay that defended the French while condemning British tyranny. He was tried for treason and outlawed from England, but he had long since slipped quietly back into France. At first, the French welcomed him with open arms, made him a citizen, and named him to the National Convention. But Paine was appalled by the unnecessary bloodshed of the revolution and, as usual, spoke his mind. Soon he was dismissed from the convention, stripped of his citizenship, and imprisoned. The American minister to France, James Monroe, came to his rescue and claimed him as an American citizen, so that soon, with the help of President Thomas Jefferson, Paine returned to the United States.

The first pamphlet of *The Crisis* opens with the memorable lines, "These are the times that try men's souls. The summer soldier and the sunshine patriot will, in this crisis, shrink from the service of his country; but he that stands it *now,* deserves the love and thanks of man and woman." Paine goes on to develop the antithesis of the glory of national triumph and the disgrace of cowardice. He describes his participation in one exercise of the war, then proceeds to attack the Tories who secretly and sometimes not so secretly supported the British. Paine's voice was a piercing cry for the patriot's cause, and his words were read by citizens throughout the colonies, who rallied to his call and to the aid of General George Washington.

1 These are the times that try men's souls. The summer soldier and the sunshine patriot will, in this crisis, shrink from the service of his country; but he that stands it *now,* deserves the love and thanks of man and woman. Tyranny, like hell, is not easily conquered; yet we have this consolation with us, that the harder the conflict, the more glorious the triumph. What we obtain too cheap, we esteem too lightly: it is dearness only that gives everything its value. Heaven knows how to put a proper price upon its goods; and it would be strange indeed if so celestial an article as FREEDOM should not be highly rated. Britain, with an army to enforce her tyranny, has declared that she has a right (*not only to* TAX) but "to BIND *us in* ALL CASES WHATSOEVER"; and if being *bound in that manner* is not slavery, then is there not such a thing as slavery upon earth. Even the expression is impious; for so unlimited a power can belong only to God.

2 Whether the independence of the continent was declared too soon, or delayed too long, I will not now enter into as an argument; my own simple opinion is, that had it been eight months earlier it would have been much better. We did not make a proper use of last winter; neither could we, while we were in a dependent state. However, the fault, if it were one, was all our own; we have none to blame but ourselves. But no great deal is lost yet. All that Howe has been doing for this month past is rather a ravage than a conquest, which the spirit of the Jerseys a year ago would have quickly repulsed, and which time and a little resolution will soon recover.

3 I have as little superstition in me as any man living; but my secret opinion has ever been, and still is, that God Almighty will not give up a people to military destruction, or leave them unsupportedly to perish, who have so earnestly and so repeatedly sought to avoid the calamities of war, by every decent method which wisdom could invent. Neither have I so much of the infidel in me as to suppose that he has relinquished the government of the world, and given us up to the care of devils; and as I do not, I cannot see on what grounds the king of Britain can look up to heaven for help against us: a common murderer, a highwayman, or a housebreaker, has as good a pretense as he.

4 It is surprising to see how rapidly a panic will sometimes run through a country. All nations and ages have been subject to them: Britain has trembled like an ague at the report of a French fleet of flat-bottomed boats; and in the fourteenth century the whole English army, after ravaging the kingdom of France, was driven back like men petrified with fear; and this brave exploit was performed by a few broken forces collected and headed by a woman, Joan of Arc. Would that heaven might inspire some Jersey maid to spirit up her countrymen, and save her fair fellow sufferers from ravage and ravishment! Yet panics, in some cases, have their uses; they produce as much good as hurt. Their duration is always short; the mind soon grows through them, and acquires a firmer habit than before. But their peculiar advantage is, that they are the touchstones of sincerity and hypocrisy, and bring things and men to light, which might otherwise have lain forever undiscovered. In fact, they have the same effect on secret traitors which an imaginary apparition would have upon a private murderer. They sift out the hidden thoughts of man, and hold them up in public to the world. Many a disguised tory has lately shown his head, that shall penitentially solemnize with curses the day on which Howe arrived upon the Delaware.

5 As I was with the troops at Fort Lee, and marched with them to the edge of Pennsylvania, I am well acquainted with many circumstances which those who live at a distance know but little or nothing of. Our situation there was exceedingly cramped, the place being a narrow neck of land between the North River and the Hackensack. Our force was inconsiderable, being not one-fourth so great as Howe could bring against us. We had no army at hand to have relieved the garrison, had we shut ourselves up and stood on our defense. Our ammunition, light artillery, and the best part of our stores, had

been removed, on the apprehension that Howe would endeavor to penetrate the Jerseys, in which case Fort Lee could be of no use to us; for it must occur to every thinking man, whether in the army or not, that these kind of field forts are only for temporary purposes, and last in use no longer than the enemy directs his force against the particular object which such forts are raised to defend. Such was our situation and condition at Fort Lee on the morning of the 20th of November, when an officer arrived with information that the enemy with 200 boats had landed about seven miles above. Major General Green, who commanded the garrison, immediately ordered them under arms, and sent express to General Washington at the town of Hackensack, distant by the way of the ferry, six miles. Our first object was to secure the bridge over the Hackensack, which laid up the river between the enemy and us, about six miles from us, three from them. General Washington arrived in about three-quarters of an hour, and marched at the head of the troops towards the bridge, which place I expected we should have a brush for; however, they did not choose to dispute it with us, and the greatest part of our troops went over the bridge, the rest over the ferry, except some which passed at a mill on a small creek between the bridge and the ferry, and made their way through some marshy grounds up to the town of Hackensack, and there passed the river. We brought off as much baggage as the wagons could contain, the rest was lost. The simple object was to bring off the garrison and march them on till they could be strengthened by the Jersey or Pennsylvania militia, so as to be enabled to make a stand. We staid four days at Newark, collected our outposts with some of the Jersey militia, and marched out twice to meet the enemy on being informed that they were advancing, though our numbers were greatly inferior to theirs. Howe, in my little opinion, committed a great error in generalship in not throwing a body of forces off from Staten Island through Amboy, by which means he might have seized all our stores at Brunswick and intercepted our march into Pennsylvania; but if we believe the power of hell to be limited, we must likewise believe that their agents are under some providential control.

6 I shall not now attempt to give all the particulars of our retreat to the Delaware; suffice it for the present to say that both officers and men, though greatly harassed and fatigued, frequently without rest, covering, or provision—the inevitable consequences of a long retreat—bore it with a manly and martial spirit. All their wishes

centered in one; which was, that the country would turn out and help them to drive the enemy back. Voltaire has remarked that King William never appeared to full advantage but in difficulties and in action; the same remark may be made on General Washington, for the character fits him. There is a natural firmness in some minds which cannot be unlocked by trifles, but which, when unlocked, discovers a cabinet of fortitude; and I reckon it among those kinds of public blessings, which we do not immediately see, that God hath blessed him with uninterrupted health, and given him a mind that can even flourish upon care.

7 I shall conclude this paper with some miscellaneous remarks on the state of our affairs; and shall begin with asking the following question, Why is it that the enemy have left the New England provinces, and made these middle ones the seat of war? The answer is easy: New England is not infested with tories, and we are. I have been tender in raising the cry against these men, and used numberless arguments to show them their danger, but it will not do to sacrifice a world either to their folly or their baseness. The period is now arrived in which either they or we must change our sentiments, or one or both must fall. And what is a tory? Good God! what is he? I should not be afraid to go with a hundred Whigs against a thousand tories, were they to attempt to get into arms. Every tory is a coward; for servile, slavish, self-interested fear is the foundation of toryism; and a man under such influence, though he may be cruel, never can be brave.

8 But, before the line of irrecoverable separation be drawn between us, let us reason the matter together: Your conduct is an invitation to the enemy, yet not one in a thousand of you has heart enough to join him. Howe is as much deceived by you as the American cause is injured by you. He expects you will all take up arms and flock to his standard with muskets on your shoulders. Your opinions are of no use to him unless you support him personally, for it is soldiers, and not tories, that he wants.

9 I once felt all that kind of anger, which a man ought to feel, against the mean principles that are held by the tories: A noted one, who kept a tavern at Amboy, was standing at his door, with as pretty a child in his hand, about eight or nine years old, as I ever saw, and after speaking his mind as freely as he thought was prudent, finished with this unfatherly expression, *"Well! give me peace in my day."* Not a man lives on the continent but fully believes that a separation

must some time or other finally take place, and a generous parent should have said, *"If there must be trouble, let it be in my day, that my child may have peace;"* and this single reflection, well applied, is sufficient to awaken every man to duty. Not a place upon earth might be so happy as America. Her situation is remote from all the wrangling world, and she has nothing to do but to trade with them. A man can distinguish himself between temper and principle; and I am as confident as I am that God governs the world, that America will never be happy till she gets clear of foreign dominion. Wars, without ceasing, will break out till that period arrives, and the continent must in the end be conqueror; for though the flame of liberty may sometimes cease to shine, the coal can never expire.

10 America did not, nor does not want force; but she wanted a proper application of that force. Wisdom is not the purchase of a day, and it is no wonder that we should err at the first setting off. From an excess of tenderness, we were unwilling to raise an army, and trusted our cause to the temporary defense of a well-meaning militia. A summer's experience has now taught us better; yet with those troops, while they were collected, we were able to set bounds to the progress of the enemy, and thank God! they are again assembling. I always considered militia as the best troops in the world for a sudden exertion, but they will not do for a long campaign. Howe, it is probable, will make an attempt on this city; should he fail on this side the Delaware, he is ruined. If he succeeds, our cause is not ruined. He stakes all on his side against a part on ours; admitting he succeeds, the consequences will be that armies from both ends of the continent will march to assist their suffering friends in the middle states; for he cannot go everywhere—it is impossible. I consider Howe as the greatest enemy the tories have; he is bringing a war into their country, which, had it not been for him and partly for themselves, they had been clear of. Should he now be expelled, I wish with all the devotion of a Christian, that the names of Whig and Tory may never more be mentioned; but should the tories give him encouragement to come, or assistance if he come, I as sincerely wish that our next year's arms may expel them from the continent, and the Congress appropriate their possessions to the relief of those who have suffered in well-doing. A single successful battle next year will settle the whole. America could carry on a two years' war by the confiscation of the property of disaffected persons, and be made happy by their expulsion. Say not that this is revenge; call it rather the soft resentment

of a suffering people, who, having no object in view but the *good* of *all,* have staked their *own all* upon a seemingly doubtful event. Yet it is folly to argue against determined hardness; eloquence may strike the ear, and the language of sorrow draw forth the tear of compassion, but nothing can reach the heart that is steeled with prejudice.

11 Quitting this class of men, I turn with the warm ardor of a friend to those who have nobly stood, and are yet determined to stand the matter out: I call not upon a few, but upon all: not on *this* State or *that* State, but on *every* State: up and help us; lay your shoulders to the wheel; better have too much force than too little, when so great an object is at stake. Let it be told to the future world, that in the depth of winter, when nothing but hope and virtue could survive, that the city and the country, alarmed at one common danger, came forth to meet and to repulse it. Say not that thousands are gone—turn out your tens of thousands; throw not the burden of the day upon Providence, but *"show your faith by your works,"* that God may bless you. It matters not where you live, or what rank of life you hold, the evil or the blessing will reach you all. The far and the near, the home counties and the back, the rich and the poor, will suffer or rejoice alike. The heart that feels not now is dead; the blood of his children will curse his cowardice who shrinks back at a time when a little might have saved the whole and made *them* happy. I love the man that can smile in trouble, that can gather strength from distress and grow brave by reflection. It is the business of little minds to shrink; but he whose heart is firm, and whose conscience approves his conduct, will pursue his principles unto death. My own line of reasoning is to myself as straight and clear as a ray of light. Not all the treasures of the world, so far as I believe, could have induced me to support an offensive war, for I think it murder; but if a thief breaks into my house, burns and destroys my property, and kills or threatens to kill me or those that are in it, and to *"bind me in all cases whatsoever"* to his absolute will, am I to suffer it? What signifies it to me whether he who does it is a king or a common man; my countryman or not my countryman; whether it be done by an individual villain, or an army of them? If we reason to the root of things we shall find no difference; neither can any just cause be assigned why we should punish in the one case and pardon in the other. Let them call me rebel and welcome—I feel no concern from it; but I should suffer the misery of devils, were I to make a whore of my soul by swearing allegiance to one whose character is that of

a sottish, stupid, stubborn, worthless, brutish man. I conceive likewise a horrid idea in receiving mercy from a being, who at the last day shall be shrieking to the rocks and mountains to cover him, and fleeing with terror from the orphan, the widow, and the slain of America.

12 There are cases which cannot be overdone by language, and this is one. There are persons, too, who see not the full extent of the evil which threatens them; they solace themselves with hopes that the enemy, if he succeed, will be merciful. It is the madness of folly, to expect mercy from those who have refused to do justice; and even mercy, where conquest is the object, is only a trick of war. The cunning of the fox is as murderous as the violence of the wolf, and we ought to guard equally against both. Howe's first object is, partly by threats and partly by promises, to terrify or seduce the people to deliver up their arms and receive mercy. The ministry recommended the same plan to Gage, and this is what the tories call making their peace, *"a peace which passeth all understanding," indeed!* A peace which would be the immediate forerunner of a worse ruin than any we have yet thought of. Ye men of Pennsylvania, do reason upon these things! Were the back counties to give up their arms, they would fall an easy prey to the Indians, who are all armed: this perhaps is what some tories would not be sorry for. Were the home counties to deliver up their arms, they would be exposed to the resentment of the back counties, who would then have it in their power to chastise their defection at pleasure. And were any one State to give up its arms, *that* State must be garrisoned by all Howe's army of Britons and Hessians to preserve it from the anger of the rest. Mutual fear is the principal link in the chain of mutual love; and woe be to that State that breaks the compact. Howe is mercifully inviting you to barbarous destruction, and men must be either rogues or fools that will not see it. I dwell not upon the vapors of imagination; I bring reason to your ears, and, in language as plain as A B C, hold up truth to your eyes.

13 I thank God that I fear not. I see no real cause for fear. I know our situation well, and can see the way out of it. While our army was collected, Howe dared not risk a battle; and it is no credit to him that he decamped from the White Plains, and waited a mean opportunity to ravage the defenseless Jerseys; but it is great credit to us, that with a handful of men, we sustained an orderly retreat for near a hundred miles, brought off our ammunition, all our field-

pieces, the greatest part of our stores, and had four rivers to pass. None can say that our retreat was precipitate; for we were near three weeks in performing it, that the country might have time to come in. Twice we marched back to meet the enemy, and remained out till dark. The sign of fear was not seen in our camp, and had not some of the cowardly and disaffected inhabitants spread false alarms through the country, the Jerseys had never been ravaged. Once more we are again collected and collecting, our new army at both ends of the continent is recruiting fast, and we shall be able to open the next campaign with sixty thousand men, well-armed and clothed. This is our situation, and who will may know it. By perseverance and fortitude we have the prospect of a glorious issue; by cowardice and submission, the sad choice of a variety of evils: a ravaged country—a depopulated city—habitations without safety, and slavery without hope—our homes turned into barracks and bawdy-houses for Hessians—and a future race to provide for, whose fathers we shall doubt of. Look on this picture and weep over it! and if there yet remains one thoughtless wretch who believes it not, let him suffer it unlamented.

from A Vindication of the Rights of Woman

MARY WOLLSTONECRAFT

Mary Wollstonecraft (1759–1797) was born in Hoxton, England. From an early age, she was forced to earn her own way in the world. Her first novel, *Mary, A Fiction* (1788), commemorated the death of her childhood friend Fanny Blood. She translated several works that were illustrated by William Blake, who himself became a literary giant. In 1792, she went to Paris to investigate for herself the French revolution; there she witnessed firsthand the Reign of Terror. In France, she met an American military captain, Gilbert Imlay, by whom she had a daughter named Fanny. She referred to herself as Mary Imlay, but there is no evidence of a marriage. Imlay ended the relationship in 1795, and Wollstonecraft tried unsuccessfully to drown herself. Later, she married William Godwin, a liberal social reformer who published his *Political Justice* in 1793. The marriage was short-lived because she died soon after giving birth to their daughter, Mary, who was to become the wife of the poet Percy Bysshe Shelley and the author of *Frankenstein*.

In *A Vindication of the Rights of Woman* (1792), Wollstonecraft wished to "persuade women to endeavour to acquire strength, both of mind and body" and to remember that "the first object of laudable ambition is to obtain a character as a human being." She wanted women to be more than mere playthings for their husbands or, worse, mere servants. In order to contribute to society and her family and to be a true companion to her husband, Wollstonecraft believed a woman needed a good education. This essay, then, argues that a female's education should equal that awarded to males. She encouraged women to enter the professions of medicine, law, and business so that they "would not then marry for a support."

1 . . . The preposterous distinctions of rank, which render civilization a curse, by dividing the world between voluptuous tyrants and cunning envious dependents, corrupt, almost equally, every class of people, because respectability is not attached to the discharge of the relative duties of life, but to the station, and when the duties are not fulfilled the affections cannot gain sufficient strength to fortify the virtue of which they are the natural reward. Still there are some loop-holes out of which a man may creep, and dare to think and act for himself; but for a woman it is an herculean task, because she has difficulties peculiar to her sex to overcome, which require almost superhuman powers.

2 A truly benevolent legislator always endeavours to make it the interest of each individual to be virtuous; and thus private virtue becoming the cement of public happiness, an orderly whole is consolidated by the tendency of all the parts towards a common centre. But the private or public virtue of woman is very problematical, for Rousseau, and a numerous list of male writers, insist that she should all her life be subjected to a severe restraint, that of propriety. Why subject her to propriety—blind propriety—if she be capable of acting from a nobler spring, if she be an heir of immortality? Is sugar always to be produced by vital blood? Is one half of the human species, like the poor African slaves, to be subjected to prejudices that brutalize them, when principles would be a surer guard, only to sweeten the cup of man? Is not this indirectly to deny woman reason? for a gift is a mockery, if it be unfit for use.

3 Women are, in common with men, rendered weak and luxurious

by the relaxing pleasures which wealth procures; but added to this they are made slaves to their persons, and must render them alluring that man may lend them his reason to guide their tottering steps aright. Or should they be ambitious, they must govern their tyrants by sinister tricks, for without rights there cannot be any incumbent duties. The laws respecting woman . . . make an absurd unit of a man and his wife; and then, by the easy transition of only considering him as responsible, she is reduced to a mere cipher.

4 The being who discharges the duties of its station is independent; and, speaking of women at large, their first duty is to themselves as rational creatures, and the next, in point of importance, as citizens, is that, which includes so many, of a mother. The rank in life which dispenses with their fulfilling this duty, necessarily degrades them by making them mere dolls. Or should they turn to something more important than merely fitting drapery upon a smooth block, their minds are only occupied by some soft platonic attachment; or the actual management of an intrigue may keep their thoughts in motion; for when they neglect domestic duties, they have it not in their power to take the field and march and counter-march like soldiers, or wrangle in the senate to keep their faculties from rusting.

5 I know that, as a proof of the inferiority of the sex, Rousseau has exultingly exclaimed, How can they leave the nursery for the camp! And the camp has by some moralists been proved the school of the most heroic virtues; though I think it would puzzle a keen casuist to prove the reasonableness of the greater number of wars that have dubbed heroes. I do not mean to consider this question critically; because, having frequently viewed these freaks of ambition as the first natural mode of civilization, when the ground must be torn up, and the woods cleared by fire and sword, I do not choose to call them pests; but surely the present system of war has little connection with virtue of any denomination, being rather the school of *finesse* and effeminacy than of fortitude.

6 Yet, if defensive war, the only justifiable war, in the present advanced state of society, where virtue can show its face and ripen amidst the rigours which purify the air on the mountain's top, were alone to be adopted as just and glorious, the true heroism of antiquity might again animate female bosoms. But fair and softly, gentle reader, male or female, do not alarm thyself, for though I have compared the character of a modern soldier with that of a civilized woman, I am not going to advise them to turn their distaff into a musket,

though I sincerely wish to see the bayonet converted into a pruning-hook. I only re-created an imagination, fatigued by contemplating the vices and follies which all proceed from a feculent stream of wealth that has muddied the pure rills of natural affection, by supposing that society will some time or other be so constituted, that man must necessary fulfil the duties of a citizen, or be despised, and that while he was employed in any of the departments of civil life, his wife, also an active citizen, should be equally intent to manage her family, educate her children, and assist her neighbours.

7 But to render her really virtuous and useful, she must not, if she discharge her civil duties, want individually the protection of civil laws; she must not be dependent on her husband's bounty for her subsistence during his life, or support after his death; for how can a being be generous who has nothing of its own? or virtuous who is not free? The wife, in the present state of things, who is faithful to her husband, and neither suckles nor educates her children, scarcely deserves the name of a wife, and has no right to that of a citizen. But take away natural rights, and duties become null.

8 Women then must be considered as only the wanton solace of men, when they become so weak in mind and body that they cannot exert themselves unless to pursue some frothy pleasure, or to invent some frivolous fashion. What can be a more melancholy sight to a thinking mind, than to look into the numerous carriages that drive helter-skelter about this metropolis in a morning full of pale-faced creatures who are flying from themselves! I have often wished, with Dr Johnson, to place some of them in a little shop with half a dozen children looking up to their languid countenances for support. I am much mistaken, if some latent vigour would not soon give health and spirit to their eyes, and some lines drawn by the exercise of reason on the blank cheeks, which before were only undulated by dimples, might restore lost dignity to the character, or rather enable it to attain the true dignity of its nature. Virtue is not to be acquired even by speculation, much less by the negative supineness that wealth naturally generates.

9 Besides, when poverty is more disgraceful than even vice, is not morality cut to the quick? Still to avoid misconstruction, though I consider that women in the common walks of life are called to fulfill the duties of wives and mothers, by religion and reason, I cannot help lamenting that women of a superior cast have not a road open by which they can pursue more extensive plans of usefulness and

independence. I may excite laughter, by dropping a hint, which I mean to pursue, some future time, for I really think that women ought to have representatives, instead of being arbitrarily governed without having any direct share allowed them in the deliberations of government.

10 But, as the whole system of representation is now, in this country, only a convenient handle for despotism, they need not complain, for they are as well represented as a numerous class of hard-working mechanics, who pay for the support of royalty when they can scarcely stop their children's mouths with bread. How are they represented whose very sweat supports the splendid stud of an heir-apparent, or varnishes the chariot of some female favourite who looks down on shame? Taxes on the very necessaries of life, enable an endless tribe of idle princes and princesses to pass with stupid pomp before a gaping crowd, who almost worship the very parade which costs them so dear. This is mere gothic grandeur, something like the barbarous useless parade of having sentinels on horseback at Whitehall, which I could never view without a mixture of contempt and indignation.

11 How strangely must the mind be sophisticated when this sort of state impresses it! But, till these monuments of folly are levelled by virtue, similar follies will leaven the whole mass. For the same character, in some degree, will prevail in the aggregate of society; and the refinements of luxury, or the vicious repinings of envious poverty, will equally banish virtue from society, considered as the characteristic of that society, or only allow it to appear as one of the stripes of the harlequin coat, worn by the civilized man.

12 In the superior ranks of life, every duty is done by deputies, as if duties could ever be waived, and the vain pleasures which consequent idleness forces the rich to pursue, appear so enticing to the next rank, that the numerous scramblers for wealth sacrifice everything to tread on their heels. The most sacred trusts are then considered as sinecures, because they were procured by interest, and only sought to enable a man to keep *good company*. Women, in particular, all want to be ladies. Which is simply to have nothing to do, but listlessly to go they scarcely care where, for they cannot tell what.

13 But what have women to do in society? I may be asked, but to loiter with easy grace; surely you would not condemn them all to suckle fools and chronicle small beer! No. Women might certainly study the art of healing and be physicians as well as nurses. And midwifery, decency seems to allot to them though I am afraid the

word midwife, in our dictionaries, will soon give place to *accoucheur*, and one proof of the former delicacy of the sex be effaced from the language.

14 They might also study politics, and settle their benevolence on the broadest basis; for the reading of history will scarcely be more useful than the perusal of romances, if read as mere biography; if the character of the times, the political improvements, arts, etc., be not observed. In short, if it be not considered as the history of man; and not of particular men, who filled a niche in the temple of fame, and dropped into the black rolling stream of time, that silently sweeps all before it into the shapeless void called—eternity.—For shape, can it be called, "that shape hath none"?

15 Business of various kinds, they might likewise pursue, if they were educated in a more orderly manner, which might save many from common and legal prostitution. Women would not then marry for a support, as men accept of places under Government, and neglect the implied duties; nor would an attempt to earn their own subsistence, a most laudable one! sink them almost to the level of those poor abandoned creatures who live by prostitution. For are not milliners and mantuamakers reckoned the next class? The few employments open to women, so far from being liberal, are menial; and when a superior education enables them to take charge of the education of children as governesses, they are not treated like the tutors of sons, though even clerical tutors are not always treated in a manner calculated to render them respectable in the eyes of their pupils, to say nothing of the private comfort of the individual. But as women educated like gentlewomen, are never designed for the humiliating situation which necessity sometimes forces them to fill; these situations are considered in the light of a degradation; and they know little of the human heart, who need to be told, that nothing so painfully sharpens sensibility as such a fall in life.

16 Some of these women might be restrained from marrying by a proper spirit of delicacy, and others may not have had it in their power to escape in this pitiful way from servitude; is not that Government then very defective, and very unmindful of the happiness of one-half of its members, that does not provide for honest, independent women, by encouraging them to fill respectable stations? But in order to render their private virtue a public benefit, they must have a civil existence in the State, married or single; else we shall continually see some worthy woman, whose sensibility has been rendered painfully

acute by undeserved contempt, droop like "the lily broken down by a plowshare."

17 It is a melancholy truth; yet such is the blessed effect of civilization! the most respectable women are the most oppressed; and, unless they have understandings far superior to the common run of understandings, taking in both sexes, they must, from being treated like contemptible beings, become contemptible. How many women thus waste life away the prey of discontent, who might have practised as physicians, regulated a farm, managed a shop, and stood erect, supported by their own industry, instead of hanging their heads surcharged with the dew of sensibility, that consumes the beauty to which it at first gave lustre; nay, I doubt whether pity and love are so near akin as poets feign, for I have seldom seen much compassion excited by the helplessness of females, unless they were fair; then, perhaps, pity was the soft handmaid of love, or the harbinger of lust.

18 How much more respectable is the woman who earns her own bread by fulfilling any duty, than the most accomplished beauty! —beauty did I say!—so sensible am I of the beauty of moral loveliness, or the harmonious propriety that attunes the passions of a well-regulated mind, that I blush at making the comparison; yet I sigh to think how few women aim at attaining this respectability by withdrawing from the giddy whirl of pleasure, or the indolent calm that stupefies the good sort of women it sucks in.

19 Proud of their weakness, however, they must always be protected, guarded from care, and all the rough toils that dignify the mind. If this be the fiat of fate, if they will make themselves insignificant and contemptible, sweetly to waste "life away," let them not expect to be valued when their beauty fades, for it is the fate of the fairest flowers to be admired and pulled to pieces by the careless hand that plucked them. In how many ways do I wish, from the purest benevolence, to impress this truth on my sex; yet I fear that they will not listen to a truth that dear bought experience has brought home to many an agitated bosom, nor willingly resign the privileges of rank and sex for the privileges of humanity, to which those have no claim who do not discharge its duties.

20 Those writers are particularly useful, in my opinion, who make man feel for man, independent of the station he fills, or the drapery of factitious sentiments. I then would fain convince reasonable men of the importance of some of my remarks; and prevail on them to weigh dispassionately the whole tenor of my observations. I appeal

to their understandings; and, as a fellow-creature, claim, in the name of my sex, some interest in their hearts. I entreat them to assist to emancipate their companion, to make her a *helpmeet* for them.

21 Would men but generously snap our chains, and be content with rational fellowship instead of slavish obedience, they would find us more observant daughters, more affectionate sisters, more faithful wives, more reasonable mothers—in a word, better citizens. We should then love them with true affection, because we should learn to respect ourselves; and the peace of mind of a worthy man would not be interrupted by the idle vanity of his wife, nor the babes sent to nestle in a strange bosom, having never found a home in their mother's.

Grace before Meat

CHARLES LAMB

Charles Lamb (1775–1834) was a British essayist and literary critic. He was educated at Christ's Hospital school where he became close friends with Samuel Taylor Coleridge. He earned his living working for the East India Company, never married, and lived with and cared for his mentally ill sister, Mary. He published most of his successful essays in *The London Magazine* from about 1820 to 1825. He republished them as *Essays of Elia* (1823) and *Last Essays of Elia* (1833). In his prose style, Lamb displays a whimsical nature colored by a warm and gentle love of life, friendship, and the simple pleasures. His style and view of life enabled him to delight audiences on such topics as "A Dissertation upon Roast Pig," "Dream Children," or "A Bachelor's Complaint of the Behavior of Married People."

In "Grace before Meat," Lamb brings his special and delightful focus to the practice of saying grace before meals but not for other blessings, many of which are more important. He wonders why we do not have "grace before Shakespeare" or grace before "a moonlight ramble." He suggests that a prayer before a plain meal of mutton with turnips might be appropriate, but that a rich table laden with savory food seems an inappropriate time: "You are startled at the injustice of returning thanks—for what?—for having too much, while so many starve. It is to praise the Gods amiss."

1 The custom of saying grace at meals had, probably, its origin in the early times of the world, and the hunter-state of man, when dinners were precarious things, and a full meal was something more than a common blessing; when a belly-full was a windfall, and looked like a special providence. In the shouts and triumphal songs with which, after a season of sharp abstinence, a lucky booty of deer's or goat's flesh would naturally be ushered home, existed, perhaps, the germ of the modern grace. It is not otherwise easy to be understood, why the blessing of food—the act of eating—should have had a particular expression of thanksgiving annexed to it, distinct from that implied and silent gratitude with which we are expected to enter upon the enjoyment of the many other various gifts and good things of existence.

2 I own that I am disposed to say grace upon twenty other occasions in the course of the day besides my dinner. I want a form for setting out upon a pleasant walk, for a moonlight ramble, for a friendly meeting, or a solved problem. Why have we none for books, those spiritual repasts—a grace before Milton—a grace before Shakespeare—a devotional exercise proper to be said before reading the Fairy Queen?—but, the received ritual having prescribed these forms to the solitary ceremony of manducation, I shall confine my observations to the experience which I have had of the grace, properly so called; commending my new scheme for extension to a niche in the grand philosophical, poetical, and perchance in part heretical, liturgy, now compiling by my friend Homo Humanus, for the use of a certain snug congregation of Utopian Rabelæsian Christians, no matter where assembled.

3 The form then of the benediction before eating has its beauty at a poor man's table, or at the simple and unprovocative repasts of children. It is here that the grace becomes exceedingly graceful. The indigent man, who hardly knows whether he shall have a meal the next day or not, sits down to his fare with a present sense of the blessing which can be but feebly acted by the rich, into whose minds the conception of wanting a dinner could never, but by some extreme theory, have entered. The proper end of food—the animal sustenance—is barely contemplated by them. The poor man's bread is his daily bread, literally his bread for the day. Their courses are perennial.

4 Again, the plainest diet seems the fittest to be preceded by the grace. That which is least stimulative to appetite, leaves the mind

most free for foreign considerations. A man may feel thankful, heartily thankful, over a dish of plain mutton with turnips, and have leisure to reflect upon the ordinance and institution of eating; when he shall confess a perturbation of mind, inconsistent with the purposes of the grace, at the presence of venison or turtle. When I have sate (a *rarus hospes**) at rich men's tables, with the savoury soup and messes steaming up the nostrils, and moistening the lips of the guests with desire and a distracted choice, I have felt the introduction of that ceremony to be unseasonable. With the ravenous orgasm upon you, it seems impertinent to interpose a religious sentiment. It is a confusion of purpose to mutter out praises from a mouth that waters. The heats of epicurism put out the gentle flame of devotion. The incense which rises round is pagan, and the belly-god intercepts it for his own. The very excess of the provision beyond the needs, takes away all sense of proportion between the end and means. The giver is veiled by his gifts. You are startled at the injustice of returning thanks—for what?—for having too much, while so many starve. It is to praise the Gods amiss.

5 I have observed this awkwardness felt, scarce consciously perhaps, by the good man who says the grace. I have seen it in clergymen and others—a sort of shame—a sense of the co-presence of circumstances which unhallow the blessing. After a devotional tone put on for a few seconds, how rapidly the speaker will fall into his common voice, helping himself or his neighbour, as if to get rid of some uneasy sensation of hypocrisy. Not that the good man was a hypocrite, or was not most conscientious in the discharge of the duty; but he felt in his inmost mind the incompatibility of the scene and the viands before him with the exercise of a calm and rational gratitude.

6 I hear somebody exclaim,—Would you have Christians sit down at table, like hogs to their troughs, without remembering the Giver?—no—I would have them sit down as Christians, remembering the Giver, and less like hogs. Or if their appetites must run riot, and they must pamper themselves with delicacies for which east and west are ransacked, I would have them postpone their benediction to a fitter season, when appetite is laid; when the still small voice can be heard, and the reason of the grace returns—with temperate diet and restricted dishes. Gluttony and surfeiting are

* Rare host.

no proper occasions for thanksgiving. When Jeshurun waxed fat, we read that he kicked. Virgil knew the harpy-nature better, when he put into the mouth of Celæno any thing but a blessing. We may be gratefully sensible of the deliciousness of some kinds of food beyond others, though that is a meaner and inferior gratitude: but the proper object of the grace is sustenance, not relishes; daily bread, not delicacies; the means of life, and not the means of pampering the carcass. With what frame or composure, I wonder, can a city chaplain pronounce his benediction at some great Hall feast, when he knows that his last concluding pious word—and that, in all probability, the sacred name which he preaches—is but the signal for so many impatient harpies to commence their foul orgies, with as little sense of true thankfulness (which is temperance) as those Virgilian fowl! It is well if the good man himself does not feel his devotions a little clouded, those foggy sensuous steams mingling with and polluting the pure altar sacrifice.

7 The severest satire upon full tables and surfeits is the banquet which Satan, in the Paradise Regained, provides for a temptation in the wilderness:—

> A table richly spread in real mode,
> With dishes piled, and meats of noblest sort
> And savour; beasts of chase, or fowl of game,
> In pastry built, or from the spit, or boiled,
> Gris-amber-steamed; all fish from sea or shore,
> Freshet or purling brook, for which was drained
> Pontus, and Lucrine bay, and Afric coast.

8 The Tempter, I warrant you, thought these cates would go down without the recommendatory preface of a benediction. They are like to be short graces where the devil plays the host.—I am afraid the poet wants his usual decorum in this place. Was he thinking of the old Roman luxury, or of a gaudy day at Cambridge? This was a temptation fitter for a Heliogabalus. The whole banquet is too civic and culinary, and the accompaniments altogether a profanation of that deep, abstracted, holy scene. The mighty artillery of sauces, which the cook-fiend conjures up, is out of proportion to the simple wants and plain hunger of the guest. He that disturbed him in his dreams, from his dreams might have been taught better. To the temperate fantasies of the famished Son of God, what sort of feasts presented themselves?—He dreamed indeed,

——— As appetite is wont to dream,
Of meats and drinks, nature's refreshment sweet.

But what meats?—

Him thought, he by the brook of Cherith stood,
And saw the ravens with their horny beaks
Food to Elijah bringing, even and morn;
Though ravenous, taught to abstain from what they brought:
He saw the prophet also how he fled
Into the desert, and how there he slept
Under a juniper; then how awaked
He found his supper on the coals prepared,
And by the angel was bid rise and eat,
And ate the second time after repose,
The strength whereof sufficed him forty days:
Sometimes, that with Elijah he partook,
Or as a guest with Daniel at his pulse.

Nothing in Milton is finelier fancied than these temperate dreams of the divine Hungerer. To which of these two visionary banquets, think you, would the introduction of what is called the grace have been most fitting and pertinent?

9 Theoretically I am no enemy to graces; but practically I own that (before meat especially) they seem to involve something awkward and unseasonable. Our appetites, of one or another kind, are excellent spurs to our reason, which might otherwise but feebly set about the great ends of preserving and continuing the species. They are fit blessings to be contemplated at a distance with a becoming gratitude: but the moment of appetite (the judicious reader will apprehend me) is, perhaps, the least fit season for that exercise. The Quakers, who go about their business, of every description, with more calmness than we, have more title to the use of these benedictory prefaces. I have always admired their silent grace, and the more because I have observed their applications to the meat and drink following to be less passionate and sensual than ours. They are neither gluttons nor wine-bibbers as a people. They eat, as a horse bolts his chopt hay, with indifference, calmness, and cleanly circumstances. They neither grease nor slop themselves. When I see a citizen in his bib and tucker, I cannot imagine it a surplice.

I am no Quaker at my food. I confess I am not indifferent to the kinds of it. Those unctuous morsels of deer's flesh were not made to be received with dispassionate services. I hate a man who swallows it affecting not to know what he is eating. I suspect his taste in higher matters. I shrink instinctively from one who professes to like minced veal. There is a physiognomical character in the tastes for food. C— holds that a man cannot have a pure mind who refuses apple-dumplings. I am not certain but he is right. With the decay of my first innocence, I confess a less and less relish daily for these innocuous cates. The whole vegetable tribe have lost their gust with me. Only I stick to asparagus, which still seems to inspire gentle thoughts. I am impatient and querulous under culinary disappointments, as to come home at the dinner hour, for instance, expecting some savoury mess, and to find one quite tasteless and sapidless. Butter ill melted —that commonest of kitchen failures—puts me beside my tenour.—The author of the Rambler used to make inarticulate animal noises over a favourite food. Was this the music quite proper to be preceded by the grace? or would the pious man have done better to postpone his devotions to a season when the blessing might be contemplated with less perturbation? I quarrel with no man's tastes, nor would set my thin face against those excellent things, in their way, jollity and feasting. But as these exercises, however laudable, have little in them of grace or gracefulness, a man should be sure, before he ventures so to grace them, that while he is pretending his devotions otherwise, he is not secretly kissing his hand to some great fish—his Dagon—with a special consecration of no ark but the fat tureen before him. Graces are the sweet preluding strains to the banquets of angels and children: to the roots and severer repasts of the Chartreuse; to the slender, but not slenderly acknowledged, refection of the poor and humble man: but at the heaped-up boards of the pampered and the luxurious they become of dissonant mood, less timed and tuned to the occasion, methinks, than the noise of those better befitting organs would be, which children hear tales of, at Hog's Norton. We sit too long at our meals, or are too curious in the study of them, or too disordered in our application to them, or engross too great a portion of these good things (which should be common) to our share, to be able with any grace to say grace. To be thankful for what we grasp exceeding our proportion is to add hypocrisy to injustice. A lurking sense of this truth is what makes the performance of this duty so cold and spiritless a service at most tables. In houses where the grace is as indispensable as the napkin, who has not seen that never-settled question arise, as to *who shall say it;* while the good man of the house and the visitor clergyman, or some other guest belike of next authority from years or gravity, shall be bandying about the office between them as a matter of compliment, each of them not unwilling to shift the awkward burthen of an equivocal duty from his own shoulders?

11 I once drank tea in company with two Methodist divines of different persuasions, whom it was my fortune to introduce to each other for the first time that evening. Before the first cup was handed round, one of these reverend gentlemen put it to the other, with all due solemnity, whether he chose to *say any thing.* It seems it is the custom with some sectaries to put up a short prayer before this meal also. His reverend brother did not at first quite apprehend him, but upon an explanation, with little less importance he made answer, that it was not a custom known in his church: in which courteous evasion the other acquiescing for good manners' sake, or in compliance with a weak brother, the supplementary or tea-grace was waived altogether. With what spirit might not Lucian have painted two priests, of *his* religion, playing into each other's hands the compliment of performing or omitting a sacrifice,—the hungry God meantime, doubtful of his incense, with expectant nostrils hovering over the two flamens, and (as between two stools) going away in the end without his supper.

12 A short form upon these occasions is felt to want reverence; a long one, I am afraid, cannot escape the charge of impertinence. I do not quite approve of the epigrammatic conciseness with which that equivocal wag (but my pleasant school-fellow) C. V. L., when importuned for a grace, used to inquire, first slily leering down the table, "Is there no clergyman here?"—significantly adding, "Thank G—." Nor do I think our old form at school quite pertinent, where we were used to preface our bald bread and cheese suppers with a preamble, connecting with that humble blessing a recognition of benefits the most awful and overwhelming to the imagination which religion has to offer. *Non tunc illis erat locus.** I remember we were put to it to reconcile the phrase "good creatures," upon which the blessing rested, with the fare set before us, wilfully understanding

* There was no place for them.

that expression in a low and animal sense,—till some one recalled a legend, which told how in the golden days of Christ's, the young Hospitallers were wont to have smoking joints of roast meat upon their nightly boards, till some pious benefactor, commiserating the decencies, rather than the palates, of the children, commuted our flesh for garments, and gave us—*horresco referens**—trowsers instead of mutton.

* I am horrified to recollect.

On the Feeling of Immortality in Youth

WILLIAM HAZLITT

William Hazlitt (1778–1830) was a British literary critic and essayist. As a youngster, he studied to be an artist, even spending time at the Louvre in Paris. In 1798, he became friends with Samuel Taylor Coleridge; he also built close relationships with other prominent writers of the age—William Wordsworth, Charles Lamb, Leigh Hunt, William Godwin, and others. These writers influenced his writing career, so that by 1821 he had established a distinguished career as a critic and essayist with such works as *The Round Table* (a series of essays), *Table Talk; or Original Essays on Men and Manners*, and *Lectures on the English Poets.* Hazlitt's positions were highly subjective and often intense and impassioned, so he developed enemies and sometimes alienated his friends, even Coleridge and Wordsworth.

In his essay "On the Feeling of Immortality in Youth," Hazlitt demonstrates his vigorous rhetorical style. While recognizing youthful exuberance for life, the essay is actually an argument against growing old. His talent for turns of phrase comes into play when he contemplates bodily infirmity: "We do not in the regular couse of nature die all at once: we have mouldered away gradually long before; faculty after faculty, attachment after attachment, we are torn from ourselves piece-meal while living, year after year takes something away from us; and death only consigns the last remnant of what we were to the grave."

1 No young man believes he shall ever die. It was a saying of my brother's, and a fine one. There is a feeling of Eternity in youth, which makes us amends for every thing. To be young is to be as one of the Immortal Gods. One half of time indeed is flown—the other half remains in store for us with all its countless treasures; for there is no line drawn, and we see no limit to our hopes and wishes. We make the coming age our own.—

"The vast, the unbounded prospect lies before us."

Death, old age, are words without a meaning, that pass by us like the idle air which we regard not. Others may have undergone, or may still be liable to them—we "bear a charmed life," which laughs to scorn all such sickly fancies. As in setting out on a delightful journey, we strain our eager gaze forward—

"Bidding the lovely scenes at distance hail,"—

and see no end to the landscape, new objects presenting themselves as we advance; so, in the commencement of life, we set no bounds to our inclinations, nor to the unrestricted opportunities of gratifying them. We have as yet found no obstacle, no disposition to flag; and it seems that we can go on so for ever. We look round in a new world, full of life, and motion, and ceaseless progress; and feel in ourselves all the vigour and spirit to keep pace with it, and do not foresee from any present symptoms how we shall be left behind in the natural course of things, decline into old age, and drop into the grave. It is the simplicity, and as it were *abstractedness* of our feelings in youth, that (so to speak) identifies us with nature, and (our experience being slight and our passions strong) deludes us into a belief of being immortal like it. Our short-lived connection with existence, we fondly flatter ourselves, is an indissoluble and lasting union—a honey-moon that knows neither coldness, jar, nor separation. As infants smile and sleep, we are rocked in the cradle of our wayward fancies, and lulled into security by the roar of the universe around us—we quaff the cup of life with eager haste without draining it, instead of which it only overflows the more—objects press around us, filling the mind with their magnitude and with the throng of desires that wait upon them, so that we have no room for the thoughts of death. From that plentitude of our being, we cannot change all at once to dust and ashes, we cannot imagine "this sensible, warm motion, to become a kneaded clod"—we are too much dazzled by the brightness of the waking dream around us to look into the darkness of the tomb. We no more see our end than our beginning: the one is lost in oblivion and vacancy, as the other is hid from us by the crowd and hurry of approaching events. Or the grim shadow is seen lingering in the horizon, which we are doomed never to overtake, or whose last, faint, glimmering outline touches upon Heaven and translates us to the skies! Nor would the hold that life has taken of us permit us to detach our thoughts from present objects and pursuits, even if we would. What is there more opposed to health, than sickness; to strength and beauty, than decay and dissolution; to the active search of knowledge than mere oblivion? Or is there none of the usual advantage to bar the approach of Death, and mock his idle threats; Hope supplies their place, and draws a veil over the abrupt termination of all our cherished schemes. While the spirit of youth remains unimpaired, ere the "wine of life is drank up," we are like people intoxicated or in a fever, who are hurried away by the violence of their own sensations: it is only as present objects begin to pall upon the sense, as we have been disappointed in our favourite pursuits, cut off from our closest ties, that passion loosens its hold upon the breast, that we by degrees become weaned from the world, and allow ourselves to contemplate, "as in a glass, darkly," the possibility of parting with it for good. The example of others, the voice of experience, has no effect upon us whatever. Casualties we must avoid: the slow and deliberate advances of age we can play at *hide-and-seek* with. We think ourselves too lusty and too nimble for that blear-eyed decrepid old gentleman to catch us. Like the foolish fat scullion, in Sterne, when she hears that Master Bobby is dead, our only reflection is—"So am not I!" The idea of death, instead of staggering our confidence, rather seems to strengthen and enhance our possession and our enjoyment of life. Others may fall around us like leaves, or be mowed down like flowers by the scythe of Time: these are but tropes and figures to the unreflecting ears and overweening presumption of youth. It is not till we see the flowers of Love, Hope, and Joy, withering around us, and our own pleasures cut up by the roots, that we bring the moral home to ourselves, that we abate something of the wanton extravagance of our pretensions, or that the emptiness and dreariness of the prospect before us reconciles us to the stillness of the grave!

> "Life! thou strange thing, that hast a power to feel
> Thou art, and to perceive that others are."

Well might the poet begin his indignant invective against an art, whose professed object is its destruction, with this animated apostrophe to life. Life is indeed a strange gift, and its privileges are most miraculous. Nor is it singular that when the splendid boon is first granted us, our gratitude, our admiration, and our delight should prevent us from reflecting on our own nothingness, or from thinking it will ever be recalled. Our first and strongest impressions are taken from the mighty scene that is opened to us, and we very innocently transfer its durability as well as magnificence to ourselves. So newly found, we cannot make up our minds to parting with it yet and at least put off that consideration to an indefinite term. Like a clown at a fair, we are full of amazement and rapture, and have no thoughts of going home, or that it will soon be night. We know our existence only from external objects, and we measure it by them. We can never be satisfied with gazing; and nature will still want us to look on and applaud. Otherwise, the sumptuous entertainment, "the feast of reason and the flow of soul," to which they were invited, seems little better than a mockery and a cruel insult. We do not go from a play till the scene is ended, and the lights are ready to be extinguished. But the fair face of things still shines on; shall we be called away, before the curtain falls, or ere we have scarce had a glimpse of what is going on? Like children, our stepmother Nature holds us up to see the raree-show of the universe; and then, as if life were a burthen to support, lets us instantly down again. Yet in that short interval, what "brave sublunary things" does not the spectacle unfold; like a bubble, at one minute reflecting the universe, and the next, shook to air!—To see the golden sun and the azure sky, the outstretched ocean, to walk upon the green earth, and to be lord of a thousand creatures, to look down giddy precipices or over distant flowery vales, to see the world spread out under one's finger in a map, to bring the stars near, to view the smallest insects in a microscope, to read history, and witness the revolutions of empires and the succession of generations, to hear of the glory of Sidon and Tyre, of Babylon and Susa, as of a faded pageant, and to say all these were, and are now nothing, to think that we exist in such a point of time, and in such a corner of space, to be at once spectators and a part of the moving scene, to watch the return of the seasons, of spring and autumn, to hear

—"The stockdove plain amid the forest deep,
That drowsy rustles to the sighing gale"—

to traverse desert wildernesses, to listen to the midnight choir, to visit lighted halls, or plunge into the dungeon's gloom, or sit in crowded theatres and see life itself mocked, to feel heat and cold, pleasure and pain, right and wrong, truth and falsehood, to study the works of art and refine the sense of beauty to agony, to worship fame and to dream of immortality, to have read Shakespeare and belong to the same species as Sir Isaac Newton; to be and to do all this, and then in a moment to be nothing, to have it all snatched from one like a juggler's ball or a phantasmagoria; there is something revolting and incredible to sense in the transition, and no wonder that, aided by youth and warm blood, and the flush of enthusiasm, the mind contrives for a long time to reject it with disdain and loathing as a monstrous and improbable fiction, like a monkey on a house-top, that is loath, amidst its fine discoveries and specious antics, to be tumbled head-long into the street, and crushed to atoms, the sport and laughter of the multitude!

2 The change, from the commencement to the close of life, appears like a fable, after it has taken place; how should we treat it otherwise than as a chimera before it has come to pass? There are some things that happened so long ago, places or persons we have formerly seen, of which such dim traces remain, we hardly know whether it was sleeping or waking they occurred; they are like dreams within the dream of life, a mist, a film before the eye of memory, which, as we try to recall them more distinctly, elude our notice altogether. It is but natural that the lone interval that we thus look back upon, should have appeared long and endless in prospect. There are others so distinct and fresh, they seem but of yesterday—their very vividness might be deemed a pledge of their permanence. Then, however far

back our impressions may go, we find others still older (for our years are multiplied in youth); descriptions of scenes that we had read, and people before our time, Priam and the Trojan war; and even then, Nestor was old and dwelt delighted on his youth, and spoke of the race, of heroes that were no more;—what wonder that, seeing this long line of being pictured in our minds, and reviving as it were in us, we should give ourselves involuntary credit for an indeterminate period of existence? In the Cathedral at Peterborough there is a monument to Mary, Queen of Scots, at which I used to gaze when a boy, while the events of the period, all that had happened since, passed in review before me. If all this mass of feeling and imagination could be crowded into a moment's compass, what might not the whole of life be supposed to contain? We are heirs of the past; we count upon the future as our natural reversion. Besides, there are some of our early impressions so exquisitely tempered, it appears that they must always last—nothing can add to or take away from their sweetness and purity—the first breath of spring, the hyacinth dipped in the dew, the mild lustre of the evening-star, the rainbow after a storm—while we have the full enjoyment of these, we must be young; and what can ever alter us in this respect? Truth, friendship, love, books, are also proof against the canker of time; and while we live, but for them, we can never grow old. We take out a new lease of existence from the objects on which we set our affections, and become abstracted, impassive, immortal in them. We cannot conceive how certain sentiments should ever decay or grow cold in our breasts; and, consequently, to maintain them in their first youthful glow and vigour, the flame of life must continue to burn as bright as ever, or rather, they are the fuel that feed the sacred lamp, that kindle "the purple light of love," and spread a golden cloud around our heads! Again, we not only flourish and survive in our affections (in which we will not listen to the possibility of a change, any more than we foresee the wrinkles on the brow of a mistress), but we have a farther guarantee against the thoughts of death in our favourite studies and pursuits, and in their continual advance. Art we know is long; life, we feel, should be so too. We see no end of the difficulties we have to encounter: perfection is slow of attainment, and we must have time to accomplish it in. Rubens complained that when he had just learnt his art, he was snatched away from it: we trust we shall be more fortunate! A wrinkle in an old head takes whole days to finish it properly: but to catch "the Raphael grace, the Guido air," no limit should be put to our endeavours. What a prospect for the future! What a task we have entered upon! and shall we be arrested in the middle of it? We do not reckon our time thus employed lost, or our pains thrown away, or our progress slow—we do not droop or grow tired, but "gain new vigour at our endless task;"—and shall Time grudge us the opportunity to finish what we have auspiciously begun, and have formed a sort of compact with nature to achieve? The fame of the great names we look up to is also imperishable; and shall not we, who contemplate it with such intense yearnings, imbibe a portion of ethereal fire, the *divinæ particula auræ*, which nothing can extinguish? I remember to have looked at a print of Rembrandt for hours together, without being conscious of the flight of time, trying to resolve it into its component parts, to connect its strong and sharp gradations, to learn the secret of its reflected lights, and found neither satiety nor pause in the prosecution of my studies. The print over which I was poring would last long enough; why should the idea in my mind, which was finer, more impalpable, perish before it? At this, I redoubled the ardour of my pursuit, and by the very subtlety and refinement of my inquiries, seemed to bespeak for them an exemption from corruption and the rude grasp of Death.

3 Objects, on our first acquaintance with them, have that singleness and integrity of impression that it seems as if nothing could destroy or obliterate them, so firmly are they stamped and rivetted on the brain. We repose on them with a sort of voluptuous indolence, in full faith and boundless confidence. We are absorbed in the present moment, or return to the same point—idling away a great deal of time in youth, thinking we have enough and to spare. There is often a local feeling in the air, which is as fixed as if it were of marble; we loiter in dim cloisters, losing ourselves in thought and in their glimmering arches; a winding road before us seems as long as the journey of life, and as full of events. Time and experience dissipate this illusion; and by reducing them to detail, circumscribe the limits of our expectations. It is only as the pageant of life passes by and the masques turn their backs upon us, that we see through the deception, or believe that the train will have an end. In many cases, the slow progress and monotonous texture of our lives, before we mingle with the world and are embroiled in its affairs, has a tendency to aid the same feeling. We have a difficulty, when left to ourselves, and without the resource of books or some more lively pursuit, to "beguile the slow and creeping hours of time," and argue that if it

moves on always at this tedious snail's-pace, it can never come to an end. We are willing to skip over certain portions of it that separate us from favourite objects, that irritate ourselves at the unnecessary delay. The young are prodigal of life from a superabundance of it; the old are tenacious on the same score, because they have little left, and cannot enjoy even what remains of it.

4 For my part, I set out in life with the French Revolution, and that event had considerable influence on my early feelings, as on those of others. Youth was then doubly such. It was the dawn of a new era, a new impulse had been given to men's minds, and the sun of Liberty rose upon the sun of Life in the same day, and both were proud to run their race together. Little did I dream, while my first hopes and wishes went hand in hand with those of the human race, that long before my eyes should close, that dawn would be overcast, and set once more in the night of despotism—"total eclipse!" Happy that I did not. I felt for years, and during the best part of my existence, *heart-whole* in that cause, and triumphed in the triumphs over the enemies of man! At that time, while the fairest aspirations of the human mind seemed about to be realized, ere the image of man was defaced and his breast mangled in scorn, philosophy took a higher, poetry could afford a deeper range. At that time, to read the "ROBBERS," was indeed delicious, and to hear

> "From the dungeon of the tower time-rent,
> That fearful voice, a famish'd father's cry,"

could be borne only amidst the fulness of hope, the crash of the fall of the strong holds of power, and the exulting sounds of the march of human freedom. What feelings the death-scene in Don Carlos sent into the soul! In that headlong career of lofty enthusiasm, and the joyous opening of the prospects of the world and our own, the thought of death crossing it, smote doubly cold upon the mind; there was a stifling sense of oppression and confinement, an impatience of our present knowledge, a desire to grasp the whole of our existence in one strong embrace, to sound the mystery of life and death, and in order to put an end to the agony of doubt and dread, to burst through our prison-house, and confront the King of Terrors in his grisly palace! . . . As I was writing out this passage, my miniature-picture when a child lay on the mantle-piece, and I took it out of the case to look at it. I could perceive few traces of myself in it; but there was the same placid brow, the dimpled mouth, the same timid, inquisitive glance as ever. But its careless smile did not seem to reproach me with having become a recreant to the sentiments that were then sown in my mind, or with having written a sentence that could call up a blush in this image of ingenuous youth!

"That time is past with all its giddy raptures." Since the future was barred to my progress, I have turned for consolation to the past, gathering up the fragments of my early recollections, and putting them into a form that might live. It is thus, that when we find our personal and substantial identity vanishing from us, we strive to gain a reflected and substituted one in our thoughts: we do not like to perish wholly, and wish to bequeath our names at least to posterity. As long as we can keep alive our cherished thoughts and nearest interests in the minds of others, we do not appear to have retired altogether from the stage, we still occupy a place in the estimation of mankind, exercise a powerful influence over them, and it is only our bodies that are trampled into dust or dispersed to air. Our darling speculations still find favour and encouragement, and we make as good a figure in the eyes of our descendants, nay, perhaps, a better than we did in our life-time. This is one point gained; the demands of our self-love are so far satisfied. Besides, if by the proofs of intellectual superiority we survive ourselves in this world, by exemplary virtue or unblemished faith, we are taught to ensure an interest in another and a higher state of being, and to anticipate at the same time the applauses of men and angels.

> "Even from the tomb the voice of nature cries;
> Even in our ashes live their wonted fires."

As we advance in life, we acquire a keener sense of the value of time. Nothing else, indeed, seems of any consequence; and we become misers in this respect. We try to arrest its few last tottering steps, and to make it linger on the brink of the grave. We can never leave off wondering how that which has ever been should cease to be, and would still live on, that we may wonder at our own shadow, and when "all the life of life is flown," dwell on the retrospect of the past. This is accompanied by a mechanical tenaciousness of whatever we possess, by a distrust and a sense of fallacious hollowness in all we see. Instead of the full, pulpy feeling of youth, every thing is flat and insipid. The world is a painted witch, that puts us off with false shews and tempting appearances. The ease, the jocund gaiety, the unsuspecting security of youth are fled: nor can we, without flying in the face of common sense,

> "From the last dregs of life, hope to receive
> What its first sprightly runnings could not give."

If we can slip out of the world without notice or mischance, can tamper with bodily infirmity, and frame our minds to the becoming composure of *still-life*, before we sink into total insensibility, it is as much as we ought to expect. We do not in the regular course of nature die all at once: we have mouldered away gradually long before; faculty after faculty, attachment after attachment, we are torn from ourselves piece-meal while living; year after year takes something from us; and death only consigns the last remnant of what we were to the grave. The revulsion is not so great, and a quiet *euthanasia* is a winding-up of the plot, that is not out of reason or nature.

6 That we should thus in a manner outlive ourselves, and dwindle imperceptibly into nothing, is not surprising, when even in our prime the strongest impressions leave so little traces of themselves behind, and the last object is driven out by the succeeding one. How little effect is produced on us at any time by the books we have read, the scenes we have witnessed, the sufferings we have gone through! Think only of the variety of feelings we experience in reading an interesting romance, or being present at a fine play—what beauty, what sublimity, what soothing, what heart-rending emotions! You would suppose these would last for ever, or at least subdue the mind to a correspondent tone and harmony—while we turn over the page, while the scene is passing before us, it seems as if nothing could ever after shake our resolution, that "treason domestic, foreign levy, nothing could touch us farther!" The first splash of mud we get, on entering the street, the first pettifogging shop-keeper that cheats us out of two-pence, and the whole vanishes clean out of our remembrance, and we become the idle prey of the most petty and annoying circumstances. The mind soars by an effort to the grand and lofty: it is at home, in the grovelling, the disagreeable, and the little. This happens in the height and hey-day of our existence, when novelty gives a stronger impulse to the blood and takes a faster hold of the brain, (I have known the impression on coming out of a gallery of pictures then last half a day)—as we grow old, we become more feeble and querulous, every object "reverbs its own hollowness," and both worlds are not enough to satisfy the peevish importunity

and extravagant presumption of our desires! There are a few superior, happy beings, who are born with a temper exempt from every trifling annoyance. This spirit sits serene and smiling as in its native skies, and a divine harmony (whether heard or not) plays around them. This is to be at peace. Without this, it is in vain to fly into deserts, or to build a hermitage on the top of rocks, if regret and ill-humour follow us there: and with this, it is needless to make the experiment. The only true retirement is that of the heart; the only true leisure is the repose of the passions. To such persons it makes little difference whether they are young or old; and they die as they have lived, with graceful resignation.

Nature

RALPH WALDO EMERSON

Ralph Waldo Emerson (1803–1882) was born in Boston; his early life was one of poverty. His genius was recognized, however, and, with help of relatives and friends, he earned a degree from Harvard in 1821. He then entered divinity school, was ordained, and preached for a time, but he soon abandoned this profession. After a year in Europe, he returned to America to become an essayist, poet, orator, and critic. Thoughtful and well-educated, he took his philosophy directly to the American people, urging them toward self-reliance and the integrity of every individual. In 1836, his first book, *Nature,* advanced his theories on transcendentalism and won for him an immediate following. The Transcendental Club advanced his theories, and for a few years Emerson edited the club's magazine, *The Dial.* His 1837 address at Harvard, "The American Scholar," further defined his views on humanism and asserted independence from Britain for America's writers and scholars. In 1838, his "Divinity School Address" challenged the authority of "historical Christianity" and advanced his new religion, which was based on a close identity with nature and an intuitive knowledge of God.

In *Nature,* Emerson encourages his readers to step outside and contemplate the glory and grandeur of the life around them. He says, "Standing on the bare ground,—my head bathed by the blithe air, and uplifted into infinite space,—all mean egotism vanishes. I become a transparent eye-ball. I am nothing. I see all. The currents of the Universal Being circulate through me; I am part or particle of God." With that pronouncement, he builds his philosophy. Nature provides as "commodities" all the advantages gained by our senses.

It offers beauty to delight our imaginations. It contributes to our language because "words are signs of natural facts" and thereby "convey a spiritual import." Finally, nature is a form of discipline because it takes us into a school of understanding that trains us in universal truths. Ultimately, he asserts that "idealism sees the world in God" because nature presents "the world in precisely that view which is most desirable to the mind."

1 To go into solitude, a man needs to retire as much from his chamber as from society. I am not solitary whilst I read and write, though nobody is with me. But if a man would be alone, let him look at the stars. The rays that come from those heavenly worlds, will separate between him and vulgar things. One might think the atmosphere was made transparent with this design, to give man, in the heavenly bodies, the perpetual presence of the sublime. Seen in the streets of cities, how great they are! If the stars should appear one night in a thousand years, how would men believe and adore; and preserve for many generations the remembrance of the city of God which had been shown! But every night come out these preachers of beauty, and light the universe with their admonishing smile.

2 The stars awaken a certain reverence, because though always present, they are always inaccessible; but all natural objects make a kindred impression, when the mind is open to their influence. Nature never wears a mean appearance. Neither does the wisest man extort all her secret, and lose his curiosity by finding out all her perfection. Nature never became a toy to a wise spirit. The flowers, the animals, the mountains, reflected all the wisdom of his best hour, as much as they had delighted the simplicity of his childhood.

3 When we speak of nature in this manner, we have a distinct but most poetical sense in the mind. We mean the integrity of impression made by manifold natural objects. It is this which distinguishes the stick of timber of the wood-cutter, from the tree of the poet. The charming landscape which I saw this morning, is indubitably made up of some twenty or thirty farms. Miller owns this field, Locke that, and Manning the woodland beyond. But none of them owns the

landscape. There is a property in the horizon which no man has but he whose eye can integrate all the parts, that is, the poet. This is the best part of these men's farms, yet to this their land-deeds give them no title.

4 To speak truly, few adult persons can see nature. Most persons do not see the sun. At least they have a very superficial seeing. The sun illuminates only the eye of the man, but shines into the eye and the heart of the child. The lover of nature is he whose inward and outward senses are still truly adjusted to each other; who has retained the spirit of infancy even into the era of manhood. His intercourse with heaven and earth, becomes part of his daily food. In the presence of nature, a wild delight runs through the man, in spite of real sorrows. Nature says,—he is my creature, and maugre all his impertinent griefs, he shall be glad with me. Not the sun or the summer alone, but every hour and season yields its tribute of delight; for every hour and change corresponds to and authorizes a different state of the mind, from breathless noon to grimmest midnight. Nature is a setting that fits equally well a comic or a mourning piece. In good health, the air is a cordial of incredible virtue. Crossing a bare common, in snow puddles, at twilight, under a clouded sky, without having in my thoughts any occurrence of special good fortune, I have enjoyed a perfect exhilaration. Almost I fear to think how glad I am. In the woods too, a man casts off his years, as the snake his slough, and at what period soever of life, is always a child. In the woods, is perpetual youth. Within these plantations of God, a decorum and sanctity reign, a perennial festival is dressed, and the guest sees not how he should tire of them in a thousand years. In the woods, we return to reason and faith. There I feel that nothing can befal me in life,—no disgrace, no calamity, (leaving me my eyes,) which nature cannot repair. Standing on the bare ground,—my head bathed by the blithe air, and uplifted into infinite space,—all mean egotism vanishes. I become a transparent eye-ball. I am nothing. I see all. The currents of the Universal Being circulate through me; I am part or particle of God. The name of the nearest friend sounds then foreign and accidental. To be brothers, to be acquaintances,—master or servant, is then a trifle and a disturbance. I am the lover of uncontained and immortal beauty. In the wilderness, I find something more dear and connate than in streets or villages. In the tranquil landscape, and especially in the distant line of the horizon, man beholds somewhat as beautiful as his own nature.

5 The greatest delight which the fields and woods minister, is the suggestion of an occult relation between man and the vegetable. I am not alone and unacknowledged. They nod to me and I to them. The waving of the boughs in the storm, is new to me and old. It takes me by surprise, and yet is not unknown. Its effect is like that of a higher thought or a better emotion coming over me, when I deemed I was thinking justly or doing right.

6 Yet it is certain that the power to produce this delight, does not reside in nature, but in man, or in a harmony of both. It is necessary to use these pleasures with great temperance. For, nature is not always tricked in holiday attire, but the same scene which yesterday breathed perfume and glittered as for the frolic of the nymphs, is overspread with melancholy today. Nature always wears the colors of the spirit. To a man laboring under calamity, the heat of his own fire hath sadness in it. Then, there is a kind of contempt of the landscape felt by him who has just lost by death a dear friend. The sky is less grand as it shuts down over less worth in the population.

Genius and Originality

JOHN STUART MILL

John Stuart Mill (1806–1873) was a British businessman, philosopher, and writer. He was educated at home by his father, learning Greek and Latin before age fourteen. At a young age, he published essays in *Westminster, Monthly Repository, London Review*, and other magazines. In his book *Logic*, he developed his theories of Utilitarianism, which advocated the dignity of each person and required a new examination of production, distribution, socialist solutions, and the role of the working class, especially the condition of women. In particular, Mill believed that we should exercise our human reason, investigating for ourselves and not blindly accepting what we might find in books or in the lectures of others. In that sense, he endorsed the empirical school of philosophy and advocated the search for evidence as a necessary step toward reaching conclusions.

In "Genius and Originality," Mill defends the role and scope of people who advance new and sometimes radical ideas, inventions, and methods. He writes, "Genius can only breathe freely in an *atmosphere* of freedom." Yet the unoriginal minds of the world do not understand persons with genius and would impede them. Without originality, the mediocrity of the masses would become "the ascendant power among mankind." His words play well still today, especially when he notes, "In this age the mere example of nonconformity, the mere refusal to bend the knee to custom, is itself a service. . . . That so few now dare to be eccentric, marks the chief danger of the time."

1 It will not be denied by anybody, that originality is a valuable element in human affairs. There is always need of persons not only to discover new truths, and point out when what were once truths are true no longer, but also to commence new practices, and set the example of more enlightened conduct, and better taste and sense in human life. This cannot well be gainsaid by anybody who does not believe that the world has already attained perfection in all its ways and practices. It is true that this benefit is not capable of being rendered by everybody alike: there are but few persons, in comparison with the whole of mankind, whose experiments, if adopted by others, would be likely to be any improvement on established practice. But these few are the salt of the earth; without them, human life would become a stagnant pool. Not only is it they who introduce good things which did not before exist; it is they who keep the life in those which already existed. If there were nothing new to be done, would human intellect cease to be necessary? Would it be a reason why those who do the old things should forget why they are done, and do them like cattle, not like human beings? There is only too great a tendency in the best beliefs and practices to degenerate into the mechanical; and unless there were a succession of persons whose ever-recurring originality prevents the grounds of those beliefs and practices from becoming merely traditional, such dead matter would not resist the smallest shock from anything really alive, and there would be no reason why civilization should not die out, as in the Byzantine Empire. Persons of genius, it is true, are, and are always likely to be, a small minority; but in order to have them, it is necessary to preserve the soil in which they grow. Genius can only breathe freely in an *atmosphere* of freedom. Persons of genius are, *ex vi termini* [by definition], *more* individual than any other people—less capable, consequently, of fitting themselves, without hurtful compression, into any of the small number of moulds which society provides in order to save its members the trouble of forming their own character. If from timidity they consent to be forced into one of these moulds, and to let all that part of themselves which cannot expand under the

pressure remain unexpanded, society will be little the better for their genius. If they are of a stronger character, and break their fetters, they become a mark for the society which has not succeeded in reducing them to commonplace, to point at with solemn warning as "wild," "erratic," and the like; much as if one should complain of the Niagra river for not flowing smoothly between its banks like a Dutch canal.

2 I insist thus emphatically on the importance of genius, and the necessity of allowing it to unfold itself freely both in thought and in practice, being well aware that no one will deny the position in theory, but knowing also that almost every one, in reality, is totally indifferent to it. People think genius a fine thing if it enables a man to write an exciting poem, or paint a picture. But in its true sense, that of originality in thought and action, though no one says that it is not a thing to be admired, nearly all, at heart, think that they can do very well without it. Unhappily this is too natural to be wondered at. Originality is the one thing which unoriginal minds cannot feel the use of. They cannot see what it is to do for them: how should they? If they could see what it would do for them, it would not be originality. The first service which originality has to render them, is that of opening their eyes: which being once fully done, they would have a chance of being themselves original. Meanwhile, recollecting that nothing was ever yet done which some one was not the first to do, and that all good things which exist are the fruits of originality, let them be modest enough to believe that there is something still left for it to accomplish, and assure themselves that they are more in need of originality, the less they are conscious of the want.

3 In sober truth, whatever homage may be professed, or even paid, to real or supposed mental superiority, the general tendency of things throughout the world is to render mediocrity the ascendant power among mankind. In ancient history, in the Middle Ages, and in a diminishing degree through the long transition from feudality to the present time, the individual was a power in himself; and if he had either great talents or a high social position, he was a considerable power. At present individuals are lost in the crowd. In politics it is almost a triviality to say that public opinion now rules the world. The only power deserving the name is that of masses, and of governments while they make themselves the organ of the tendencies and instincts of masses. This is as true in the moral and social relations of private life as in public transactions. Those whose opinions go by

the name of public opinion, are not always the same sort of public: in America, they are the whole white population; in England, chiefly the middle class. But they are always a mass, that is to say, collective mediocrity. And what is a still greater novelty, the mass do not now take their opinions from dignitaries in Church or State, from ostensible leaders, or from books. Their thinking is done for them by men much like themselves, addressing them or speaking in their name, on the spur of the moment, through the newspapers. I am not complaining of all this. I do not assert that anything better is compatible, as a general rule, with the present low state of the human mind. But that does not hinder the government of mediocrity from being mediocre government. No government by a democracy or a numerous aristocracy, either in its political acts or in the opinions, qualities, and tone of mind which it fosters, ever did or could rise above mediocrity, except in so far as the sovereign. Many have let themselves be guided (which in their best times they always have done) by the counsels and influence of a more highly gifted and instructed One or Few. The initiation of all wise or noble things, comes and must come from individuals; generally at first from some one individual. The honor and glory of the average man is that he is capable of following that initiative; that he can respond internally to wise and noble things, and be led to them with his eyes open. I am not countenancing the sort of "hero-worship" which applauds the strong man of genius for forcibly seizing on the government of the world and making it do his bidding in spite of itself. All he can claim is, freedom to point out the way. The power of compelling others into it, is not only inconsistent with the freedom and development of all the rest, but corrupting to the strong man himself. It does seem, however, that when the opinions of masses of merely average men are everywhere become or becoming the dominant power, the counterpoise and corrective to that tendency would be, the more and more pronounced individuality of those who stand on the higher eminences of thought. It is in these circumstances most especially, that exceptional individuals, instead of being deterred, should be encouraged in acting differently from the mass. In other times there was no advantage in their doing so, unless they acted not only differently, but better. In this age, the mere example of nonconformity, the mere refusal to bend the knee to custom, is itself a service. Precisely because the tyranny of opinion is such as to make eccentricity a reproach, it is desirable, in order to break through that tyranny, that people should be eccentric. Eccentricity has always abounded when and where strength of character has abounded; and the amount of eccentricity in a society has generally been proportional to the amount of genius, mental vigor, and moral courage which it contained. That so few now dare to be eccentric, marks the chief danger of the time.

from "Civil Disobedience"

HENRY DAVID THOREAU

Henry David Thoreau (1817–1862) was born in Concord, Massachusetts, the son of a father who made pencils and a mother who took in boarders. His parents helped him to earn a degree from Harvard College in 1837. Thoreau is best known for *Walden,* a lengthy essay on the role of humans in relation to the environment, in particular the necessity for human beings to respect, preserve, and—on occasion—worship nature. Thoreau spent about two years living alone at Walden Pond, where his spirit was nourished by daily contact with the outdoors. Thoreau came to believe that citizens must speak out and act against immoral behavior by social and political institutions. He felt that every individual must be free of government restraint and unnecessary taxation. He even spent a night in jail in 1846 when he refused to pay poll taxes in opposition to slavery, which had become an issue during the Mexican War.

"Civil Disobedience" develops his ideas on *passive resistance,* by which citizens assert their independence by ignoring or disobeying unjust regulations. He writes, "There will never be a really free and enlightened State until the State comes to recognize the individual as a higher and independent power, from which all its own power and authority are derived, and treats him accordingly." He attacks the idea of a standing army, in which "the mass of men serve the state thus, not as men mainly, but as machines, with their bodies." He argues that if just one person stands firm against injustice, the world will take notice, for "what is once well done is done forever."

His theories in this essay influenced the thinking of Leo Tolstoy, Mahatma Gandhi, and Martin Luther King, Jr.

1 I heartily accept the motto,—"That government is best which governs least"; and I should like to see it acted up to more rapidly and systematically. Carried out, it finally amounts to this, which also I believe,—"That government is best which governs not at all"; and when men are prepared for it, that will be the kind of government which they will have. Government is at best but an expedient; but most governments are usually, and all governments are sometimes, inexpedient. The objections which have been brought against a standing army, and they are many and weighty, and deserve to prevail, may also at last be brought against a standing government. The standing army is only an arm of the standing govenment. The government itself, which is only the mode which the people have chosen to execute their will, is equally liable to be abused and perverted before the people can act through it. Witness the present Mexican war, the work of comparatively a few individuals using the standing government as their tool; for, in the outset, the people would not have consented to this measure.

2 This American government,—what is it but a tradition, though a recent one, endeavoring to transmit itself unimpaired to posterity, but each instant losing some of its integrity? It has not the vitality and force of a single living man; for a single man can bend it to his will. It is a sort of wooden gun to the people themselves. But it is not the less necessary for this; for the people must have some complicated machinery or other, and hear its din, to satisfy that idea of government which they have. Governments show thus how successfully men can be imposed on, even impose on themselves, for their own advantage. It is excellent, we must all allow. Yet this government never of itself furthered any enterprise, but by the alacrity with which it got out of its way. *It* does not keep the country free. *It* does not settle the West. *It* does not educate. The character inherent in the American people has done all that has been accomplished; and it would have done somewhat more, if the government had not sometimes got in its way. For government is an expedient by which men would fain succeed in letting one another alone; and, as has been said, when it

is most expedient, the governed are most let alone by it. Trade and commerce, if they were not made of India-rubber, would never manage to bounce over the obstacles which legislators are continually putting in their way; and, if one were to judge these men wholly by the effects of their actions and not partly by their intentions, they would deserve to be classed and punished with those mischievous persons who put obstructions on the railroads.

3 But, to speak practically and as a citizen, unlike those who call themselves no-government men, I ask for, not at once no government, but *at once* a better government. Let every man make known what kind of government would command his respect, and that will be one step toward obtaining it.

4 After all, the practical reason why, when the power is once in the hands of the people, a majority are permitted, and for a long period continue, to rule is not because they are most likely to be in the right, nor because this seems fairest to the minority, but because they are physically the strongest. But a government in which the majority rule in all cases cannot be based on justice, even as far as men understand it. Can there not be a government in which majorities do not virtually decide right and wrong, but conscience?—in which majorities decide only those questions to which the rule of expediency is applicable? Must the citizen ever for a moment, or in the least degree, resign his conscience to the legislator? Why has every man a conscience, then? I think that we should be men first, and subjects afterward. It is not desirable to cultivate a respect for the law, so much as for the right. The only obligation which I have a right to assume is to do at any time what I think right. It is truly enough said, that a corporation has no conscience; but a corporation of conscientious men is a corporation *with* a conscience. Law never made men a whit more just; and, by means of their respect for it, even the well-disposed are daily made the agents of injustice. A common and natural result of an undue respect for law is, that you may see a file of soldiers, colonel, captain, corporal, privates, powder-monkeys, and all, marching in admirable order over hill and dale to the wars, against their wills, ay, against their common sense and consciences, which makes it very steep marching indeed, and produces a palpitation of the heart. They have no doubt that it is a damnable business in which they are concerned; they are all peaceably inclined. Now, what are they? Men at all? Or small movable forts and magazines, at the service of some unscrupulous man in power?

Visit the Navy-Yard, and behold a marine, such a man as an American government can make, or such as it can make a man with its black arts,—a mere shadow and reminiscence of humanity, a man laid out alive and standing, and already, as one may say, buried under arms with funeral accompaniments, though it may be,—

> Not a drum was heard, not a funeral note,
>   As his corse to the rampart we hurried;
> Not a soldier discharged his farewell shot
>   O'er the grave where our hero we buried.

5 The mass of men serve the state thus, not as men mainly, but as machines, with their bodies. They are the standing army, and the militia, jailors, constables, posse comitatus, etc. In most cases there is no free exercise whatever of the judgment or of the moral sense; but they put themselves on a level with wood and earth and stones; and wooden men can perhaps be manufactured that will serve the purpose as well. Such command no more respect than men of straw or a lump of dirt. They have the same sort of worth only as horses and dogs. Yet such as these even are commonly esteemed good citizens. Others—as most legislators, politicians, lawyers, ministers, and office-holders—serve the state chiefly with their heads; and, as they rarely make any moral distinctions, they are as likely to serve the Devil, without *intending* it, as God. A very few, as heroes, patriots, martyrs, reformers in the great sense, and *men,* serve the state with their consciences also, and so necessarily resist it for the most part; and they are commonly treated as enemies by it. A wise man will only be useful as a man, and will not submit to be "clay," and "stop a hole to keep the wind away," but leave that office to his dust at least:

> I am too high-born to be propertied,
> To be a secondary at control,
> Or useful serving-man and instrument
> To any sovereign state throughout the world.

6 He who gives himself entirely to his fellow-men appears to them useless and selfish; but he who gives himself partially to them is pronounced a benefactor and philanthropist.

7 How does it become a man to behave toward this American government to-day? I answer, that he cannot without disgrace be associated with it. I cannot for an instant recognize that political organization as *my* government which is the *slave's* government also.

8 All men recognize the right of revolution; that is, the right to refuse allegiance to, and to resist, the government, when its tyranny or its inefficiency are great and unendurable. But almost all say that such is not the case now. But such was the case, they think, in the Revolution of '75. If one were to tell me that this was a bad government because it taxed certain foreign commodities brought to its ports, it is most probable that I should not make an ado about it, for I can do without them. All machines have their friction; and possibly this does enough good to counterbalance the evil. At any rate, it is a great evil to make a stir about it. But when the friction comes to have its machine, and oppression and robbery are organized, I say, let us not have such a machine any longer. In other words, when a sixth of the population of a nation which has undertaken to be the refuge of liberty are slaves, and a whole country is unjustly overrun and conquered by a foreign army, and subjected to military law, I think that it is not too soon for honest men to rebel and revolutionize. What makes this duty the more urgent is the fact that the country so overrun is not our own, but ours is the invading army. . . .

9 Practically speaking, the opponents to a reform in Massachusetts are not a hundred thousand politicians at the South, but a hundred thousand merchants and farmers here, who are more interested in commerce and agriculture than they are in humanity, and are not prepared to do justice to the slave and to Mexico, *cost what it may.* I quarrel not with far-off foes, but with those who, near at home, coöperate with, and do the bidding of, those far away, and without whom the latter would be harmless. We are accustomed to say, that the mass of men are unprepared, but improvement is slow, because the few are not materially wiser or better than the many. It is not so important that many should be as good as you, as that there be some absolute goodness somewhere; for that will leaven the whole lump. There are thousands who are *in opinion* opposed to slavery and to the war, who yet in effect do nothing to put an end to them; who, esteeming themselves children of Washington and Franklin, sit down with their hands in their pockets, and say that they know not what to do, and do nothing; who even postpone the question of freedom to the question of free-trade, and quietly read the prices-current along with the latest advices from Mexico, after dinner, and, it may be, fall asleep over them both. What is the price-current of an honest man and patriot to-day? They hesitate, and they regret,

and sometimes they petition; but they do nothing in earnest and with effect. They will wait, well disposed, for others to remedy the evil, that they may no longer have it to regret. At most, they give only a cheap vote, and a feeble countenance and Godspeed, to the right, as it goes by them. There are nine hundred and ninety-nine patrons of virtue to one virtuous man. But it is easier to deal with the real possessor of a thing than with the temporary guardian of it.

10 All voting is a sort of gaming, like checkers or backgammon, with a slight moral tinge to it, a playing with right and wrong, with moral questions; and betting naturally accompanies it. The character of the voters is not staked. I cast my vote, perchance, as I think right; but I am not vitally concerned that that right should prevail. I am willing to leave it to the majority. Its obligation, therefore, never exceeds that of expediency. Even voting *for the right* is *doing* nothing for it. Is it only expressing to men feebly your desire that it should prevail. A wise man will not leave the right to the mercy of chance, nor wish it to prevail through the power of the majority. There is but little virtue in the action of masses of men. When the majority shall at length vote for the abolition of slavery, it will be because they are indifferent to slavery, or because there is but little slavery left to be abolished by their vote. *They* will then be the only slaves. Only *his* vote can hasten the abolition of slavery who asserts his own freedom by his vote.

11 I hear of a convention to be held at Baltimore, or elsewhere, for the selection of a candidate for the Presidency, made up chiefly of editors, and men who are politicians by profession; but I think, what is it to any independent, intelligent, and respectable man what decision they may come to? Shall we not have the advantage of his wisdom and honesty, nevertheless? Can we not count upon some independent votes? Are there not many individuals in the country who do not attend conventions? But no: I find that the respectable man, so called, has immediately drifted from his position, and despairs of his country, when his country has more reason to despair of him. He forthwith adopts one of the candidates thus selected as the only *available* one, thus proving that he is himself *available* for any purposes of the demagogue. His vote is of no more worth than that of any unprincipled foreigner or hireling native, who may have been bought. O for a man who is a *man*, and, as my neighbor says, has a bone in his back which you cannot pass your hand through! Our statistics are at fault: The population has been returned too large.

How many *men* are there to a square thousand miles in this country? Hardly one. Does not America offer any inducement for men to settle here? The American has dwindled into an Odd Fellow,—one who may be known by the development of his organ of gregariousness, and a manifest lack of intellect and cheerful self-reliance; whose first and chief concern, on coming into the world, is to see that the Alms-houses are in good repair; and, before yet he has lawfully donned the virile garb, to collect a fund for the support of the widows and orphans that may be; who, in sort, ventures to live only by the aid of the Mutual Insurance company, which has promised to bury him decently.

12 It is not a man's duty, as a matter of course, to devote himself to the eradication of any, even the most enormous wrong; he may still properly have other concerns to engage him; but it is his duty, at least, to wash his hands of it, and, if he gives it no thought longer, not to give it practically his support. If I devote myself to other pursuits and contemplations, I must first see, at least, that I do not pursue them sitting upon another man's shoulders. I must get off him first, that he may pursue his contemplations too. See what gross inconsistency is tolerated. I have heard some of my townsmen say, "I should like to have them order me out to help put down an insurrection of the slaves, or to march to Mexico;—see if I would go"; and yet these very men have each, directly by their allegiance, and so indirectly, at least, by their money, furnished a substitute. The soldier is applauded who refuses to serve in an unjust war by those who do not refuse to sustain the unjust government which makes the war; is applauded by those whose own act and authority he disregards and sets at naught; as if the state were penitent and to that degree that it hired one to scourge it while it sinned, but not to that degree that it left off sinning for a moment. Thus, under the name of Order and Civil Government, we are all made at last to pay homage to and support our own meanness. After the first blush of sin comes its indifference, and from immoral it becomes, as it were, *un*moral, and not quite unnecessary to that life which we have made.

13 The broadest and most prevalent error requires the most disinterested virtue to sustain it. The slight reproach to which the virtue of patriotism is commonly liable, the noble are most likely to incur. Those who, while they disapprove of the character and measures of a government, yield to it their allegiance and support are undoubtedly its most conscientious supporters, and so frequently the most serious

obstacles to reform. Some are petitioning the state to dissolve the Union, to disregard the requisitions of the President. Why do they not dissolve it themselves,—the union between themselves and the state,—and refuse to pay their quota into its treasury? Do not they stand in the same relation to the state that the state does to the Union? And have not the same reasons prevented the state from resisting the Union which have prevented them from resisting the state?

14 How can a man be satisfied to entertain an opinion merely, and enjoy *it?* Is there any enjoyment in it, if his opinion is that he is aggrieved? If you are cheated out of a single dollar by your neighbor, you do not rest satisfied with knowing that you are cheated, or with saying that you are cheated, or even with petitioning him to pay you your due; but you take effectual steps at once to obtain the full amount, and see that you are never cheated again. Action from principle, the perception and the performance of right, changes things and relations; it is essentially revolutionary, and does not consist wholly with anything which was. It not only divides states and churches, it divides families; ay, it divides the *individual,* separating the diabolical in him from the divine.

15 Unjust laws exist: shall we be content to obey them, or shall we endeavor to amend them, and obey them until we have succeeded, or shall we transgress them at once? Men generally, under such a government as this, think that they ought to wait until they have persuaded the majority to alter them. They think that, if they should resist, the remedy would be worse than the evil. But it is the fault of the government itself that the remedy *is* worse than the evil. *It* makes it worse. Why is it not more apt to anticipate and provide for reform? Why does it not cherish its wise minority? Why does it cry and resist before it is hurt? Why does it not encourage its citizens to be on the alert to point out its faults and *do* better than it would have them? Why does it always crucify Christ, and excommunicate Copernicus and Luther, and pronounce Washington and Franklin rebels? . . .

16 I meet this American government, or its representative, the state government, directly, and face to face, once a year—no more—in the person of its tax-gatherer; this is the only mode in which a man situated as I am necessarily meets it; and it then says distinctly, Recognize me; and the simplest, most effectual, and, in the present posture of affairs, the indispensablest mode of treating with it on

this head, of expressing your little satisfaction with and love for it, is to deny it then. My civil neighbor, the tax-gatherer, is the very man I have to deal with,—for it is, after all, with men and not with parchment that I quarrel,—and he has voluntarily chosen to be an agent of the government. How shall he ever know well what he is and does as an officer of the government, or as a man, until he is obliged to consider whether he shall treat me, his neighbor, for whom he has respect, as a neighbor and well-disposed man, or as a maniac and disturber of the peace, and see if he can get over this obstruction to his neighborliness without a ruder and more impetuous thought or speech corresponding with his action. I know this well, that if one thousand, if one hundred, if ten men whom I could name,—if ten *honest* men only,—ay, if *one* HONEST man, in this State of Massachusetts, *ceasing to hold slaves,* were actually to withdraw from this co-partnership, and be locked up in the county jail therefor, it would be the abolition of slavery in America. For it matters not how small the beginning may seem to be: what is once well done is done forever. But we love better to talk about it: that we say is our mission. Reform keeps many scores of newspapers in its service, but not one man. If my esteemed neighbor, the State's ambassador, who will devote his days to the settlement of the question of human rights in the Council Chamber, instead of being threatened with the prisons of Carolina, were to sit down the prisoner of Massachusetts, that State which is so anxious to foist the sin of slavery upon her sister,—though at present she can discover only an act of inhospitality to be the ground of a quarrel with her,—the Legislature would not wholly waive the subject the following winter.

17 Under a government which imprisons any unjustly, the true place for a just man is also a prison. The proper place to-day, the only place which Massachusetts has provided for her freer and less desponding spirits, is in her prisons, to be put out and locked out of the State by her own act, as they have already put themselves out by their principles. It is there that the fugitive slave, and the Mexican prisoner on parole, and the Indian come to plead the wrongs of his race should find them; on that separate, but more free and honorable ground, where the State places those who are not *with* her, but *against* her,—the only house in a slave State in which a free man can abide with honor. If any think that their influence would be lost there, and their voices no longer afflict the ear of the State, that they would not be as an enemy within its walls, they do not know by

how much truth is stronger than error, nor how much more eloquently and effectively he can combat injustice who has experienced a little in his own person. Cast your whole vote, not a strip of paper merely, but your whole influence. A minority is powerless while it conforms to the majority; it is not even a minority then; but it is irresistible when it clogs by its whole weight. If the alternative is to keep all just men in prison, or give up war and slavery, the State will not hesitate which to choose. If a thousand men were not to pay their tax bills this year, that would not be a violent and bloody measure, as it would be to pay them, and enable the State to commit violence and shed innocent blood. This is, in fact, the definition of a peaceable revolution, if any such is possible. If the tax-gatherer, or any other public officer, asks me, as one has done, "But what shall I do?" my answer is, "If you really wish to do anything, resign your office." When the subject has refused allegiance, and the officer has resigned his office, then the revolution is accomplished. But even suppose blood should flow. Is there not a sort of blood shed when the conscience is wounded? Through this wound a man's real manhood and immortality flow out, and he bleeds to an everlasting death. I see this blood flowing now. . . .

18 I have paid no poll-tax for six years. I was put into a jail once on this account, for one night; and, as I stood considering the walls of solid stone, two or three feet thick, the door of wood and iron, a foot thick, and the iron grating which strained the light, I could not help being struck with the foolishness of that institution which treated me as if I were mere flesh and blood and bones, to be locked up. I wondered that it should have concluded at length that this was the best use it could put me to, and had never thought to avail itself of my services in some way. I saw that, if there was a wall of stone between me and my townsmen, there was a still more difficult one to climb or break through before they could get to be as free as I was. I did not for a moment feel confined, and the walls seemed a great waste of stone and mortar. I felt as if I alone of all my townsmen had paid my tax. They plainly did not know how to treat me, but behaved like persons who are underbred. In every threat and in every compliment there was a blunder; for they thought that my chief desire was to stand the other side of that stone wall. I could not but smile to see how industriously they locked the door on my meditations, which followed them out again without let or hindrance, and *they* were really all that was dangerous. As they could not reach

me, they had resolved to punish my body; just as boys, if they cannot come at some person against whom they have a spite, will abuse his dog. I saw that the State was half-witted, that it was timid as a lone woman with her silver spoons, and that it did not know its friends from its foes, and I lost all my remaining respect for it, and pitied it.

19 Thus the State never intentionally confronts a man's sense, intellectual or moral, but only his body, his senses. It is not armed with superior wit or honesty, but with superior physical strength. I was not born to be forced. I will breathe after my own fashion. Let us see who is the strongest. What force has a multitude? They only can force me who obey a higher law than I. They force me to become like themselves. I do not hear of *men* being *forced* to live this way or that by masses of men. What sort of life were that to live? When I meet a government which says to me, "Your money or your life," why should I be in haste to give it my money? It may be in a great strait, and not know what to do: I cannot help that. It must help itself: do as I do. It is not worth the while to snivel about it. I am not responsible for the successful working of the machinery of society. I am not the son of the engineer. I perceive that when an acorn and a chestnut fall side by side, the one does not remain inert to make way for the other, but both obey their own laws, and spring and grow and flourish as best they can, till one, perchance, overshadows and destroys the other. If a plant cannot live according to its nature, it dies; and so a man.

from *The Narrative of the Life of Frederick Douglass, an American Slave*

FREDERICK DOUGLASS

Frederick Douglass (1817–1895) was born a slave in Tuckahoe, Maryland, and was sent at age eight to work for his master's relatives in Baltimore. There, he secretly started a self-education program that continued into his adult life. In 1838, at age twenty-one, he escaped and fled to New Bedford, Massachusetts. To avoid bounty hunters, he changed his name (from Frederick Augustus Washington Bailey) and existed by working a variety of jobs—"saw wood, shovel coal, carry the hod, sweep the chimney, or roll oil casks."

The turning point of his life came in 1841 when he was invited to speak at a meeting of the Massachusetts Antislavery Society. His discourse, which explained what freedom meant to him, so influenced the audience that the Society hired him for a lecture series. In 1845, he published *The Narrative of the Life of Frederick Douglass*, an autobiography that exposed his identity. He fled to Europe, continued his lectures, and raised enough money to buy his freedom. *My Bondage and My Freedom* (1855) and *Life and Times of Frederick Douglass* (1881) are expanded versions of his 1845 autobiography.

He returned to the United States in 1847 to found *North Star*, an antislavery newspaper in which he launched a campaign not only against slavery but against racism in northern businesses, churches, schools, and public facilities. During the Civil War, he recruited blacks for the Union Army. He even discussed the war effort with President Lincoln on several occasions. Later, during the administration of Benjamin Harrison, he served as U.S. minister to Haiti.

The portion of Douglass's *Narrative* reprinted below uncovers Douglass's wisdom, voices the conditions of bondage, and shows the human spirit searching with determination for its independence.

1 I now come to that part of my life during which I planned, and finally succeeded in making, my escape from slavery. But before narrating any of the peculiar circumstances, I deem it proper to make known my intention not to state all the facts connected with the transaction. My reasons for pursuing this course may be understood from the following: First, were I to give a minute statement of all the facts, it is not only possible, but quite probable, that others would thereby be involved in the most embarrassing difficulties. Secondly, such a statement would most undoubtedly induce greater vigilance on the part of slaveholders than has existed heretofore among them; which would, of course be the means of guarding a door whereby some dear brother bondman might escape his galling chains. I deeply regret the necessity that impels me to suppress any thing of importance connected with my experience in slavery. It would afford me great pleasure indeed, as well as materially add to the interest of my narrative, were I at liberty to gratify a curiosity, which I know exists in the minds of many, by an accurate statement of all the facts

pertaining to my most fortunate escape. But I must deprive myself of this pleasure, and the curious of the gratification which such a statement would afford. I would allow myself to suffer under the greatest imputations which evil-minded men might suggest, rather than exculpate myself, and thereby run the hazard of closing the slightest avenue by which a brother slave might clear himself of the chains and fetters of slavery.

2 I have never approved of the very public manner in which some of our western friends have conducted what they call the *underground railroad*, but which, I think, by their open declarations, has been made most emphatically the *upperground railroad*. I honor those good men and women for their noble daring, and applaud them for willingly subjecting themselves to bloody persecution, by openly avowing their participation in the escape of slaves. I, however, can see very little good resulting from such a course, either to themselves or the slaves escaping; while, upon the other hand, I see and feel assured that those open declarations are a positive evil to the slaves remaining, who are seeking to escape. They do nothing towards enlightening the slave, whilst they do much towards enlightening the master. They stimulate him to greater watchfulness, and enhance his power to capture his slave. We owe something to the slaves south of the line as well as to those north of it; and in aiding the latter on their way to freedom, we should be careful to do nothing which would be likely to hinder the former from escaping from slavery. I would keep the merciless slaveholder profoundly ignorant of the means of flight adopted by the slave. I would leave him to imagine himself surrounded by myriads of invisible tormentors, ever ready to snatch from his infernal grasp his trembling prey. Let him be left to feel his way in the dark; let darkness commensurate with his crime hover over him; and let him feel that at every step he takes, in pursuit of the flying bondman, he is running the frightful risk of having his hot brains dashed out by an invisible agency. Let us render the tyrant no aid; let us not hold the light by which he can trace the footprints of our flying brother. But enough of this. I will now proceed to the statement of those facts, connected with my escape, for which I am alone responsible, and for which no one can be made to suffer but myself.

3 In the early part of the year 1838, I became quite restless. I could see no reason why I should, at the end of each week, pour the reward of my toil into the purse of my master. When I carried to him my weekly wages, he would, after counting the money, look me in the

face with a robber-like fierceness, and ask, "Is this all?" He was satisfied with nothing less than the last cent. He would, however, when I made him six dollars, sometimes give me six cents, to encourage me. It had the opposite effect. I regarded it as a sort of admission of my right to the whole. The fact that he gave me any part of my wages was proof, to my mind, that he believed me entitled to the whole of them. I always felt worse for having received any thing; for I feared that the giving me a few cents would ease his conscience, and make him feel himself to be a pretty honorable sort of robber. My discontent grew upon me. I was ever on the look-out for means of escape; and, finding no direct means, I determined to try to hire my time, with a view of getting money with which to make my escape. In the spring of 1838, when Master Thomas came to Baltimore to purchase his spring goods, I got an opportunity, and applied to him to allow me to hire my time. He unhesitatingly refused my request, and told me this was another stratagem by which to escape. He told me I could go nowhere but that he could get me; and that, in the event of my running away, he should spare no pains in his efforts to catch me. He exhorted me to content myself, and be obedient. He told me, if I would be happy, I must lay out no plans for the future. He said, if I behaved myself properly, he would take care of me. Indeed, he advised me to complete thoughtlessness of the future, and taught me to depend solely upon him for happiness. He seemed to see fully the pressing necessity of setting aside my intellectual nature, in order to contentment in slavery. But in spite of him, and even in spite of myself, I continued to think, and to think about the injustice of my enslavement, and the means of escape.

4 About two months after this, I applied to Master Hugh for the privilege of hiring my time. He was not acquainted with the fact that I had applied to Master Thomas, and had been refused. He too, at first, seemed disposed to refuse; but, after some reflection, he granted me the privilege, and proposed the following term: I was to be allowed all my time, make all contracts with those for whom I worked, and find my own employment; and, in return for this liberty, I was to pay him three dollars at the end of each week; find myself in calking tools, and in board and clothing. My board was two dollars and a half per week. This, with the wear and tear of clothing and calking tools, made my regular expenses about six dollars per week. This amount I was compelled to make up, or relinquish the privilege of hiring my time. Rain or shine, work or no work, at the end of

each week the money must be forthcoming, or I must give up my privilege. This arrangement, it will be perceived, was decidedly in my master's favor. It relieved him of all need of looking after me. His money was sure. He received all the benefits of slaveholding without its evils; while I endured all the evils of a slave, and suffered all the care and anxiety of a freeman. I found it a hard bargain. But, hard as it was, I thought it better than the old mode of getting along. It was a step towards freedom to be allowed to bear the responsibilities of a freeman, and I was determined to hold on upon it. I bent myself to the work of making money. I was ready to work at night as well as day, and by the most untiring perseverance and industry, I made enough to meet my expenses, and lay up a little money every week. I went on thus from May till August. Master Hugh then refused to allow me to hire my time longer. The ground for his refusal was a failure on my part, one Saturday night, to pay him for my week's time. This failure was occasioned by my attending a camp meeting about ten miles from Baltimore. During the week, I had entered into an engagement with a number of young friends to start from Baltimore to the camp ground early Saturday evening; and being detained by my employer, I was unable to get down to Master Hugh's without disappointing the company. I knew that Master Hugh was in no special need of the money that night. I therefore decided to go to camp meeting, and upon my return pay him the three dollars. I staid at the camp meeting one day longer than I intended when I left. But as soon as I returned, I called upon him to pay him what he considered his due. I found him very angry; he could scarce restrain his wrath. He said he had a great mind to give me a severe whipping. He wished to know how I dared go out of the city without asking his permission. I told him I hired my time, and while I paid him the price which he asked for it, I did not know that I was bound to ask him when and where I should go. This reply troubled him; and, after reflecting a few moments, he turned to me, and said I should hire my time no longer; that the next thing he should know of, I would be running away. Upon the same plea, he told me to bring my tools and clothing home forthwith. I did so; but instead of seeking work, as I had been accustomed to do previously to hiring my time, I spent the whole week without the performance of a single stroke of work. I did this in retaliation. Saturday night, he called upon me as usual for my week's wages. I told him I had no wages; I had done no work that week. Here we were upon the point of coming to blows. He raved, and swore his determination to get hold of me. I did not allow myself a single word; but was resolved, if he laid the weight of his hand upon me, it should be blow for blow. He did not strike me, but told me that he would find me in constant employment in future. I thought the matter over during the next day, Sunday, and finally resolved upon the third day of September, as the day upon which I would make a second attempt to secure my freedom. I now had three weeks during which to prepare for my journey. Early on Monday morning, before Master Hugh had time to make any engagement for me, I went out and got employment of Mr. Butler, at his ship-yard near the drawbridge, upon what is called the City Block, thus making it unnecessary for him to seek employment for me. At the end of the week, I brought him between eight and nine dollars. He seemed very well pleased, and asked me why I did not do the same the week before. He little knew what my plans were. My object in working steadily was to remove any suspicion he might entertain of my intent to run away; and in this I succeeded admirably. I suppose he thought I was never better satisfied with my condition than at the very time during which I was planning my escape. The second week passed, and again I carried him my full wages; and so well pleased was he, that he gave me twenty-five cents (quite a large sum for a slaveholder to give a slave) and bade me to make a good use of it. I told him I would.

5 Things went on without very smoothly indeed, but within there was trouble. It is impossible for me to describe my feelings as the time of my contemplated start drew near. I had a number of warm-hearted friends in Baltimore—friends that I loved almost as I did my life—and the thought of being separated from them forever was painful beyond expression. It is my opinion that thousands would escape from slavery, who now remain, but for the strong cords of affection that bind them to their friends. The thought of leaving my friends was decidedly the most painful thought with which I had to contend. The love of them was my tender point, and shook my decision more than all things else. Besides the pain of separation, the dread and apprehension of a failure exceeded what I had experienced at my first attempt. The appalling defeat I then sustained returned to torment me. I felt assured that, if I failed in this attempt, my case would be a hopeless one—it would seal my fate as a slave forever. I could not hope to get off with any thing less than the severest punishment, and being placed beyond the means of escape.

It required no very vivid imagination to depict the most frightful scenes through which I should have to pass, in case I failed. The wretchedness of slavery, and the blessedness of freedom, were perpetually before me. It was life and death with me. But I remained firm, and, according to my resolution, on the third day of September, 1838, I left my chains, and succeeded in reaching New York without the slightest interruption of any kind. How I did so—what means I adopted—what direction I travelled, and by what mode of conveyance—I must leave unexplained, for the reasons before mentioned.

6 I have been frequently asked how I felt when I found myself in a free State. I have never been able to answer the question with any satisfaction to myself. It was a moment of the highest excitement I ever experienced. I suppose I felt as one may imagine the unarmed mariner to feel when he is rescued by a friendly man-of-war from the pursuit of a pirate. In writing to a dear friend, immediately after my arrival at New York, I said I felt like one who had escaped a den of hungry lions. This state of mind, however, very soon subsided; and I was again seized with a feeling of great insecurity and loneliness. I was yet liable to be taken back, and subjected to all the tortures of slavery. This in itself was enough to damp the ardor of my enthusiasm. But the loneliness overcame me. There I was in the midst of thousands, and yet a perfect stranger; without home and without friends, in the midst of thousands of my own brethren—children of a common Father, and yet I dared not to unfold to any one of them my sad condition. I was afraid to speak to any one for fear of speaking to the wrong one, and thereby falling into the hands of money-loving kidnappers, whose business it was to lie in wait for the panting fugitive, as the ferocious beasts of the forest lie in wait for their prey. The motto which I adopted when I started from slavery was this—"Trust no man!" I saw in every white man an enemy, and in almost every colored man cause for distrust. It was a most painful situation; and, to understand it, one must needs experience it, or imagine himself in similar circumstances. Let him be a fugitive slave in a strange land—a land given up to be the hunting-ground for slaveholders—whose inhabitants are legalized kidnappers—where he is every moment subjected to the terrible liability of being seized upon by his fellow-men, as the hideous crocodile seizes upon his prey!—I say, let him place himself in my situation—without home or friends—without money or credit—wanting shelter, and no one to give it—wanting bread, and no money to buy it—and at the same

time let him feel that he is pursued by merciless men-hunters, and in total darkness as to what to do, where to go, or where to stay—perfectly helpless both as to the means of defense and means of escape—in the midst of plenty, yet suffering the terrible gnawings of hunger—in the midst of houses, yet having no home—among fellow-men, yet feeling as if in the midst of wild beasts, whose greediness to swallow up the trembling and half-famished fugitive is only equalled by that with which the monsters of the deep swallow up the helpless fish upon which they subsist—I say, let him be placed in this most trying situation—the situation in which I was placed—then, and not till then, will he fully appreciate the hardships of, and know how to sympathize with, the toil-worn and whip-scarred fugitive slave.

7 Thank Heaven, I remained but a short time in this distressed situation. I was relieved from it by the humane hand of Mr. David Ruggles, whose vigilance, kindness, and perseverance, I shall never forget. I am glad of an opportunity to express, as far as words can, the love and gratitude I bear him. Mr. Ruggles is now afflicted with blindness, and is himself in need of the same kind offices which he was once so forward in the performance of toward others. I had been in New York but a few days, when Mr. Ruggles sought me out, and very kindly took me to his boarding-house at the corner of Church and Lespenard Streets. Mr. Ruggles was then very deeply engaged in the memorable *Darg* case, as well as attending to a number of other fugitive slaves, devising ways and means for their successful escape; and, though watched and hemmed in on almost every side, he seemed to be more than a match for his enemies.

8 Very soon after I went to Mr. Ruggles, he wished to know of me where I wanted to go; as he deemed in unsafe for me to remain in New York. I told him I was a calker, and should like to go where I could get work. I thought of going to Canada; but he decided against it, and in favor of my going to New Bedford, thinking I should be able to get work there at my trade. At this time, Anna, my intended wife, came on; for I wrote to her immediately after my arrival at New York (notwithstanding my homeless, houseless, and helpless condition) informing her of my successful flight, and wishing her to come on forthwith. In a few days after her arrival, Mr. Ruggles called in the Rev. J. W. C. Pennington, who, in the presence of Mr. Ruggles, Mrs. Michaels, and two or three others, performed the marriage

ceremony, and gave us a certificate, of which the following is an exact copy:

> This may certify, that I joined together in holy matrimony Frederick Johnson and Anna Murray, as man and wife, in the presence of Mr. David Ruggles and Mrs. Michaels.
>
> JAMES W. C. PENNINGTON
> *New York, Sept. 15, 1838*

9 Upon receiving this certificate, and a five-dollar bill from Mr. Ruggles, I shouldered one part of our baggage, and Anna took up the other, and we set out forthwith to take passage on board of the steamboat John W. Richmond for Newport, on our way to New Bedford. Mr. Ruggles gave me a letter to a Mr. Shaw in Newport, and told me, in case my money did not serve me to New Bedford, to stop in Newport and obtain further assistance; but upon our arrival at Newport, we were so anxious to get to a place of safety, that, notwithstanding we lacked the necessary money to pay our fare, we decided to take seats in the stage, and promise to pay when we got to New Bedford. We were encouraged to do this by two excellent gentlemen, residents of New Bedford, whose names I afterward ascertained to be Joseph Ricketson and William C. Taber. They seemed at once to understand our circumstances, and gave us such assurance of their friendliness as put us fully at ease in their presence. It was good indeed to meet with such friends, at such a time. Upon reaching New Bedford, we were directed to the house of Mr. Nathan Johnson, by whom we were kindly received, and hospitably provided for. Both Mr. and Mrs. Johnson took a deep and lively interest in our welfare. They proved themselves quite worthy of the name of abolitionists. When the stage-driver found us unable to pay our fare, he held on upon our baggage as security for the debt. I had but to mention the fact to Mr. Johnson, and he forthwith advanced the money.

10 We now began to feel a degree of safety, and to prepare ourselves for the duties and responsibilities of a life of freedom. On the morning after our arrival at New Bedford, while at the breakfast-table, the question arose as to what name I should be called by. The name given me by my mother was, "Frederick Augustus Washington Bailey." I, however, had dispensed with the two middle names long before I left Maryland so that I was generally known by the name of "Frederick Bailey." I started from Baltimore bearing the name of "Stanley."

When I got to New York, I again changed my name to "Frederick Johnson," and thought that would be the last change. But when I got to New Bedford, I found it necessary again to change my name. The reason of this necessity was, that there were so many Johnsons in New Bedford, it was already quite difficult to distinguish between them. I gave Mr. Johnson the privilege of choosing me a name, but told him he must not take from me the name of "Frederick." I must hold on to that, to preserve a sense of my identity. Mr. Johnson had just been reading the "Lady of the Lake," and at once suggested that my name be "Douglass." From that time until now I have been called "Frederick Douglass"; and as I am more widely known by that name than by either of the others, I shall continue to use it as my own.

11 I was quite disappointed at the general appearance of things in New Bedford. The impression which I had received respecting the character and condition of the people of the north, I found to be singularly erroneous. I had very strangely supposed, while in slavery, that few of the comforts, and scarcely any of the luxuries, of life were enjoyed at the north, compared with what were enjoyed by the slaveholders of the south. I probably came to this conclusion from the fact that northern people owned no slaves. I supposed that they were about upon a level with the non-slaveholding population of the south. I knew *they* were exceedingly poor, and I had been accustomed to regard their poverty as the necessary consequence of their being non-slaveholders. I had somehow imbibed the opinion that, in the absence of slaves, there could be no wealth, and very little refinement. And upon coming to the north, I expected to meet with a rough, hard-handed, and uncultivated population, living in the most Spartan-like simplicity, knowing nothing of the ease, luxury, pomp, and grandeur of southern slaveholders. Such being my conjectures, any one acquainted with the appearance of New Bedford may very readily infer how palpably I must have seen my mistake.

12 In the afternoon of the day when I reached New Bedford, I visited the wharves, to take a view of the shipping. Here I found myself surrounded with the strongest proofs of wealth. Lying at the wharves, and riding in the stream, I saw many ships of the finest model, in the best order, and of the largest size. Upon the right and left, I was walled in by granite warehouses of the widest dimensions, stowed to their utmost capacity with the necessaries and comforts of life. Added to this, almost every body seemed to be at work, but noiselessly

so, compared with what I had been accustomed to in Baltimore. There were no loud songs heard from those engaged in loading and unloading ships. I heard no deep oaths or horrid curses on the laborer. I saw no whipping of men; but all seemed to go smoothly on. Every man appeared to understand his work, and went at it with a sober, yet cheerful earnestness, which betokened the deep interest which he felt in what he was doing, as well as a sense of his own dignity as a man. To me this looked exceedingly strange. From the wharves I strolled around and over the town, gazing with wonder and admiration at the splendid churches, beautiful dwellings, and finely-cultivated gardens; evincing an amount of wealth, comfort, taste, and refinement, such as I had never seen in any part of slaveholding Maryland.

13 Every thing looked clean, new and beautiful. I saw few or no dilapidated houses, with poverty-stricken inmates; no half-naked children and barefooted women, such as I had been accustomed to see in Hillsborough, Easton, St. Michael's, and Baltimore. The people looked more able, stronger, healthier, and happier, than those of Maryland. I was for once made glad by a view of extreme wealth, without being saddened by seeing extreme poverty. But the most astonishing as well as the most interesting thing to me was the condition of the colored people, a great many of whom, like myself, had escaped thither as a refuge from the hunters of men. I found many, who had not been seven years out of their chains, living in finer houses, and evidently enjoying more of the comforts of life, than the average of slaveholders in Maryland. I will venture to assert that my friend Mr. Nathan Johnson (of whom I can say with a grateful heart, "I was hungry, and he gave me meat; I was thirsty, and he gave me drink; I was a stranger, and he took me in") lived in a neater house; dined at a better table; took, paid for, and read, more newspapers; better understood the moral, religious, and political character of the nation—than nine tenths of the slaveholders in Talbot county, Maryland. Yet Mr. Johnson was a working man. His hands were hardened by toil, and not his alone, but those also of Mrs. Johnson. I found the colored people much more spirited than I had supposed they would be. I found among them a determination to protect each other from the blood-thirsty kidnapper, at all hazards. Soon after my arrival, I was told of a circumstance which illustrated their spirit. A colored man and a fugitive slave were on unfriendly terms. The former was heard to threaten the latter with informing

his master of his whereabouts. Straightway a meeting was called among the colored people, under the stereotyped notice, "Business of importance!" The betrayer was invited to attend. The people came at the appointed hour, and organized the meeting by appointing a very religious old gentleman as president, who, I believe, made a prayer, after which he addressed the meeting as follows: *"Friends, we have got him here, and I would recommend that you young men just take him outside the door, and kill him!"* With this, a number of them bolted at him; but they were intercepted by some more timid than themselves, and the betrayer escaped their vengeance, and has not been seen in New Bedford since. I believe there have been no more such threats, and should there be hereafter, I doubt not that death would be the consequence.

14 I found employment, the third day after my arrival, in stowing a sloop with a load of oil. It was new, dirty, and hard work for me; but I went at it with a glad heart and a willing hand. I was now my own master. It was a happy moment, the rapture of which can be understood only by those who have been slaves. It was the first work, the reward of which was to be entirely my own. There was no Master Hugh standing ready, the moment I earned the money, to rob me of it. I worked that day with a pleasure I had never before experienced. I was at work for myself and newly-married wife. It was to me the starting-point of a new existence. When I got through with that job, I went in pursuit of a job of calking; but such was the strength of prejudice against color, among the white calkers, that they refused to work with me, and of course I could get no employment. Finding my trade of no immediate benefit, I threw off my calking habiliments, and prepared myself to do any kind of work I could get to do. Mr. Johnson kindly let me have his wood-horse and saw, and I very soon found myself a plenty of work. There was no work too hard—none too dirty. I was ready to saw wood, shovel coal, carry the hod, sweep the chimney, or roll oil casks—all of which I did for nearly three years in New Bedford, before I became known to the anti-slavery world.

15 In about four months after I went to New Bedford, there came a young man to me, and inquired if I did not wish to take the "Liberator." I told him I did; but, just having made my escape from slavery, I remarked that I was unable to pay for it then. I, however, finally became a subscriber to it. The paper came, and I read it from week to week with such feelings as it would be quite idle for me to

attempt to describe. The paper became my meat and my drink. My soul was set all on fire. Its sympathy for my brethren in bonds—its scathing denunciations of slaveholders—its faithful exposures of slavery—and its powerful attacks upon the upholders of the institution—sent a thrill of joy through my soul, such as I had never felt before!

16 I had not long been a reader of the "Liberator," before I got a pretty correct idea of the principles, measures and spirit of the anti-slavery reform. I took right hold of the cause. I could do but little; but what I could, I did with a joyful heart, and never felt happier than when in an anti-slavery meeting. I seldom had much to say at the meetings, because what I wanted to say was said so much better by others. But, while attending an anti-slavery convention at Nantucket, on the 11th of August, 1841, I felt strongly moved to speak, and was at the same time much urged to do so by Mr. William C. Coffin, a gentleman who had heard me speak in the colored people's meeting at New Bedford. It was a severe cross, and I took it up reluctantly. The truth was, I felt myself a slave, and the idea of speaking to white people weighed me down. I spoke but a few moments, when I felt a degree of freedom, and said what I desired with considerable ease. From that time until now, I have been engaged in pleading the cause of my brethren—with what success, and with what devotion, I leave those acquainted with my labors to decide.

Sweetness and Light

MATTHEW ARNOLD

Matthew Arnold (1822–1888) was born in Laleham, England; his father served as headmaster at Rugby, a well-known British secondary school. Arnold attended Rugby and then earned a degree at Oxford University. In 1851, he became inspector of schools. He also served as professor of poetry at Oxford from 1857 to 1867.

In addition to numerous poems, he produced two major prose works. *Essays in Criticism* (1865 and 1888, second series) focuses on literary theory and criticism. In it, he expressed concern that contemporary writers did not have the artistic talent of great writers, such as Homer or Shakespeare. *Culture and Anarchy* (1869) featured his social criticism, in which he warned his middle-class audience that anarchy among the masses could result if good reason did not prevail.

"Sweetness and Light" is an essay from *Culture and Anarchy*. In it, he defines *culture*, writing, "Culture is then properly described not as having its origin in curiosity, but as having its origin in the love of perfection, it is *a study of perfection*." Thus, he says, the "pursuit of perfection" is the search for "sweetness and light."

1 The disparagers of culture make its motive curiosity; sometimes, indeed, they make its motive mere exclusiveness and vanity. The culture which is supposed to plume itself on a smattering of Greek

and Latin is a culture which is begotten by nothing so intellectual as curiosity; it is valued either out of sheer vanity and ignorance or else as an engine of social and class distinction, separating its holder, like a badge or title, from other people who have not got it. No serious man would call this *culture,* or attach any value to it, as culture, at all. To find the real ground for the very different estimate which serious people will set upon culture, we must find some motive for culture in the terms of which may lie a real ambiguity; and such a motive the word *curiosity* gives us.

2 I have before now pointed out that we English do not, like the foreigners, use this word in a good sense as well as in a bad sense. With us the word is always used in a somewhat disapproving sense. A liberal and intelligent eagerness about the things of the mind may be meant by a foreigner when he speaks of curiosity, but with us the word always conveys a certain notion of frivolous and unedifying activity. In the *Quarterly Review,* some little time ago, was an estimate of the celebrated French critic, M. Sainte-Beuve, and a very inadequate estimate it in my judgment was. And its inadequacy consisted chiefly in this: that in our English way it left out of sight the double sense really involved in the word *curiosity,* thinking enough was said to stamp M. Sainte-Beuve with blame if it was said that he was impelled in his operations as a critic by curiosity, and omitting either to perceive that M. Sainte-Beuve himself, and many other people with him, would consider that this was praiseworthy and not blameworthy, or to point out why it ought really to be accounted worthy of blame and not of praise. For as there is a curiosity about intellectual matters which is futile, and merely a disease, so there is certainly a curiosity,—a desire after the things of the mind simply for their own sakes and for the pleasure of seeing them as they are,—which is, in an intelligent being, natural and laudable. Nay, and the very desire to see things as they are implies a balance and regulation of mind which is not often attained without fruitful effort, and which is the very opposite of the blind and diseased impulse of mind which is what we mean to blame when we blame curiosity. Montesquieu says: "The first motive which ought to impel us to study is the desire to augment the excellence of our nature, and to render an intelligent being yet more intelligent." This is the true ground to assign for the genuine scientific passion, however manifested, and for culture, viewed simply as a fruit of this passion; and it is a worthy ground, even though we let the term *curiosity* stand to describe it.

3 But there is of culture another view, in which not solely the scientific passion, the sheer desire to see things as they are, natural and proper in an intelligent being, appears as the ground of it. There is a view in which all the love of our neighbour, the impulses towards action, help, and beneficence, the desire for removing human error, clearing human confusion, and diminishing human misery, the noble aspiration to leave the world better and happier than we found it,—motives eminently such as are called social,—come in as part of the grounds of culture, and the main and pre-eminent part. Culture is then properly described not as having its origin in curiosity, but as having its origin in the love of perfection; it is *a study of perfection.* It moves by the force, not merely or primarily of the scientific passion for pure knowledge, but also of the moral and social passion for doing good. As, in the first view of it, we took for its worthy motto Montesquieu's words: "To render an intelligent being yet more intelligent!" so, in the second view of it, there is no better motto which it can have than these words of Bishop Wilson: "To make reason and the will of God prevail!"

4 Only, whereas the passion for doing good is apt to be overhasty in determining what reason and the will of God say, because its turn is for acting rather than thinking and it wants to be beginning to act; and whereas it is apt to take its own conceptions, which proceed from its own state of development and share in all the imperfections and immaturities of this, for a basis of action; what distinguishes culture is, that it is possessed by the scientific passion as well as by the passion of doing good; that it demands worthy notions of reason and the will of God, and does not readily suffer its own crude conceptions to substitute themselves for them. And knowing that no action or institution can be salutary and stable which is not based on reason and the will of God, it is not so bent on acting and instituting, even with the great aim of diminishing human error and misery ever before its thoughts, but that it can remember that acting and instituting are of little use, unless we know how and what we ought to act and to institute.

5 This culture is more interesting and more far-reaching than that other, which is founded solely on the scientific passion for knowing. But it needs times of faith and ardour, times when the intellectual horizon is opening and widening all round us, to flourish in. . . . The danger now is, not that people should obstinately refuse to allow anything but their old routine to pass for reason and the will of God,

but either that they should allow some novelty or other to pass for these too easily, or else that they should under-rate the importance of them altogether, and think it enough to follow action for its own sake, without troubling themselves to make reason and the will of God prevail therein. . . .

6 The moment this view of culture is seized, the moment it is regarded not solely as the endeavour to see things as they are, to draw towards a knowledge of the universal order which seems to be intended and aimed at in the world, and which it is a man's happiness to go along with or his misery to go counter to,—to learn, in short, the will of God,—the moment, I say, culture is considered not merely as the endeavour to *see* and *learn* this, but as the endeavour, also, to make it *prevail*, the moral, social, and beneficent character of culture becomes manifest. . . .

7 And religion, the greatest and most important of the efforts by which the human race has manifested its impulse to perfect itself,—religion, that voice of the deepest human experience,—does not only enjoin and sanction the aim which is the great aim of culture, the aim of setting ourselves to ascertain what perfection is and to make it prevail; but also, in determining generally in what human perfection consists, religion comes to a conclusion identical with that which culture,—culture seeking the determination of this question through *all* the voices of human experience which have been heard upon it, of art, science, poetry, philosophy, history, as well as of religion, in order to give a greater fulness and certainty to its solution,—likewise reaches. Religion says: *The kingdom of God is within you;* and culture, in like manner, places human perfection in an *internal* condition, in the growth and predominance of our humanity proper, as distinguished from our animality. It places it in the ever-increasing efficacy and in the general harmonious expansion of those gifts of thought and feeling, which make the peculiar dignity, wealth, and happiness of human nature. . . . Not a having and a resting, but a growing and a becoming, is the character of perfection as culture conceives it; and here, too, it coincides with religion. . . .

8 Faith in machinery is, I said, our besetting danger; often in machinery most absurdly disproportioned to the end which this machinery, if it is to do any good at all, is to serve; but always in machinery, as if it had a value in and for itself. What is freedom but machinery? what is population but machinery? what is coal but machinery? what are railroads but machinery? what is wealth but machinery? what are,

even, religious organisations but machinery? Now almost every voice in England is accustomed to speak of these things as if they were precious ends in themselves, and therefore had some of the characters of perfection indisputably joined to them. I have before now noticed Mr. Roebuck's stock argument for proving the greatness and happiness of England as she is, and for quite stopping the mouths of all gainsayers. Mr. Roebuck is never weary of reiterating this argument of his, so I do not know why I should be weary of noticing it. "May not every man in England say what he likes?"—Mr. Roebuck perpetually asks; and that, he thinks, is quite sufficient, and when every man may say what he likes, our aspirations ought to be satisfied. But the aspirations of culture, which is the study of perfection, are not satisfied, unless what men say, when they may say what they like, is worth saying,—has good in it, and more good than bad. In the same way the *Times*, replying to some foreign strictures on the dress, looks, and behaviour of the English abroad, urges that the English ideal is that every one should be free to do and to look just as he likes. But culture indefatigably tries, not to make what each raw person may like the rule by which he fashions himself; but to draw ever nearer to a sense of what is indeed beautiful, graceful, and becoming, and to get the raw person to like that. . . .

9 Wealth, again, that end to which our prodigious works for material advantage are directed,—the commonest of commonplaces tells us how men are always apt to regard wealth as a precious end in itself; and certainly they have never been so apt thus to regard it as they are in England at the present time. Never did people believe anything more firmly than nine Englishmen out of ten at the present day believe that our greatness and welfare are proved by our being so very rich. Now, the use of culture is that it helps us, by means of its spiritual standard of perfection, to regard wealth as but machinery, and not only to say as a matter of words that we regard wealth as but machinery, but really to perceive and feel that it is so. If it were not for this purging effect wrought upon our minds by culture, the whole world, the future as well as the present, would inevitably belong to the Philistines. The people who believe most that our greatness and welfare are proved by our being very rich, and who most give their lives and thoughts to becoming rich, are just the very people whom we call Philistines. Culture says: "Consider these people, then, their way of life, their habits, their manners, the very tones of their voice; look at them attentively; observe the literature

they read, the things which give them pleasure, the words which come forth out of their mouths, the thoughts which make the furniture of their minds; would any amount of wealth be worth having with the condition that one was to become just like these people by having it?" And thus culture begets a dissatisfaction which is of the highest possible value in stemming the common tide of men's thoughts in a wealthy and industrial community, and which saves the future, as one may hope, from being vulgarised, even if it cannot save the present.

10 Population, again, and bodily health and vigour, are things which are nowhere treated in such an unintelligent, misleading, exaggerated way as in England. Both are really machinery; yet how many people all around us do we see rest in them and fail to look beyond them! Why, one has heard people, fresh from reading certain articles of the *Times* on the Registrar-General's returns of marriages and births in this country, who would talk of our large English families in quite a solemn strain, as if they had something in itself beautiful, elevating, and meritorious in them; as if the British Philistine would have only to present himself before the Great Judge with his twelve children, in order to be received among the sheep as a matter of right!

11 But bodily health and vigour, it may be said, are not to be classed with wealth and population as mere machinery; they have a more real and essential value. . . . Every one with anything like an adequate idea of human perfection has distinctly marked this subordination to higher and spiritual ends of the cultivation of bodily vigour and activity. "Bodily exercise profiteth little; but godliness is profitable unto all things," says the author of the Epistle to Timothy. And the utilitarian Franklin says just as explicitly:—"Eat and drink such an exact quantity as suits the constitution of thy body, *in reference to the services of the mind*." But the point of view of culture, keeping the mark of human perfection simply and broadly in view, and not assigning to this perfection, as religion or utilitarianism assigns to it, a special and limited character, this point of view, I say, of culture is best given by these words of Epictetus:—"It is a sign of ἀφυΐα." says he,—that is, of a nature not finely tempered,—"to give yourselves up to things which relate to the body; to make, for instance, a great fuss about exercise, a great fuss about eating, a great fuss about drinking, a great fuss about walking, a great fuss about riding. All these things ought to be done merely by the way: the formation of the spirit and character must be our real concern." This is admirable;

and, indeed, the Greek word εὐφυΐα, a finely tempered nature, gives exactly the notion of perfection as culture brings us to conceive it: a harmonious perfection, a perfection in which the characters of beauty and intelligence are both present, which unites "the two noblest of things,"—as Swift, who of one of the two, at any rate, had himself all too little, most happily calls them in his *Battle of the Books,*—"the two noblest of things, *sweetness and light.*" The εὐφυής, is the man who tends towards sweetness and light; the ἀφυής, on the other hand, is our Philistine. The immense spiritual significance of the Greeks is due to their having been inspired with this central and happy idea of the essential character of human perfection; and Mr. Bright's misconception of culture, as a smattering of Greek and Latin, comes itself, after all, from this wonderful significance of the Greeks having affected the very machinery of our education, and is in itself a kind of homage to it.

12 In thus making sweetness and light to be characters of perfection, culture is of like spirit with poetry, follows one law with poetry. Far more than on our freedom, our population, and our industrialism, many amongst us rely upon our religious organisations to save us. I have called religion a yet more important manifestation of human nature than poetry, because it has worked on a broader scale for perfection, and with greater masses of men. But the idea of beauty and of a human nature perfect on all its sides, which is the dominant idea of poetry, is a true and invaluable idea, though it has not yet had the success that the idea of conquering the obvious faults of our animality, and of a human nature perfect on the moral side,—which is the dominant idea of religion,—has been enabled to have; and it is destined, adding to itself the religious idea of a devout energy, to transform and govern the other.

13 The best art and poetry of the Greeks, in which religion and poetry are one, in which the idea of beauty and of a human nature perfect on all sides adds to itself a religious and devout energy, and works in the strength of that, is on this account of such surpassing interest and instructiveness for us, though it was,—as, having regard to the human race in general, and, indeed, having regard to the Greeks themselves, we must own,—a premature attempt, an attempt which for success needed the moral and religious fibre in humanity to be more braced and developed than it had yet been. But Greece did not err in having the idea of beauty, harmony, and complete human perfection, so present and paramount. It is impossible to have this

idea too present and paramount; only, the moral fibre must be braced too. And we, because we have braced the moral fibre, are not on that account in the right way, if at the same time the idea of beauty, harmony, and complete human perfection, is wanting or misapprehended amongst us; and evidently it *is* wanting or misapprehended at present. And when we rely as we do on our religious organisations, which in themselves do not and cannot give us this idea, and think we have done enough if we make them spread and prevail, then, I say, we fall into our common fault of overvaluing machinery. . . .

14 The impulse of the English race towards moral development and self-conquest has nowhere so powerfully manifested itself as in Puritanism. Nowhere has Puritanism found so adequate an expression as in the religious organisation of the Independents. The modern Independents have a newspaper, the *Nonconformist,* written with great sincerity and ability. The motto, the standard, the profession of faith which this organ of theirs carries aloft, is: "The Dissidence of Dissent and the Protestantism of the Protestant religion." There is sweetness and light, and an ideal of complete harmonious human perfection! One need not go to culture and poetry to find language to judge it. Religion, with its instinct for perfection, supplies language to judge it, language, too, which is in our mouths every day. "Finally, be of one mind, united in feeling," says St. Peter. There is an ideal which judges the Puritan ideal: "The Dissidence of Dissent and the Protestantism of the Protestant religion!" And religious organisations like this are what people believe in, rest in, would give their lives for! . . .

15 But men of culture and poetry, it will be said, are again and again failing, and failing conspicuously, in the necessary first stage to a harmonious perfection, in the subduing of the great obvious faults of our animality, which it is the glory of these religious organisations to have helped us to subdue. True, they do often so fail. They have often been without the virtues as well as the faults of the Puritan; it has been one of their dangers that they so felt the Puritan's faults that they too much neglected the practice of his virtues. I will not, however, exculpate them at the Puritan's expense. They have often failed in morality, and morality is indispensable. And they have been punished for their failure, as the Puritan has been rewarded for his performance. They have been punished wherein they erred; but their ideal of beauty, of sweetness and light, and a human nature complete on all its sides, remains the true ideal of perfection still; just as the Puritan's ideal of perfection remains narrow and inadequate,

although for what he did well he has been richly rewarded. Notwithstanding the mighty results of the Pilgrim Fathers' voyage, they and their standard of perfection are rightly judged when we figure to ourselves Shakespeare or Virgil,—souls in whom sweetness and light, and all that in human nature is most humane, were eminent,—accompanying them on their voyage, and think what intolerable company Shakespeare and Virgil would have found them! In the same way let us judge the religious organisations which we see all around us. . . . Look at the life imaged in such a newspaper as the *Nonconformist,*—a life of jealousy of the Establishment, disputes, tea-meetings, openings of chapels, sermons; and then think of it as an ideal of a human life completing itself on all sides, and aspiring with all its organs after sweetness, light, and perfection!

16 Another newspaper, representing, like the *Nonconformist,* one of the religious organisations of this country, was a short time ago giving an account of the crowd at Epsom on the Derby day, and of all the vice and hideousness which was to be seen in that crowd; and then the writer turned suddenly round upon Professor Huxley, and asked him how he proposed to cure all this vice and hideousness without religion. I confess I felt disposed to ask the asker this question: and how do you propose to cure it with such a religion as yours? How is the ideal of a life so unlovely, so unattractive, so incomplete, so narrow, so far removed from a true and satisfying ideal of human perfection, as is the life of your religious organisation as you yourself reflect it, to conquer and transform all this vice and hideousness? . . . And I say that the English reliance on our religious organisations and on their ideas of human perfection just as they stand, is like our reliance on freedom, on muscular Christianity, on population, on coal, on wealth,—mere belief in machinery, and unfruitful; and that it is wholesomely counteracted by culture, bent on seeing things as they are, and on drawing the human race onwards to a more complete, a harmonious perfection.

17 Culture, however, shows its single-minded love of perfection, its desire simply to make reason and the will of God prevail, its freedom from fanaticism, by its attitude towards all this machinery, even while it insists that it *is* machinery. Fanatics, seeing the mischief men do themselves by their blind belief in some machinery or other,—whether it is wealth and industrialism, or whether it is the cultivation of bodily strength and activity, or whether it is a political organisation,—or whether it is a religious organisation,—oppose with might and main

the tendency to this or that political and religious organisation, or to games and athletic exercises, or to wealth and industrialism, and try violently to stop it. But the flexibility which sweetness and light give, and which is one of the rewards of culture pursued in good faith, enables a man to see that a tendency may be necessary, and even, as a preparation for something in the future, salutary, and yet that the generations or individuals who obey this tendency are sacrificed to it, that they fall short of the hope of perfection by following it; and that its mischiefs are to be criticised, lest it should take too firm a hold and last after it has served its purpose. . . .

18 Oxford, the Oxford of the past, has many faults; and she has heavily paid for them in defeat, in isolation, in want of hold upon the modern world. Yet we in Oxford, brought up amidst the beauty and sweetness of that beautiful place, have not failed to seize one truth,—the truth that beauty and sweetness are essential characters of a complete human perfection. When I insist on this, I am all in the faith and tradition of Oxford. I say boldly that this our sentiment for beauty and sweetness, our sentiment against hideousness and rawness, has been at the bottom of our attachment to so many beaten causes, of our opposition to so many triumphant movements. And the sentiment is true, and has never been wholly defeated, and has shown its power even in its defeat. We have not won our political battles, we have not carried our main points, we have not stopped our adversaries' advance, we have not marched victoriously with the modern world; but we have told silently upon the mind of the country, we have prepared currents of feeling which sap our adversaries' position when it seems gained, we have kept up our own communications with the future. Look at the course of the great movement which shook Oxford to its centre some thirty years ago! It was directed, as any one who reads Dr. Newman's *Apology* may see, against what in one word may be called "Liberalism." Liberalism prevailed, it was the appointed force to do the work of the hour; it was necessary, it was inevitable that it should prevail. The Oxford movement was broken, it failed: our wrecks are scattered on every shore:—

Quæ regio in terris nostri non plena laboris?*

But what was it, this liberalism, as Dr. Newman saw it, and as it really broke the Oxford movement? It was the great middle-class

* Who in the kingdom of our earth does not labor?

liberalism, which had for the cardinal points of its belief the Reform Bill of 1832, and local self-government, in politics; in the social sphere, free-trade, unrestricted competition, and the making of large industrial fortunes; in the religious sphere, the Dissidence of Dissent and the Protestantism of the Protestant religion. I do not say that other and more intelligent forces than this were not opposed to the Oxford movement: but this was the force which really beat it; this was the force which Dr. Newman felt himself fighting with; this was the force which till only the other day seemed to be the paramount force in this country, and to be in possession of the future; this was the force whose achievements fill Mr. Lowe with such inexpressible admiration, and whose rule he was so horror-struck to see threatened. And where is this great force of Philistinism now? It is thrust into the second rank, it is become a power of yesterday, it has lost the future. A new power has suddenly appeared, a power which it is impossible yet to judge fully, but which is certainly a wholly different force from middle-class liberalism; different in its cardinal points of belief, different in its tendencies in every sphere. It loves and admires neither the legislation of middle-class Parliaments, nor the local self-government of middle-class vestries, nor the unrestricted competition of middle-class industrialists, nor the dissidence of middle-class Dissent and the Protestantism of middle-class Protestant religion. I am not now praising this new force, or saying that its own ideals are better; all I say is, that they are wholly different. And who will estimate how much the currents of feeling created by Dr. Newman's movements, the keen desire for beauty and sweetness which it nourished, the deep aversion it manifested to the hardness and vulgarity of middle-class liberalism, the strong light it turned on the hideous and grotesque illusions of middle-class Protestantism,—who will estimate how much all these contributed to swell the tide of secret dissatisfaction which has mined the ground under self-confident liberalism of the last thirty years, and has prepared the way for its sudden collapse and supersession? It is in this manner that the sentiment of Oxford for beauty and sweetness conquers, and in this manner long may it continue to conquer! . . .

19 Mr. Bright, who has a foot in both worlds, the world of middle-class liberalism and the world of democracy, but who brings most of his ideas from the world of middle-class liberalism in which he was bred, always inclines to inculcate that faith in machinery to which, as we have seen, Englishmen are so prone, and which has been

the bane of middle-class liberalism. He complains with a sorrowful indignation of people who "appear to have no proper estimate of the value of the franchise"; he leads his disciples to believe,—what the Englishman is always too ready to believe,—that the having a vote, like the having a large family, or a large business, or large muscles, has in itself some edifying and perfecting effect upon human nature. Or else he cries out to the democracy,—"the men," as he calls them, "upon whose shoulders the greatness of England rests," —he cries out to them: "See what you have done! I look over this country and see the cities you have built, the railroads you have made, the manufactures you have produced, the cargoes which freight the ships of the greatest mercantile navy the world has ever seen! I see that you have converted by your labours what was once a wilderness, these islands, into a fruitful garden; I know that you have created this wealth, and are a nation whose name is a word of power throughout all the world." Why, this is just the very style of laudation with which Mr. Roebuck or Mr. Lowe debauches the minds of the middle classes, and makes such Philistines of them. It is the same fashion of teaching a man to value himself not on what he *is*, not on his progress in sweetness and light, but on the number of the railroads he has constructed, or the bigness of the tabernacle he has built. . . .

20 Other well-meaning friends of this new power are for leading it, not in the old ruts of middle-class Philistinism, but in ways which are naturally alluring to the feet of democracy, though in this country they are novel and untried ways. I may call them the ways of Jacobinism. Violent indignation with the past, abstract systems of renovation applied wholesale, a new doctrine drawn up in black and white for elaborating down to the very smallest details a rational society for the future,—these are the ways of Jacobinism. . . . A current in people's minds sets towards new ideas; people are dissatisfied with their old narrow stock of Philistine ideas, Anglo-Saxon ideas, or any other; and some man, some Bentham or Comte, who has the real merit of having early and strongly felt and helped the new current, but who brings plenty of narrowness and mistakes of his own into his feeling and help of it, is credited with being the author of the whole current, the fit person to be entrusted with its regulation and to guide the human race. . . .

21 The pursuit of perfection, then, is the pursuit of sweetness and light. He who works for sweetness and light, works to make reason and the will of God prevail. He who works for machinery, he who

works for hatred, works only for confusion. Culture looks beyond machinery, culture hates hatred; culture has one great passion, the passion for sweetness and light. It has one even yet greater!—the passion for making them *prevail.* It is not satisfied till we *all* come to a prefect man; it knows that the sweetness and light of the few must be imperfect until the raw and unkindled masses of humanity are touched with sweetness and light. If I have not shrunk from saying that we must work for sweetness and light, so neither have I shrunk from saying that we must have a broad basis, must have sweetness and light for as many as possible. Again and again I have insisted how those are the happy moments of humanity, how those are the marking epochs of a people's life, how those are the flowering times for literature and art and all the creative power of genius, when there is a *national* glow of life and thought, when the whole of society is in the fullest measure permeated by thought, sensible to beauty, intelligent and alive. Only it must be *real* thought and *real* beauty; *real* sweetness and *real* light. Plenty of people will try to give the masses, as they call them, an intellectual food prepared and adapted in the way they think proper for the actual condition of the masses. The ordinary popular literature is an example of this way of working on the masses. Plenty of people will try to indoctrinate the masses with the set of ideas and judgments constituting the creed of their own profession or party. Our religious and political organisations give an example of this way of working on the masses. I condemn neither way; but culture works differently. It does not try to teach down to the level of inferior classes; it does not try to win them for this or that sect of its own, with ready-made judgments and watchwords. It seeks to do away with classes; to make the best that has been thought and known in the world current everywhere; to make all men live in an atmosphere of sweetness and light, where they may use ideas, as it uses them itself, freely,—nourished, and not bound by them.

22 This is the *social idea;* and the men of culture are the true apostles of equality. The great men of culture are those who have had a passion for diffusing, for making prevail, for carrying from one end of society to the other, the best knowledge, the best ideas of their time; who have laboured to divest knowledge of all that was harsh, uncouth, difficult, abstract, professional, exclusive; to humanise it, to make it efficient outside the clique of the cultivated and learned, yet still remaining the *best* knowledge and thought of the time, and a true source, therefore, of sweetness and light.

A Liberal Education

THOMAS HENRY HUXLEY

Thomas Henry Huxley (1825–1895) was a self-educated British scientist, surgeon, and writer. After medical college, he spent four years as a surgeon in the British Navy on tour in the Indian Ocean and the East Indies. He wrote a scientific study of jellyfish that established his fame as a zoologist. His scientific studies drew him into the debate on evolution and the findings of Charles Darwin. Although he disagreed with Darwin on several points, he nevertheless joined the debate, defending Darwin but meeting censure by many learned people of his age. He did recognize the findings of modern science, that life in every species is the "struggle for existence" more than a gradual transmutation implied by "natural selection." He also asserted that modern humans have ended their struggle for existence and now participate in the "struggle for enjoyment."

Among other words, he coined the term *agnostic* to describe a person who thinks that God's existence cannot be proved and the term *biogenesis* to argue that life develops only from previous life.

For a time he served on the London School Board where he left his mark by arguing for new scholastic methods, such as less rote memory work and more reading, writing, arithmetic, and the study of physical science. "A Liberal Education" is an excerpt from his long essay, "A Liberal Education; and Where to Find It," which was published in his *Lay Sermons* (1870). In this essay, he uses an analogy to compare life with a game of chess. He explains that learning the rules to play a good game of chess is like learning the game of life, which demands that we know the laws of physical science. In particular, we must learn to read carefully and write accurately.

1 Suppose it were perfectly certain that the life and fortune of every one of us would, one day or other, depend upon his winning or losing a game at chess. Don't you think that we should all consider it to be a primary duty to learn at least the names and the moves of the pieces; to have a notion of a gambit, and a keen eye for all the means of giving and getting out of check? Do you not think that we should look with a disapprobation amounting to scorn upon the father who allowed his son, or the state which allowed its members, to grow up without knowing a pawn from a knight?

2 Yet, it is a very plain and elementary truth that the life, the fortune, and the happiness of every one of us, and, more or less, of those who are connected with us, do depend upon our knowing something of the rules of a game infinitely more difficult and complicated than chess. It is a game which has been played for untold ages, every man and woman of us being one of the two players in a game of his or her own. The chess-board is the world, the pieces are the phenomena of the universe, the rules of the game are what we call the laws of Nature. The player on the other side is hidden from us. We know that his play is always fair, just and patient. But also we know, to our cost, that he never overlooks a mistake, or makes the smallest allowance for ignorance. To the man who plays well, the highest stakes are paid, with that sort of overflowing generosity with which the strong shows delight in strength. And one who plays ill is checkmated—without haste, but without remorse.

3 My metaphor will remind some of you of the famous picture in which Retzsch has depicted Satan playing at chess with man for his soul. Substitute for the mocking fiend in that picture a calm, strong angel who is playing for love, as we say, and would rather lose than win—and I should accept it as an image of human life.

4 Well, what I mean by Education is learning the rules of this mighty game. In other words, education is the instruction of the intellect in the laws of Nature, under which name I include not merely things

and their forces, but men and their ways; and the fashioning of the affections and of the will into an earnest and loving desire to move in harmony with those laws. For me, education means neither more nor less than this. Anything which professes to call itself education must be tried by this standard, and if it fails to stand the test, I will not call it education, whatever may be the force of authority or of numbers upon the other side.

Shadow Lake

JOHN MUIR

John Muir (1838–1914) was born in Scotland, but his family moved to Wisconsin when he was eleven. After he left the University of Wisconsin, he had a fear that he might not live to see "all of God's beauty." Therefore, he set out on walking tours that inspired several books, such as *The Mountains of California* (1894), *My First Summer in the Sierra* (1911), and *The Yosemite* (1912). In 1892, he founded the Sierra Club, a powerful environmental and conservation organization. By his efforts, he became known as the father of the National Park System, for he influenced Congress to establish both Yosemite National Park and Sequoia National Park, and he convinced President Theodore Roosevelt to preserve 148 million acres of forestland.

In "Shadow Lake," written as part of *The Mountains of California*, he describes the environment that he visited for the first time in 1872. Its pristine beauty enraptured him, until one day he found the footprints and staff markings of a shepherd. Returning later, he found that, indeed, the "gardens and meadows were destroyed" by the roaming herds of sheep in the most beautiful of valleys.

1 The color-beauty about Shadow Lake during the Indian summer is much richer than one could hope to find in so young and so glacial a wilderness. Almost every leaf is tinted then, and the goldenrods are in bloom; but most of the color is given by the ripe grasses, willows, and aspens. At the foot of the lake you stand in a trembling aspen grove, every leaf painted like a butterfly, and away to right

and left round the shores sweeps a curving ribbon of meadow, red and brown dotted with pale yellow, shading off here and there into hazy purple. The walls, too, are dashed with bits of bright color that gleam out on the neutral granite gray. But neither the walls, nor the margin meadow, nor yet the gay, fluttering grove in which you stand, nor the lake itself, flashing with spangles, can long hold your attention; for at the head of the lake there is a gorgeous mass of orange-yellow, belonging to the main aspen belt of the basin, which seems the very fountain whence all the color below it had flowed, and here your eye is filled and fixed. This glorious mass is about thirty feet high, and extends across the basin nearly from wall to wall. Rich bosses of willow flame in front of it, and from the base of these the brown meadow comes forward to the water's edge, the whole being relieved against the unyielding green of the coniferae, while thick sun-gold is poured over all.

2 During these blessed color-days no cloud darkens the sky, the winds are gentle, and the landscape rests, hushed everywhere, and indescribably impressive. A few ducks are usually seen sailing on the lake, apparently more for pleasure than anything else, and the ouzels at the head of the rapids sing always; while robins, grosbeaks, and the Douglas squirrels are busy in the groves, making delightful company, and intensifying the feeling of grateful sequestration without ruffling the deep, hushed calm and peace.

3 This autumnal mellowness usually lasts until the end of November. Then come days of quite another kind. The winter clouds grow, and bloom, and shed their starry crystals on every leaf and rock, and all the colors vanish like a sunset. The deer gather and hasten down their well-known trails, fearful of being snow-bound. Storm succeeds storm, heaping snow on the cliffs and meadows, and bending the slender pines to the ground in wide arches, one over the other, clustering and interlacing like lodged wheat. Avalanches rush and boom from the shelving heights, piling immense heaps upon the frozen lake, and all the summer glory is buried and lost. Yet in the midst of this hearty winter the sun shines warm at times, calling the Douglas squirrel to frisk in the snowy pines and seek out his hidden stores; and the weather is never so severe as to drive away the grouse and little nut-hatches and chickadees.

4 Toward May, the lake begins to open. The hot sun sends down innumerable streams over the cliffs, streaking them round and round with foam. The snow slowly vanishes, and the meadows show tintings

of green. Then spring comes on apace; flowers and flies enrich the air and the sod, and the deer come back to the upper groves like birds to an old nest.

I first discovered this charming lake in the autumn of 1872, while on my way to the glaciers at the head of the river. It was rejoicing then in its gayest colors, untrodden, hidden in the glorious wilderness like unmined gold. Year after year I walked its shores without discovering any other trace of humanity than the remains of an Indian camp-fire, and the thigh-bones of a deer that had been broken to get at the marrow. It lies out of the regular ways of Indians, who love to hunt in more accessible fields adjacent to trails. Their knowledge of deer-haunts had probably enticed them here some hunger-time when they wished to make sure of a feast; for hunting in this lake-hollow is like hunting in a fenced park. I had told the beauty of Shadow Lake only to a few friends, fearing it might come to be trampled and "improved" like Yosemite. On my last visit, as I was sauntering along the shore on the strip of sand between the water and sod, reading the tracks of the wild animals that live here, I was startled by a human track, which I at once saw belonged to some shepherd; for each step was turned out 35° or 40° from the general course pursued, and was also run over in an uncertain sprawling fashion at the heel, while a row of round dots on the right indicated the staff that shepherds carry. None but a shepherd could make such a track, and after tracing it a few minutes I began to fear that he might be seeking pasturage; for what else could he be seeking? Returning from the glaciers shortly afterward, my worst fears were realized. A trail had been made down the mountain-side from the north, and all the gardens and meadows were destroyed by a horde of hoofed locusts, as if swept by a fire. The money-changers were in the temple.

Apollonianism and Dionysianism

FRIEDRICH NIETZSCHE

Friedrich Nietzsche (1844–1900) was a German poet, philosopher, and classicist. He was born in Saxony to a Protestant minister. He attended universities in Bonn and Leipzig. At twenty-four, he became professor of classics at the University of Basel in Switzerland. It was there that he became a friend of the composer Richard Wagner. In Wagner's music, he found a synthesis for human passion and reason, which he developed into his first major work, *The Birth of Tragedy from the Spirit of Music* (1872). Nietzsche caused a sensation with his *Thus Spake Zarathustra* (1883–1885) in which he announced that "God is dead," meaning that religion no longer served as a moral basis for human behavior. In *Beyond Good and Evil* (1886) and *Genealogy of Morals* (1887), he examined definitions of good and evil, arguing that human beings and society as a whole conformed to the "will of power." Whoever has power condemns the other classes, while in truth every individual person wishes to gain control over his or her own incorrigible passions.

In "Apollonianism and Dionysianism," Nietzsche compares two psychological forces at work within every human: the Apollonian yearning for intellectual control and the Dionysian passion toward gluttony, selfishness, and sexual indulgence. He indicates that the Apollonian, while it offers control and beauty in life, must be balanced

> against the raging forces of the Dionysian. Individuals and societies keep the two balanced and stabilized most of the time. The tragedy of life occurs when these forces meet head on, relentlessly, without give and take.

1 Much will have been gained for esthetics once we have succeeded in apprehending directly—rather than merely *ascertaining*—that art owes its continuous evolution to the Apollonian–Dionysiac duality, even as the propagation of the species depends on the duality of the sexes, their constant conflicts and periodic acts of reconciliation. I have borrowed my adjectives from the Greeks, who developed their mystical doctrines of art through plausible *embodiments*, not through purely conceptual means. It is by those two art-sponsoring deities, Apollo and Dionysos, that we are made to recognize the tremendous split, as regards both origins and objectives, between the plastic, Apollonian arts and the non-visual art of music inspired by Dionysos. The two creative tendencies developed alongside one another, usually in fierce opposition, each by its taunts forcing the other to more energetic production, both perpetuating in a discordant concord that agon which the term *art* but feebly denominates: until at last, by the thaumaturgy of an Hellenic act of will, the pair accepted the yoke of marriage and, in this condition, begot Attic tragedy, which exhibits the salient features of both parents.

2 To reach a closer understanding of both these tendencies, let us begin by viewing them as the separate art realms of *dream* and *intoxication*, two physiological phenomena standing toward one another in much the same relationship as the Apollonian and Dionysiac. It was in a dream, according to Lucretius, that the marvelous gods and goddesses first presented themselves to the minds of men. That great sculptor, Phidias, beheld in a dream the entrancing bodies of more-than-human beings, and likewise, if anyone had asked the Greek poets about the mystery of poetic creation, they too would have referred him to dreams and instructed him much as Hans Sachs instructs us in *Die Meistersinger:*

> My friend, it is the poet's work
> Dreams to interpret and to mark.

Believe me that man's true conceit
In a dream becomes complete:
All poetry we ever read
Is but true dreams interpreted.

3 The fair illusion of the dream sphere, in the production of which every man proves himself an accomplished artist, is a precondition not only of all plastic art, but even, as we shall see presently, of a wide range of poetry. Here we enjoy an immediate apprehension of form, all shapes speak to us directly, nothing seems indifferent or redundant. Despite the high intensity with which these dream realities exist for us, we still have a residual sensation that they are illusions; at least such has been my experience—and the frequency, not to say normality, of the experience is borne out in many passages of the poets. Men of philosophical disposition are known for their constant premonition that our everyday reality, too, is an illusion, hiding another, totally different kind of reality. It was Schopenhauer who considered the ability to view at certain times all men and things as mere phantoms or dream images to be the true mark of philosophic talent. The person who is responsive to the stimuli of art behaves toward the reality of dream much the way the philosopher behaves toward the reality of existence: he observes exactly and enjoys his observations, for it is by these images that he interprets life, by these processes that he rehearses it. Nor is it by pleasant images only that such plausible connections are made: the whole divine comedy of life, including its somber aspects, its sudden balkings, impish accidents, anxious expectations, moves past him, not quite like a shadow play—for it is he himself, after all, who lives and suffers through these scenes—yet never without giving a fleeting sense of illusion; and I imagine that many persons have reassured themselves amidst the perils of dream by calling out, "It is a dream! I want it to go on." I have even heard of people spinning out the causality of one and the same dream over three or more successive nights. All these facts clearly bear witness that our innermost being, the common substratum of humanity, experiences dreams with deep delight and a sense of real necessity. This deep and happy sense of the necessity of dream experiences was expressed by the Greeks in the image of Apollo. Apollo is at once the god of all plastic powers and the soothsaying god. He who is etymologically the "lucent" one, the god of light, reigns also over the fair illusion of our inner world

of fantasy. The perfection of these conditions in contrast to our imperfectly understood waking reality, as well as our profound awareness of nature's healing powers during the interval of sleep and dream, furnishes a symbolic analogue to the soothsaying faculty and quite generally to the arts, which make life possible and worth living. But the image of Apollo must incorporate that thin line which the dream image may not cross, under penalty of becoming pathological, of imposing itself on us as crass reality: a discreet limitation, a freedom from all extravagant urges, the sapient tranquillity of the plastic god. His eye must be sunlike, in keeping with his origin. Even at those moments when he is angry and ill-tempered there lies upon him the consecration of fair illusion. In an eccentric way one might say of Apollo what Schopenhauer says, in the first part of *The World as Will and Idea*, of man caught in the veil of Maya: "Even as on an immense, raging sea, assailed by huge wave crests, a man sits in a little rowboat trusting his frail craft, so, amidst the furious torments of this world, the individual sits tranquilly, supported by the *principium individuationis** and relying on it." One might say that the unshakable confidence in that principle has received its most magnificent expression in Apollo, and that Apollo himself may be regarded as the marvelous divine image of the *principium individuationis*, whose looks and gestures radiate the full delight, wisdom, and beauty of "illusion."

4 In the same context Schopenhauer has described for us the tremendous awe which seizes man when he suddenly begins to doubt the cognitive modes of experience, in other words, when in a given instance the law of causation seems to suspend itself. If we add to this awe the glorious transport which arises in man, even from the very depths of nature, at the shattering of the *principium individuationis*, then we are in a position to apprehend the essence of Dionysiac rapture, whose closest analogy is furnished by physical intoxication. Dionysiac stirrings arise either through the influence of those narcotic potions of which all primitive races speak in their hymns, or through the powerful approach of spring, which penetrates with joy the whole frame of nature. So stirred, the individual forgets himself completely. It is the same Dionysiac power which in medieval Germany drove ever increasing crowds of people singing and dancing from place to place; we recognize in these St. John's and St. Vitus' dancers the bacchic choruses

* The principle of individuation.

of the Greeks, who had their precursors in Asia Minor and as far back as Babylon and the orgiastic Sacaea. There are people who, either from lack of experience or out of sheer stupidity, turn away from such phenomena, and, strong in the sense of their own sanity, label them either mockingly or pityingly "endemic diseases." These benighted souls have no idea how cadaverous and ghostly their "sanity" appears as the intense throng of Dionysiac revelers sweeps past them.

5 Not only does the bond between man and man come to be forged once more by the magic of the Dionysiac rite, but nature itself, long alienated or subjugated, rises again to celebrate the reconciliation with her prodigal son, man. The earth offers its gifts voluntarily, and the savage beasts of mountain and desert approach in peace. The chariot of Dionysos is bedecked with flowers and garlands; panthers and tigers stride beneath his yoke. If one were to convert Beethoven's "Paean to Joy" into a painting, and refuse to curb the imagination when that multitude prostrates itself reverently in the dust, one might form some apprehension of Dionysiac ritual. Now the slave emerges as a freeman; all the rigid, hostile walls which either necessity or despotism has erected between men are shattered. Now that the gospel of universal harmony is sounded, each individual becomes not only reconciled to his fellow but actually at one with him—as though the veil of Maya had been torn apart and there remained only shreds floating before the vision of mystical Oneness. Man now expresses himself through song and dance as the member of a higher community; he has forgotten how to walk, how to speak, and is on the brink of taking wing as he dances. Each of his gestures betokens enchantment; through him sounds a supernatural power, the same power which makes the animals speak and the earth render up milk and honey. He feels himself to be godlike and strides with the same elation and ecstasy as the gods he has seen in his dreams. No longer the *artist*, he has himself become a *work of art:* the productive power of the whole universe is now manifest in his transport, to the glorious satisfaction of the primordial One. The finest clay, the most precious marble—man—is here kneaded and hewn, and the chisel blows of the Dionysiac world artist are accompanied by the cry of the Eleusinian mystagogues: "Do you fall on your knees, multitudes, do you divine your creator?"

6 So far we have examined the Apollonian and Dionysiac states as the product of formative forces arising directly from nature without the mediation of the human artist. At this stage artistic urges are

satisfied directly, on the one hand through the imagery of dreams, whose perfection is quite independent of the intellectual rank, the artistic development of the individual; on the other hand, through an ecstatic reality which once again takes no account of the individual and may even destroy him, or else redeem him through a mystical experience of the collective. In relation to these immediate creative conditions of nature every artist must appear as "imitator," either as the Apollonian dream artist or the Dionysiac ecstatic artist, or, finally (as in Greek tragedy, for example) as dream and ecstatic artist in one. We might picture to ourselves how the last of these, in a state of Dionysiac intoxication and mystical self-abrogation, wandering apart from the reveling throng, sinks upon the ground, and how there is then revealed to him his own condition—complete oneness with the essence of the universe—in a dream similitude.

7 Having set down these general premises and distinctions, we now turn to the Greeks in order to realize to what degree the formative forces of nature were developed in them. Such an inquiry will enable us to assess properly the relation of the Greek artist to his prototypes or, to use Aristotle's expression, his "imitation of nature." Of the dreams the Greeks dreamed it is not possible to speak with any certainty, despite the extant dream literature and the large number of dream anecdotes. But considering the incredible accuracy of their eyes, their keen and unabashed delight in colors, one can hardly be wrong in assuming that their dreams too showed a strict consequence of lines and contours, hues and groupings, a progression of scenes similar to their best bas-reliefs. The perfection of these dream scenes might almost tempt us to consider the dreaming Greek as a Homer and Homer as a dreaming Greek; which would be as though the modern man were to compare himself in his dreaming to Shakespeare.

8 Yet there is another point about which we do not have to conjecture at all: I mean the profound gap separating the Dionysiac Greeks from the Dionysiac barbarians. Throughout the range of ancient civilization (leaving the newer civilizations out of account for the moment) we find evidence of Dionysiac celebrations which stand to the Greek type in much the same relation as the bearded satyr, whose name and attributes are derived from the he-goat, stands to the god Dionysos. The central concern of such celebrations was, almost universally, a complete sexual promiscuity overriding every form of established tribal law; all the savage urges of the mind were unleashed on those occasions until they reached that paroxysm of lust and

cruelty which has always struck me as the "witches' cauldron" *par excellence.* It would appear that the Greeks were for a while quite immune from these feverish excesses which must have reached them by every known land or sea route. What kept Greece safe was the proud, imposing image of Apollo, who in holding up the head of the Gorgon to those brutal and grotesque Dionysiac forces subdued them. Doric art has immortalized Apollo's majestic rejection of all license. But resistance became difficult, even impossible, as soon as similar urges began to break forth from the deep substratum of Hellenism itself. Soon the function of the Delphic god developed into something quite different and much more limited: all he could hope to accomplish now was to wrest the destructive weapon, by a timely gesture of pacification, from his opponent's hand. That act of pacification represents the most important event in the history of Greek ritual; every department of life now shows symptoms of a revolutionary change. The two great antagonists have been reconciled. Each feels obliged henceforth to keep to his bounds, each will honor the other by the bestowal of periodic gifts, while the cleavage remains fundamentally the same. And yet, if we examine what happened to the Dionysiac powers under the pressure of that treaty we notice a great difference: in the place of the Babylonian Sacaea, with their throwback of men to the condition of apes and tigers, we now see entirely new rites celebrated: rites of universal redemption, of glorious transfiguration. Only now has it become possible to speak of nature's celebrating an *esthetic* triumph; only now has the abrogation of the *principium individuationis* become an esthetic event. That terrible witches' brew concocted of lust and cruelty has lost all power under the new conditions. Yet the peculiar blending of emotions in the heart of the Dionysiac reveler—his ambiguity if you will—seems still to hark back (as the medicinal drug harks back to the deadly poison) to the days when the infliction of pain was experienced as joy while a sense of supreme triumph elicited cries of anguish from the heart. For now in every exuberant joy there is heard an undertone of terror, or else a wistful lament over an irrecoverable loss. It is as though in these Greek festivals a sentimental trait of nature were coming to the fore, as though nature were bemoaning the fact of her fragmentation, her decomposition into separate individuals. The chants and gestures of these revelers, so ambiguous in their motivation, represented an absolute *novum* in the world of the Homeric Greeks; their Dionysiac music, in especial, spread abroad terror and a deep shudder. It is true: music had long been familiar to the Greeks as an Apollonian art, as a regular beat like that of waves lapping the shore, a plastic rhythm expressly developed for the portrayal of Apollonian conditions. Apollo's music was a Doric architecture of sound—of barely hinted sounds such as are proper to the cithara. Those very elements which characterize Dionysiac music and, after it, music quite generally: the heart-shaking power of tone, the uniform stream of melody, the incomparable resources of harmony—all those elements had been carefully kept at a distance as being inconsonant with the Apollonian norm. In the Dionysiac dithyramb man is incited to strain his symbolic faculties to the utmost; something quite unheard of is now clamoring to be heard: the desire to tear asunder the veil of Maya, to sink back into the original oneness of nature; the desire to express the very essence of nature symbolically. Thus an entirely new set of symbols springs into being. First, all the symbols pertaining to physical features: mouth, face, the spoken word, the dance movement which coordinates the limbs and bends them to its rhythm. Then suddenly all the rest of the symbolic forces—music and rhythm as such, dynamics, harmony—assert themselves with great energy. In order to comprehend this total emancipation of all the symbolic powers one must have reached the same measure of inner freedom those powers themselves were making manifest; which is to say that the votary of Dionysos could not be understood except by his own kind. It is not difficult to imagine the awed surprise with which the Apollonian Greek must have looked on him. And that surprise would be further increased as the latter realized, with a shudder, that all this was not so alien to him after all, that his Apollonian consciousness was but a thin veil hiding from him the whole Dionysiac realm.

9 In order to comprehend this we must take down the elaborate edifice of Apollonian culture stone by stone until we discover its foundations. At first the eye is struck by the marvelous shapes of the Olympian gods who stand upon its pediments, and whose exploits, in shining bas-relief, adorn its friezes. The fact that among them we find Apollo as one god among many, making no claim to a privileged position, should not mislead us. The same drive that found its most complete representation in Apollo generated the whole Olympian world, and in this sense we may consider Apollo the father of that world. But what was the radical need out of which that illustrious society of Olympian beings sprang?

10 Whoever approaches the Olympians with a different religion in his heart, seeking moral elevation, sanctity, spirituality, loving-kindness, will presently be forced to turn away from them in ill-humored disappointment. Nothing in these deities reminds us of asceticism, high intellect, or duty: we are confronted by luxuriant, triumphant *existence*, which deifies the good and the bad indifferently. And the beholder may find himself dismayed in the presence of such overflowing life and ask himself what potion these heady people must have drunk in order to behold, in whatever direction they looked, Helen laughing back at them, the beguiling image of their own existence. But we shall call out to this beholder, who has already turned his back: Don't go! Listen first to what the Greeks themselves have to say of this life, which spreads itself before you with such puzzling serenity. An old legend has it that King Midas hunted a long time in the woods for the wise Silenus, companion of Dionysos, without being able to catch him. When he had finally caught him the king asked him what he considered man's greatest good. The daemon remained sullen and uncommunicative until finally, forced by the king, he broke into a shrill laugh and spoke: "Ephemeral wretch, begotten by accident and toil, why do you force me to tell you what it would be your greatest boon not to hear? What would be best for you is quite beyond your reach: not to have been born, not to *be*, to be *nothing*. But the second best is to die soon."

11 What is the relation of the Olympian gods to this popular wisdom? It is that of the entranced vision of the martyr to his torment.

12 Now the Olympian magic mountain opens itself before us, showing us its very roots. The Greeks were keenly aware of the terrors and horrors of existence; in order to be able to live at all they had to place before them the shining fantasy of the Olympians. Their tremendous distrust of the titanic forces of nature: *Moira*, mercilessly enthroned beyond the knowable world; the vulture which fed upon the great philanthropist Prometheus; the terrible lot drawn by wise Oedipus; the curse on the house of Atreus which brought Orestes to the murder of his mother: that whole Panic philosophy, in short, with its mythic examples, by which the gloomy Etruscans perished, the Greeks conquered—or at least hid from view—again and again by means of this artificial Olympus. In order to live at all the Greeks had to construct these deities. The Apollonian need for beauty had to develop the Olympian hierarchy of joy by slow degrees from the original titanic hierarchy of terror, as roses are seen to break from a

thorny thicket. How else could life have been borne by a race so hypersensitive, so emotionally intense, so equipped for suffering? The same drive which called art into being as a completion and consummation of existence, and as a guarantee of further existence, gave rise also to that Olympian realm which acted as a transfiguring mirror to the Hellenic will. The gods justified human life by living it themselves—the only satisfactory theodicy ever invented. To exist in the clear sunlight of such deities was now felt to be the highest good, and the only real grief suffered by Homeric man was inspired by the thought of leaving that sunlight, especially when the departure seemed imminent. Now it became possible to stand the wisdom of Silenus on its head and proclaim that it was the worst evil for man to die soon, and second worst for him to die at all. Such laments as arise now arise over short-lived Achilles, over the generations ephemeral as leaves, the decline of the heroic age. It is not unbecoming to even the greatest hero to yearn for an afterlife, though it be as a day laborer. So impetuously, during the Apollonian phase, does man's will desire to remain on earth, so identified does he become with existence, that even his lament turns to a song of praise.

13 It should have become apparent by now that the harmony with nature which we late-comers regard with such nostalgia, and for which Schiller has coined the cant term *naïve*, is by no means a simple and inevitable condition to be found at the gateway to every culture, a kind of paradise. Such a belief could have been endorsed only by a period for which Rousseau's Emile was an artist and Homer just such an artist nurtured in the bosom of nature. Whenever we encounter "naïveté" in art, we are face to face with the ripest fruit of Apollonian culture—which must always triumph first over titans, kill monsters, and overcome the somber contemplation of actuality, the intense susceptibility to suffering, by means of illusions strenuously and zestfully entertained. But how rare are the instances of true naïveté, of that complete identification with the beauty of appearance! It is this achievement which makes Homer so magnificent—Homer, who, as a single individual, stood to Apollonian popular culture in the same relation as the individual dream artist to the oneiric capacity of a race and of nature generally. The naïveté of Homer must be viewed as a complete victory of Apollonian illusion. Nature often uses illusions of this sort in order to accomplish its secret purposes. The true goal is covered over by a phantasm. We stretch out our hands to the latter, while nature, aided by our decep-

tion, attains the former. In the case of the Greeks it was the will wishing to behold itself in the work of art, in the transcendence of genius; but in order so to behold itself its creatures had first to view themselves as glorious, to transpose themselves to a higher sphere, without having that sphere of pure contemplation either challenge them or upbraid them with insufficiency. It was in that sphere of beauty that the Greeks saw the Olympians as their mirror images; it was by means of that esthetic mirror that the Greek will opposed suffering and the somber wisdom of suffering which always accompanies artistic talent. As a monument to its victory stands Homer, the naïve artist.

14 We can learn something about that naïve artist through the analogy of dream. We can imagine the dreamer as he calls out to himself, still caught in the illusion of his dream and without disturbing it, "This is a dream, and I want to go on dreaming," and we can infer, on the one hand, that he takes deep delight in the contemplation of his dream, and, on the other, that he must have forgotten the day, with its horrible importunity, so to enjoy his dream. Apollo, the interpreter of dreams, will furnish the clue to what is happening here. Although of the two halves of life—the waking and the dreaming—the former is generally considered not only the more important but the only one which is truly lived, I would, at the risk of sounding paradoxical, propose the opposite view. The more I have come to realize in nature those omnipotent formative tendencies and, with them, an intense longing for illusion, the more I feel inclined to the hypothesis that the original Oneness, the ground of Being, ever-suffering and contradictory, time and again has need of rapt vision and delightful illusion to redeem itself. Since we ourselves are the very stuff of such illusions, we must view ourselves as the truly non-existent, that is to say, as a perpetual unfolding in time, space, and causality—what we label "empiric reality." But if, for the moment, we abstract from our own reality, viewing our empiric existence, as well as the existence of the world at large, as the *idea* of the original Oneness, produced anew each instant, then our dreams will appear to us as illusions of illusions, hence as a still higher form of satisfaction of the original desire for illusion. It is for this reason that the very core of nature takes such a deep delight in the naïve artist and the naïve work of art, which likewise is merely the illusion of an illusion. Raphael, himself one of those immortal "naïve" artists, in a symbolic canvas has illustrated that reduction of illusion to further illusion

which is the original act of the naïve artist and at the same time of all Apollonian culture. In the lower half of his "Transfiguration," through the figures of the possessed boy, the despairing bearers, the helpless, terrified disciples, we see a reflection of original pain, the sole ground of being: "illusion" here is a reflection of eternal contradiction, begetter of all things. From this illusion there rises, like the fragrance of ambrosia, a new illusory world, invisible to those enmeshed in the first: a radiant vision of pure delight, a rapt seeing through wide-open eyes. Here we have, in a great symbol of art, both the fair world of Apollo and its substratum, the terrible wisdom of Silenus, and we can comprehend intuitively how they mutually require one another. But Apollo appears to us once again as the apotheosis of the *principium individuationis*, in whom the eternal goal of the original Oneness, namely its redemption through illusion, accomplishes itself. With august gesture the god shows us how there is need for a whole world of torment in order for the individual to produce the redemptive vision and to sit quietly in his rocking rowboat in mid-sea, absorbed in contemplation.

15 If this apotheosis of individuation is to be read in normative terms, we may infer that there is one norm only: the individual—or, more precisely, the observance of the limits of the individual: *sophrosyne*. As a moral deity Apollo demands self-control from his people and, in order to observe such self-control, a knowledge of self. And so we find that the esthetic necessity of beauty is accompanied by the imperatives, "Know thyself," and "Nothing too much." Conversely, excess and *hubris* come to be regarded as the hostile spirits of the non-Apollonian sphere, hence as properties of the pre-Apollonian era—the age of Titans—and the extra-Apollonian world, that is to say the world of the barbarians. It was because of his Titanic love of man that Prometheus had to be devoured by vultures; it was because of his extravagant wisdom which succeeded in solving the riddle of the Sphinx that Oedipus had to be cast into a whirlpool of crime: in this fashion does the Delphic god interpret the Greek past.

16 The effects of the Dionysiac spirit struck the Apollonian Greeks as titanic and barbaric; yet they could not disguise from themselves the fact that they were essentially akin to those deposed Titans and heroes. They felt more than that: their whole existence, with its temperate beauty, rested upon a base of suffering and *knowledge* which had been hidden from them until the reinstatement of Dionysos uncovered it once more. And lo and behold! Apollo found it

impossible to live without Dionysos. The elements of titanism and barbarism turned out to be quite as fundamental as the Apollonian element. And now let us imagine how the ecstatic sounds of the Dionysiac rites penetrated ever more enticingly into that artificially restrained and discreet world of illusion, how this clamor expressed the whole outrageous gamut of nature—delight, grief, knowledge—even to the most piercing cry; and then let us imagine how the Apollonian artist with his thin, monotonous harp music must have sounded beside the demoniac chant of the multitude! The muses presiding over the illusory arts paled before an art which enthusiastically told the truth, and the wisdom of Silenus cried "Woe!" against the serene Olympians. The individual, with his limits and moderations, forgot himself in the Dionysiac vortex and became oblivious to the laws of Apollo. Indiscreet extravagance revealed itself as truth, and contradiction, a delight born of pain, spoke out of the bosom of nature. Wherever the Dionysiac voice was heard, the Apollonian norm seemed suspended or destroyed. Yet it is equally true that, in those places where the first assault was withstood, the prestige and majesty of the Delphic god appeared more rigid and threatening than before. The only way I am able to view Doric art and the Doric state is as a perpetual military encampment of the Apollonian forces. An art so defiantly austere, so ringed about with fortifications—an education so military and exacting—a polity so ruthlessly cruel—could endure only in a continual state of resistance against the titanic and barbaric menace of Dionysos.

17 Up to this point I have developed at some length a theme which was sounded at the beginning of this essay: how the Dionysiac and Apollonian elements, in a continuous chain of creations, each enhancing the other, dominated the Hellenic mind: how from the Iron Age, with its battles of Titans and its austere popular philosophy, there developed under the aegis of Apollo the Homeric world of beauty; how this "naïve" splendor was then absorbed once more by the Dionysiac torrent, and how, face to face with this new power, the Apollonian code rigidified into the majesty of Doric art and contemplation. If the earlier phase of Greek history may justly be broken down into four major artistic epochs dramatizing the battle between the two hostile principles, then we must inquire further (lest Doric art appear to us as the acme and final goal of all these striving tendencies) what was the true end toward which that evolution moved. And our eyes will come to rest on the sublime and much

lauded achievement of the dramatic dithyramb and Attic tragedy, as the common goal of both urges; whose mysterious marriage, after long discord, ennobled itself with such a child, at once Antigone and Cassandra.

CLASSIC ESSAYS OF THE 20*th* CENTURY

Modern Masters

A Slave among Slaves

BOOKER T. WASHINGTON

Booker T. Washington (1856–1915) was born a slave in Virginia but moved to West Virginia after slaves were freed. In the main, he educated himself until he entered Hampton Institute in 1872 to learn the craft of brick mason. He made a success of his own life, so he began to preach that blacks should work hard, acquire property, and earn their civil and political rights. At the same time, he lectured whites on the necessity of providing jobs and other opportunities for the black population. His moderate political position won him a large following, and he advised several presidents, including Theodore Roosevelt. In order to demonstrate his committment to his ideals, he founded Tuskegee Institute in Tuskegee, Alabama, in 1881 to train blacks to be mechanics, tradesmen, teachers, and farmers. In 1900, he founded an alliance that helped blacks form their own businesses. His moderate position did not go unchallenged. Several prominent black politicians and writers, such as W. E. B. DuBois, argued that blacks should fight for their civil rights by public protests against discrimination.

The most famous of his writings is his autobiography, *Up from Slavery,* published in 1901. In it he traces the trials and tribulations he and his family suffered in their effort to succeed despite the scars of slavery and the discrimination thereafter. In the chapter reproduced here, "A Slave among Slaves," he meditates on conditions of slavery, especially the tiny cabin in which he lived his early years while his mother cooked for the plantation. He learned enough to know that his mother's addition to "the slave family attracted about as much attention as the purchase of a new horse or cow." He recounts his ordeals in delivering huge bags of corn to the mill; he explains the ability of slaves to know precisely how efforts for emancipation were progressing; and he describes how slaves held no great animosity toward their masters. He writes, "As a rule, not only did the members of my race entertain no feelings of bitterness against the whites before and during the war, but there are many instances of Negroes tenderly caring for their former masters and mistresses who for some reason have become poor and dependent since the war." He relates with poignant feelings the day the slaves were called to the big house to hear a stranger read the Emancipation Proclamation and tell them they were free and could go when and where they pleased. He recalls, however, that "freedom was a more serious thing than they had expected to find it."

1 I was born a slave on a plantation in Franklin County, Virginia. I am not quite sure of the exact place or exact date of my birth, but at any rate I suspect I must have been born somewhere and at some time. As nearly as I have been able to learn, I was born near a cross-roads post-office called Hale's Ford, and the year was 1858 or 1859. I do not know the month or the day. The earliest impressions I can now recall are of the plantation and the slave quarters—the latter being the part of the plantation where the slaves had their cabins.

2 My life had its beginning in the midst of the most miserable, desolate, and discouraging surroundings. This was so, however, not because my owners were especially cruel, for they were not, as compared with many others. I was born in a typical log cabin, about fourteen by sixteen feet square. In this cabin I lived with my mother and a brother and sister till after the Civil War, when we were all declared free.

3 Of my ancestry I know almost nothing. In the slave quarters, and even later, I heard whispered conversations among the coloured people of the tortures which the slaves, including, no doubt, my ancestors on my mother's side, suffered in the middle passage of the

slave ship while being conveyed from Africa to America. I have been unsuccessful in securing any information that would throw any accurate light upon the history of my family beyond my mother. She, I remember, had a half-brother and a half-sister. In the days of slavery not very much attention was given to family history and family records—that is, black family records. My mother, I suppose, attracted the attention of a purchaser who was afterward my owner and hers. Her addition to the slave family attracted about as much attention as the purchase of a new horse or cow. Of my father I know even less than of my mother. I do not even know his name. I have heard reports to the effect that he was a white man who lived on one of the near-by plantations. Whoever he was, I never heard of his taking the least interest in me or providing in any way for my rearing. But I do not find especial fault with him. He was simply another unfortunate victim of the institution which the Nation unhappily had engrafted upon it at that time.

4 The cabin was not only our living-place, but was also used as the kitchen for the plantation. My mother was the plantation cook. The cabin was without glass windows; it had only openings in the side which let in the light, and also the cold, chilly air of winter. There was a door to the cabin—that is, something that was called a door—but the uncertain hinges by which it was hung, and the large cracks in it, to say nothing of the fact that it was too small, made the room a very uncomfortable one. In addition to these openings there was, in the lower right-hand corner of the room, the "cat-hole,"—a contrivance which almost every mansion or cabin in Virginia possessed during the ante-bellum period. The "cat-hole" was a square opening, about seven by eight inches, provided for the purpose of letting the cat pass in and out of the house at will during the night. In the case of our particular cabin I could never understand the necessity for this convenience, since there were at least a half-dozen other places in the cabin that would have accommodated the cats. There was no wooden floor in our cabin, the naked earth being used as a floor. In the centre of the earthen floor there was a large, deep opening covered with boards, which was used as a place in which to store sweet potatoes during the winter. An impression of this potato-hole is very distinctly engraved upon my memory, because I recall that during the process of putting the potatoes in or taking them out I would often come into possession of one or two, which I roasted and thoroughly enjoyed. There was no cooking-stove on our

plantation, and all the cooking for the whites and slaves my mother had to do over an open fireplace, mostly in pots and "skillets." While the poorly built cabin caused us to suffer with cold in the winter, the heat from the open fireplace in summer was equally trying.

5 The early years of my life, which were spent in the little cabin, were not very different from those of thousands of other slaves. My mother, of course, had little time in which to give attention to the training of her children during the day. She snatched a few moments for our care in the early morning before her work began, and at night after the day's work was done. One of my earliest recollections is that of my mother cooking a chicken late at night, and awakening her children for the purpose of feeding them. How or where she got it I do not know. I presume, however, it was procured from our owner's farm. Some people may call this theft. If such a thing were to happen now, I should condemn it as theft myself. But taking place at the time it did, and for the reason that it did, no one could ever make me believe that my mother was guilty of thieving. She was simply a victim of the system of slavery. I cannot remember having slept in a bed until after our family was declared free by the Emancipation Proclamation. Three children—John, my older brother, Amanda, my sister, and myself—had a pallet on the dirt floor, or, to be more correct, we slept in and on a bundle of filthy rags laid upon the dirt floor.

6 I was asked not long ago to tell something about the sports and pastimes that I engaged in during my youth. Until that question was asked it had never occurred to me that there was no period of my life that was devoted to play. From the time that I can remember anything, almost every day of my life has been occupied in some kind of labour; though I think I would now be a more useful man if I had had time for sports. During the period that I spent in slavery I was not large enough to be of much service, still I was occupied most of the time in cleaning the yards, carrying water to the men in the fields, or going to the mill, to which I used to take the corn, once a week, to be ground. The mill was about three miles from the plantation. This work I always dreaded. The heavy bag of corn would be thrown across the back of the horse, and the corn divided about evenly on each side; but in some way, almost without exception, on these trips, the corn would shift as to become unbalanced and would fall off the horse, and often I would fall with it. As I was not strong enough to reload the corn upon the horse, I would have to wait, sometimes for many hours; till a chance passer-by came along who

would help me out of my trouble. The hours while waiting for some one were usually spent in crying. The time consumed in this way made me late in reaching the mill, and by the time I got my corn ground and reached home it would be far into the night. The road was a lonely one, and often led through dense forests. I was always frightened. The woods were said to be full of soldiers who had deserted from the army, and I had been told that the first thing a deserter did to a Negro boy when he found him alone was to cut off his ears. Besides, when I was late in getting home I knew I would always get a severe scolding or a flogging.

7 I had no schooling whatever while I was a slave, though I remember on several occasions I went as far as the schoolhouse door with one of my young mistresses to carry her books. The picture of several dozen boys and girls in a schoolroom engaged in study made a deep impression upon me, and I had the feeling that to get into a schoolhouse and study in this way would be about the same as getting into paradise.

8 So far as I can now recall, the first knowledge that I got of the fact that we were slaves, and that freedom of the slaves was being discussed, was early one morning before day, when I was awakened by my mother kneeling over her children and fervently praying that Lincoln and his armies might be successful, and that one day she and her children might be free. In this connection I have never been able to understand how the slaves throughout the South, completely ignorant as were the masses so far as books or newspapers were concerned, were able to keep themselves so accurately and completely informed about the great National questions that were agitating the country. From the time that Garrison, Lovejoy, and others began to agitate for freedom, the slaves throughout the South kept in close touch with the progress of the movement. Though I was a mere child during the preparation for the Civil War and during the war itself, I now recall the many late-at-night whispered discussions that I heard my mother and the other slaves on the plantation indulge in. These discussions showed that they understood the situation, and that they kept themselves informed of events by what was termed the "grape-vine" telegraph.

9 During the campaign when Lincoln was first a candidate for the Presidency, the slaves on our far-off plantation, miles from any railroad or large city or daily newspaper, knew what the issues involved were. When war was begun between the North and the South, every

slave on our plantation felt and knew that, though other issues were discussed, the primal one was that of slavery. Even the most ignorant members of my race on the remote plantations felt in their hearts, with a certainty that admitted of no doubt, that the freedom of the slaves would be the one great result of the war, if the Northern armies conquered. Every success of the Federal armies and every defeat of the Confederate forces was watched with the keenest and most intense interest. Often the slaves got knowledge of the results of great battles before the white people received it. This news was usually gotten from the coloured man who was sent to the post-office for the mail. In our case the post-office was about three miles from the plantation and the mail came once or twice a week. The man who was sent to the office would linger about the place long enough to get the drift of the conversation from the group of white people who naturally congregated there, after receiving their mail, to discuss the latest news. The mail-carrier on his way back to our master's house would as naturally retail the news that he had secured among the slaves, and in this way they often heard of important events before the white people at the "big house," as the master's house was called.

10 I cannot remember a single instance during my childhood or early boyhood when our entire family sat down to the table together, and God's blessing was asked, and the family ate a meal in a civilized manner. On the plantation in Virginia, and even later, meals were gotten by the children very much as dumb animals get theirs. It was a piece of bread here and a scrap of meat there. It was a cup of milk at one time and some potatoes at another. Sometimes a portion of our family would eat out of the skillet or pot, while some one would eat from a tin plate held on the knees, and often using nothing but the hands with which to hold the food. When I had grown to sufficient size, I was required to go to the "big house" at meal-times to fan the flies from the table by means of a large set of paper fans operated by a pulley. Naturally much of the conversation of the white people turned upon the subject of freedom and the war, and I absorbed a good deal of it. I remember that at one time I saw two of my young mistresses and some lady visitors eating ginger-cakes, in the yard. At that time those cakes seemed to me to be absolutely the most tempting and desirable things that I had ever seen; and I then and there resolved that, if I ever got free, the height of my ambition would be reached if I could get to the point where I could

secure and eat ginger-cakes in the way that I saw those ladies doing.

11 Of course as the war was prolonged the white people, in many cases, often found it difficult to secure food for themselves. I think the slaves felt the deprivation less than the white, because the usual diet for the slaves was corn bread and pork, and these could be raised on the plantation; but coffee, tea, sugar, and other articles which the whites had been accustomed to use could not be raised on the plantation, and the conditions brought about by the war frequently made it impossible to secure these things. The whites were often in great straits. Parched corn was used for coffee, and a kind of black molasses was used instead of sugar. Many times nothing was used to sweeten the so-called tea and coffee.

12 The first pair of shoes that I recall wearing were wooden ones. They had rough leather on the top, but the bottoms, which were about an inch thick, were of wood. When I walked they made a fearful noise, and besides this they were very inconvenient, since there was no yielding to the natural pressure of the foot. In wearing them one presented an exceedingly awkward appearance. The most trying ordeal that I was forced to endure as a slave boy, however, was the wearing of a flax shirt. In the portion of Virginia where I lived it was common to use flax as part of the clothing for the slaves. That part of the flax from which our clothing was made was largely the refuse, which of course was the cheapest and roughest part. I can scarcely imagine any torture, except, perhaps, the pulling of a tooth, that is equal to that caused by putting on a new flax shirt for the first time. It is almost equal to the feeling that one would experience if he had a dozen or more chestnut burrs, or a hundred small pinpoints, in contact with his flesh. Even to this day I can recall accurately the tortures that I underwent when putting on one of these garments. The fact that my flesh was soft and tender added to the pain. But I had no choice. I had to wear the flax shirt or none; and had it been left to me to choose, I should have chosen to wear no covering. In connection with the flax shirt, my brother John, who is several years older than I am, performed one of the most generous acts that I ever heard of one slave relative doing for another. On several occasions when I was being forced to wear a new flax shirt, he generously agreed to put it on in my stead and wear it for several days, till it was "broken in." Until I had grown to be quite a youth this single garment was all that I wore.

13 One may get the idea from what I have said, that there was bitter

feeling toward the white people on the part of my race, because of the fact that most of the white population was away fighting in a war which would result in keeping the Negro in slavery if the South was successful. In the case of the slaves on our place this was not true, and it was not true of any large portion of the slave population in the South where the Negro was treated with anything like decency. During the Civil War one of my young masters was killed, and two were severely wounded. I recall the feeling of sorrow which existed among the slaves when they heard of the death of "Mars' Billy." It was no sham sorrow but real. Some of the slaves had nursed "Mars' Billy"; others had played with him when he was a child. "Mars' Billy" had begged for mercy in the case of others when the overseer or master was thrashing them. The sorrow in the slave quarter was only second to that in the "big house." When the two young masters were brought home wounded, the sympathy of the slaves was shown in many ways. They were just as anxious to assist in the nursing as the family relatives of the wounded. Some of the slaves would even beg for the privilege of sitting up at night to nurse their wounded masters. This tenderness and sympathy on the part of those held in bondage was a result of their kindly and generous nature. In order to defend and protect the women and children who were left on the plantations when the white males went to war, the slaves would have laid down their lives. The slave who was selected to sleep in the "big house" during the absence of the males was considered to have the place of honour. Any one attempting to harm "young Mistress" or "old Mistress" during the night would have had to cross the dead body of the slave to do so. I do not know how many have noticed it, but I think that it will be found to be true that there are few instances, either in slavery or freedom, in which a member of my race has been known to betray a specific trust.

14 As a rule, not only did the members of my race entertain no feelings of bitterness against the whites before and during the war, but there are many instances of Negroes tenderly caring for their former masters and mistresses who for some reason have become poor and dependent since the war. I know of instances where the former masters of slaves have for years been supplied with money by their former slaves to keep them from suffering. I have known of still other cases in which the former slaves have assisted in the education of the descendants of their former owners. I know of a case on a large plantation in the South in which a young white man, the son of the

former owner of the estate, has become so reduced in purse and self-control by reason of drink that he is a pitiable creature; and yet, notwithstanding the poverty of the coloured people themselves on this plantation, they have for years supplied this young white man with the necessities of life. One sends him a little coffee or sugar, another a little meat, and so on. Nothing that the coloured people possess is too good for the son of "old Mars' Tom," who will perhaps never be permitted to suffer while any remain on the place who knew directly or indirectly of "old Mars' Tom."

15 I have said that there are few instances of a member of my race betraying a specific trust. One of the best illustrations of this which I know of is in the case of an ex-slave from Virginia whom I met not long ago in a little town in the state of Ohio. I found that this man had made a contract with his master, two or three years previous to the Emancipation Proclamation, to the effect that the slave was to be permitted to buy himself, by paying so much per year for his body; and while he was paying for himself, he was to be permitted to labour where and for whom he pleased. Finding that he could secure better wages in Ohio, he went there. When freedom came, he was still in debt to his master some three hundred dollars. Notwithstanding that the Emancipation Proclamation freed him from any obligation to his master, this black man walked the greater portion of the distance back to where his old master lived in Virginia, and placed the last dollar, with interest, in his hands. In talking to me about this, the man told me that he knew that he did not have to pay the debt, but that he had given his word to his master, and his word he had never broken. He felt that he could not enjoy his freedom till he had fulfilled his promise.

16 From some things that I have said one may get the idea that some of the slaves did not want freedom. This is not true. I have never seen one who did not want to be free, or one who would return to slavery.

17 I pity from the bottom of my heart any nation or body of people that is so unfortunate as to get entangled in the net of slavery. I have long since ceased to cherish any spirit of bitterness against the Southern white people on account of the enslavement of my race. No one section of our country was wholly responsible for its introduction, and, besides, it was recognized and protected for years by the General Government. Having once got its tentacles fastened on to the economic and social life of the Republic, it was no easy matter for the

country to relieve itself of the institution. Then, when we rid ourselves of prejudice, or racial feeling, and look facts in the face, we must acknowledge that, notwithstanding the cruelty and moral wrong of slavery, the ten million Negroes inhabiting this country, who themselves or whose ancestors went through the school of American slavery, are in a stronger and more hopeful condition, materially, intellectually, morally, and religiously, than is true of an equal number of black people in any other portion of the globe. This is so to such an extent that Negroes in this country, who themselves or whose forefathers went through the school of slavery, are constantly returning to Africa as missionaries to enlighten those who remained in the fatherland. This I say, not to justify slavery—on the other hand, I condemn it as an institution, as we all know that in America it was established for selfish and financial reasons, and not from a missionary motive—but to call attention to a fact, and to show how Providence so often uses men and institutions to accomplish a purpose. When persons ask me in these days how, in the midst of what sometimes seem hopelessly discouraging conditions, I can have such faith in the future of my race in this country, I remind them of the wilderness through which and out of which, a good Providence has already led us.

18 Ever since I have been old enough to think for myself, I have entertained the idea that, notwithstanding the cruel wrongs inflicted upon us, the black man got nearly as much out of slavery as the white man did. The hurtful influences of the institution were not by any means confined to the Negro. This was fully illustrated by the life upon our own plantation. The whole machinery of slavery was so constructed as to cause labour, as a rule, to be looked upon as a badge of degradation, of inferiority. Hence labour was something that both races on the slave plantation sought to escape. The slave system on our place, in a large measure, took the spirit of self-reliance and self-help out of the white people. My old master had many boys and girls, but not one, so far as I know, ever mastered a single trade or special line of productive industry. The girls were not taught to cook, sew or to take care of the house. All of this was left to the slaves. The slaves, of course, had little personal interest in the life of the plantation, and their ignorance prevented them from learning how to do things in the most improved and thorough manner. As a result of the system, fences were out of repair, gates were hanging half off the hinges, doors creaked, window-panes were out, plastering

had fallen but was not replaced, weeds grew in the yard. As a rule, there was food for whites and blacks, but inside the house, and on the dining-room table, there was wanting that delicacy and refinement of touch and finish which can make a home the most convenient, comfortable, and attractive place in the world. Withal there was a waste of food and other materials which was sad. When freedom came, the slaves were almost as well fitted to begin life anew as the master, except in the matter of book-learning and ownership of property. The slave owner and his sons had mastered no special industry. They unconsciously had imbibed the feeling that manual labour was not the proper thing for them. On the other hand, the slaves, in many cases, had mastered some handicraft, and none were ashamed, and few unwilling, to labour.

19 Finally the war closed, and the day of freedom came. It was a momentous and eventful day to all upon our plantation. We had been expecting it. Freedom was in the air, and had been for months. Deserting soldiers returning to their homes were to be seen every day. Others who had been discharged, or whose regiments had been paroled, were constantly passing near our place. The "grape-vine telegraph" was kept busy night and day. The news and mutterings of great events were swiftly carried from one plantation to another. In the fear of "Yankee" invasions, the silverware and other valuables were taken from the "big house," buried in the woods, and guarded by trusted slaves. Woe be to any one who would have attempted to disturb the buried treasure. The slaves would give the Yankee soldiers food, drink, clothing—anything but that which had been specifically intrusted to their care and honour. As the great day grew nearer, there was more singing in the slave quarters than usual. It was bolder, had more ring, and lasted later into the night. Most of the verses of the plantation songs had some reference to freedom. True, they had sung those same verses before, but they had been careful to explain that the "freedom" in these songs referred to the next world, and had no connection with life in this world. Now they gradually threw off the mask; and were not afraid to let it be known that the "freedom" in their songs meant freedom of the body in this world. The night before the eventful day, word was sent to the slave quarters to the effect that something unusual was going to take place at the "big house" the next morning. There was little, if any, sleep that night. All was excitement and expectancy. Early the next morning word was sent to all the slaves, old and young, to gather at the house.

In company with my mother, brother, and sister, and a large number of other slaves, I went to the master's house. All of our master's family were either standing or seated on the veranda of the house, where they could see what was to take place and hear what was said. There was a feeling of deep interest, or perhaps sadness, on their faces, but not bitterness. As I now recall the impression they made upon me, they did not at the moment seem to be sad because of the loss of property, but rather because of parting with those whom they had reared and who were in many ways very close to them. The most distinct thing that I now recall in connection with the scene was that some man who seemed to be a stranger (a United States officer, I presume) made a little speech and then read a rather long paper—the Emancipation Proclamation, I think. After the reading we were told that we were all free, and could go when and where we pleased. My mother, who was standing by my side, leaned over and kissed her children, while tears of joy ran down her cheeks. She explained to us what it all meant, that this was the day for which she had been so long praying, but fearing that she would never live to see.

For some minutes there was great rejoicing, and thanksgiving, and wild scenes of ecstasy. But there was no feeling of bitterness. In fact, there was pity among the slaves for our former owners. The wild rejoicing on the part of the emancipated coloured people lasted but for a brief period, for I noticed that by the time they returned to their cabins there was a change in their feelings. The great responsibility of being free, of having charge of themselves, of having to think and plan for themselves and their children, seemed to take possession of them. It was very much like suddenly turning a youth of ten or twelve years out into the world to provide for himself. In a few hours the great questions with which the Anglo-Saxon race had been grappling for centuries had been thrown upon these people to be solved. These were the questions of a home, a living, the rearing of children, education, citizenship, and the establishment and support of churches. Was it any wonder that within a few hours the wild rejoicing ceased and a feeling of deep gloom seemed to pervade the slave quarters? To some it seemed that, now that they were in actual possession of it, freedom was a more serious thing than they had expected to find it. Some of the slaves were seventy or eighty years old; their best days were gone. They had no strength with which to earn a living in a strange place and among strange people, even if they had been sure where to find a new place of abode. To this class the problem seemed especially hard. Besides, deep down in their hearts there was a strange and peculiar attachment to "old Marster" and "old Missus," and to their children, which they found it hard to think of breaking off. With these they had spent in some cases nearly a half-century, and it was no light thing to think of parting. Gradually, one by one, stealthily at first, the older slaves began to wander from the slave quarters back to the "big house" to have a whispered conversation with their former owners as to the future.

The Symbolism of Poetry

WILLIAM BUTLER YEATS

William Butler Yeats (1865–1939) was born in Dublin, Ireland. Both his father and his uncle were celebrated painters, so he attended the School of Art in Dublin for a time in pursuit of an art career. However, he abandoned art in favor of literature at age twenty-one. He actively built a theater company in Dublin and wrote several plays, such as *The Countess Cathleen* (1892) and *Cathleen ni Houlinhan* (1902). He also wrote several studies of Irish folklore and legend, but his greatest love was poetry, for which he received a Nobel Prize in 1923. He published several collections of essays, including *Essays and Introductions* (1916), from which this next selection is drawn.

Yeats opens "The Symbolism of Poetry" with a reference to Arthur Symons's book, *The Symbolist Movement in Literature,* which had provoked Yeats to examine his own use of symbolism. He begins by emphasizing the role of the personal philosophy of each artist, which calls "into outer life some portion of the divine life, or of the buried reality."

Yeats defines a complex, almost subjective term with a grace and style that clarifies it with rich images and fresh metaphors. He writes, for example, that symbols "call down among us certain disembodied powers, whose footsteps over our hearts we call emotions." He argues that "poets and painters and musicians . . . are continually making and unmaking mankind by identifying emotions in colour or in sound or in form."

I

1 "Symbolism, as seen in the writers of our day, would have no value if it were not seen also, under one disguise or another, in every great imaginative writer," writes Mr. Arthur Symons in *The Symbolist Movement in Literature,* a subtle book which I cannot praise as I would, because it has been dedicated to me; and he goes on to show how many profound writers have in the last few years sought for a philosophy of poetry in the doctrine of symbolism, and how even in countries where it is almost scandalous to seek for any philosophy of poetry, new writers are following them in their search. We do not know what the writers of ancient times talked of among themselves, and one bull is all that remains of Shakespeare's talk, who was on the edge of modern times; and the journalist is convinced, it seems, that they talked of wine and women and politics, but never about their art, or never quite seriously about their art. He is certain that no one, who had a philosophy of his art or a theory of how he should write, has ever made a work of art, that people have no imagination who do not write without forethought and afterthought as he writes his own articles. He says this with enthusiasm, because he has heard it at so many comfortable dinner-tables, where some one had mentioned through carelessness, or foolish zeal, a book whose difficulty had offended indolence, or a man who had not forgotten that beauty is an accusation. Those formulas and generalisations, in which a hidden sergeant has drilled the ideas of journalists and through them the ideas of all but all the modern world, have created in their turn a forgetfulness like that of soldiers in battle, so that journalists and their readers have forgotten, among many like events, that Wagner spent seven years arranging and explaining his ideas before he began his most characteristic music; that opera, and with it modern music, arose from certain talks at the house of one Giovanni Bardi of Flor-

ence; and that the Pléiade laid the foundations of modern French literature with a pamphlet. Goethe has said, "a poet needs all philosophy, but he must keep it out of his work," though that is not always necessary; and almost certainly no great art, outside England, where journalists are more powerful and ideas less plentiful than elsewhere, has arisen without a great criticism, for its herald or its interpreter and protector, and it may be for this reason that great art, now that vulgarity has armed itself and multiplied itself, is perhaps dead in England.

2 All writers, all artists of any kind, in so far as they have had any philosophical or critical power, perhaps just in so far as they have been deliberate artists at all, have had some philosophy, some criticism of their art; and it has often been this philosophy, or this criticism, that has evoked their most startling inspiration, calling into outer life some portion of the divine life, or of the buried reality, which could alone extinguish in the emotions what their philosophy or their criticism would extinguish in the intellect. They have sought for no new thing, it may be, but only to understand and to copy the pure inspiration of early times, but because the divine life wars upon our outer life, and must needs change its weapons and its movements as we change ours, inspiration has come to them in beautiful startling shapes. The scientific movement brought with it a literature, which was always tending to lose itself in externalities of all kinds, in opinion, in declamation, in picturesque writing, in word-painting, or in what Mr. Symons has called an attempt "to build in brick and mortar inside the covers of a book"; and now writers have begun to dwell upon the element of evocation, of suggestion, upon what we call the symbolism in great writers.

II

3 In "Symbolism in Painting," I tried to describe the element of symbolism that is in pictures and sculpture, and described a little the symbolism in poetry, but did not describe at all the continuous indefinable symbolism which is the substance of all style.

4 There are no lines with more melancholy beauty than these by Burns—

> The white moon is setting behind the white wave,
> And Time is setting with me, O!

and these lines are perfectly symbolical. Take from them the whiteness of the moon and of the wave, whose relation to the setting of Time is too subtle for the intellect, and you take from them their beauty. But, when all are together, moon and wave and whiteness and setting Time and the last melancholy cry, they evoke an emotion which cannot be evoked by any other arrangement of colours and sounds and forms. We may call this metaphorical writing, but it is better to call it symbolical writing, because metaphors are not profound enough to be moving, when they are not symbols, and when they are symbols they are the most perfect of all, because the most subtle, outside of pure sound, and through them one can the best find out what symbols are. If one begins the reverie with any beautiful lines that one can remember, one finds they are like those by Burns. Begin with this line by Blake—

> The gay fishes on the wave when the moon sucks
> up the dew;

or these lines by Nash—

> Queens have died young and fair,
> Brightness falls from the air,
> Dust hath closed Helen's eye;

or these lines by Shakespeare—

> Timon hath made his everlasting mansion
> Upon the beached verge of the salt flood;
> Who once a day with his embossed froth
> The turbulent surge shall cover;

or take some line that is quite simple, that gets its beauty from its place in a story, and see how it flickers with the light of the many symbols that have given the story its beauty, as a sword-blade may flicker with the light of burning towers.

5 All sounds, all colours, all forms, either because of their preordained energies or because of long association, evoke indefinable and yet precise emotions, or, as I prefer to think, call down among us certain disembodied powers, whose footsteps over our hearts we call emotions; and when sound, and colour, and form are in a musical

relation, a beautiful relation to one another, they become as it were one sound, one colour, one form, and evoke an emotion that is made out of their distinct evocations and yet is one emotion. The same relation exists between all portions of every work of art, whether it be an epic or a song, and the more perfect it is, and the more various and numerous the elements that have flowed into its perfection, the more powerful will be the emotion, the power, the god it calls among us. Because an emotion does not exist, or does not become perceptible and active among us, till it has found its expression, in colour or in sound or in form, or in all of these, and because no two modulations or arrangements of these evoke the same emotion, poets and painters and musicians, and in a less degree because their effects are momentary, day and night and cloud and shadow, are continually making and unmaking mankind. It is indeed only those things which seem useless or very feeble that have any power, and all those things that seem useful or strong, armies, moving wheels, modes of architecture, modes of government, speculations of the reason, would have been a little different if some mind long ago had not given itself to some emotion, as a woman gives herself to her lover, and shaped sounds or colours or forms, or all of these, into a musical relation, that their emotion might live in other minds. A little lyric evokes an emotion, and this emotion gathers others about it and melts into their being in the making of some great epic; and at last, needing an always less delicate body, or symbol, as it grows more powerful, it flows out, with all it has gathered, among the blind instincts of daily life, where it moves a power within powers, as one sees ring within ring in the stem of an old tree. This is maybe what Arthur O'Shaughnessy meant when he made his poets say they had built Nineveh with their sighing; and I am certainly never certain, when I hear of some war, or of some religious excitement or of some new manufacture, or of anything else that fills the ear of the world, that it has not all happened because of something that a boy piped in Thessaly. I remember once telling a seer to ask one among the gods who, as she believed, were standing about her in their symbolic bodies, what would come of a charming but seeming trivial labour of a friend, and the form answering, "the devastation of peoples and the overwhelming of cities." I doubt indeed if the crude circumstance of the world, which seems to create all our emotions, does more than reflect, as in multiplying mirrors, the emotions that have come to solitary men in moments of poetical contemplation; or that love itself would be more than an animal hunger but for the poet and his shadow the priest, for unless we believe that outer things are the reality, we must believe that the gross is the shadow of the subtle, that things are wise before they become foolish, and secret before they cry out in the market-place. Solitary men in moments of contemplation receive, as I think, the creative impulse from the lowest of the Nine Hierarchies, and so make and unmake mankind, and even the world itself, for does not "the eye altering alter all"?

> Our towns are copied fragments from our breast;
> And all man's Babylons strive but to impart
> The grandeurs of his Babylonian heart.

III

6 The purpose of rhythm, it has always seemed to me, is to prolong the moment of contemplation, the moment when we are both asleep and awake, which is the one moment of creation, by hushing us with an alluring monotony, while it holds us waking by variety, to keep us in that state of perhaps real trance, in which the mind liberated from the pressure of the will is unfolded in symbols. If certain sensitive persons listen persistently to the ticking of a watch, or gaze persistently on the monotonous flashing of a light, they fall into the hypnotic trance; and rhythm is but the ticking of a watch made softer, that one must needs listen, and various, that one may not be swept beyond memory or grow weary of listening; while the patterns of the artist are but the monotonous flash woven to take the eyes in a subtler enchantment. I have heard in meditation voices that were forgotten the moment they had spoken; and I have been swept, when in more profound meditation, beyond all memory but of those things that came from beyond the threshold of waking life. I was writing once at a very symbolical and abstract poem, when my pen fell on the ground; and as I stooped to pick it up, I remembered some phantastic adventure that yet did not seem phantastic, and then another like adventure, and when I asked myself when these things had happened, I found that I was remembering my dreams for many nights. I tried to remember what I had done the day before, and then what I had done that morning; but all my waking life had perished from me, and it was only after

a struggle that I came to remember it again, and as I did so that more powerful and startling life perished in its turn. Had my pen not fallen on the ground and so made me turn from the images that I was weaving into verse, I would never have known that meditation had become trance, for I would have been like one who does not know that he is passing through a wood because his eyes are on the pathway. So I think that in the making and in the understanding of a work of art, and the more easily if it is full of patterns and symbols and music, we are lured to the threshold of sleep, and it may be far beyond it, without knowing that we have ever set our feet upon the steps of horn or of ivory.

IV

7 Besides emotional symbols, symbols that evoke emotions alone,—and in this sense all alluring or hateful things are symbols, although their relations with one another are too subtle to delight us fully, away from rhythm and pattern,—there are intellectual symbols, symbols that evoke ideas alone, or ideas mingled with emotions; and outside the very definite traditions of mysticism and the less definite criticism of certain modern poets, these alone are called symbols. Most things belong to one or another kind, according to the way we speak of them and the companions we give them, for symbols, associated with ideas that are more than fragments of the shadows thrown upon the intellect by the emotions they evoke, are the playthings of the allegorist or the pedant, and soon pass away. If I say "white" or "purple" in an ordinary line of poetry, they evoke emotions so exclusively that I cannot say why they move me; but if I bring them into the same sentence with such obvious intellectual symbols as a cross or a crown of thorns, I think of purity and sovereignty. Furthermore, innumerable meanings, which are held to "white" or to "purple" by bonds of subtle suggestion, and alike in the emotions and in the intellect, move visibly through my mind, and move invisibly beyond the threshold of sleep, casting lights and shadows of an indefinable wisdom on what had seemed before, it may be, but sterility and noisy violence. It is the intellect that decides where the reader shall ponder over the procession of the symbols, and if the symbols are merely emotional, he gazes from amid the accidents and destinies of the world; but if the symbols are intellectual too, he becomes himself a part of pure intellect, and he is

himself mingled with the procession. If I watch a rushy pool in the moonlight, my emotion at its beauty is mixed with memories of the man that I have seen ploughing by its margin, or of the lovers I saw there a night ago; but if I look at the moon herself and remember any of her ancient names and meanings, I move among divine people, and things that have shaken off our mortality, the tower of ivory, the queen of waters, the shining stag among enchanted woods, the white hare sitting upon the hilltop, the fool of faery with his shining cup full of dreams, and it may be "make a friend of one of these images of wonder," and "meet the Lord in the air." So, too, if one is moved by Shakespeare, who is content with emotional symbols that he may come the nearer to our sympathy, one is mixed with the whole spectacle of the world; while if one is moved by Dante, or by the myth of Demeter, one is mixed into the shadow of God or of a goddess. So too one is furthest from symbols when one is busy doing this or that, but the soul moves among symbols and unfolds in symbols when trance, or madness, or deep meditation has withdrawn it from every impulse but its own. "I then saw," wrote Gérard de Nerval of his madness, "vaguely drifting into form, plastic images of antiquity, which outlined themselves, became definite, and seemed to represent symbols of which I only seized the idea with difficulty." In an earlier time he would have been of that multitude, whose souls austerity withdrew, even more perfectly than madness could withdraw his soul, from hope and memory, from desire and regret, that they might reveal those processions of symbols that men bow to before altars, and woo with incense and offerings. But being of our time, he has been like Maeterlinck, like Villiers de l'Isle Adam in *Axël*, like all who are preoccupied with intellectual symbols in our time, a foreshadower of the new sacred book, of which all the arts, as somebody has said, are begging to dream. How can the arts overcome the slow dying of men's hearts that we call the progress of the world, and lay their hands upon men's heart-strings again, without becoming the garment of religion as in old times?

V

8 If people were to accept the theory that poetry moves us because of its symbolism, what change should one look for in the manner of our poetry? A return to the way of our fathers, a casting out of

descriptions of nature for the sake of nature, of the moral law for the sake of the moral law, a casting out of all anecdotes and of that brooding over scientific opinion that so often extinguished the central flame in Tennyson, and of that vehemence that would make us do or not do certain things; or, in other words, we should come to understand that the beryl stone was enchanted by our fathers that it might unfold the pictures in its heart, and not to mirror our own excited faces, or the boughs waving outside the window. With this change of substance, this return to imagination, this understanding that the laws of art, which are the hidden laws of the world, can alone bind the imagination, would come a change of style, and we would cast out of serious poetry those energetic rhythms, as of a man running, which are the invention of the will with its eyes always on something to be done or undone; and we would seek out those wavering, meditative, organic rhythms, which are the embodiment of the imagination, that neither desires nor hates, because it has done with time, and only wishes to gaze upon some reality, some beauty; nor would it be any longer possible for anybody to deny the importance of form, in all its kinds, for although you can expound an opinion, or describe a thing when your words are not quite well chosen, you cannot give a body to something that moves beyond the senses, unless your words are as subtle, as complex, as full of mysterious life, as the body of a flower or of a woman. The form of sincere poetry, unlike the form of the popular poetry, may indeed be sometimes obscure, or ungrammatical as in some of the best of the Songs of Innocence and Experience, but it must have the perfections that escape analysis, the subtleties that have a new meaning every day, and it must have all this whether it be but a little song made out of a moment of dreamy indolence, or some great epic made out of the dreams of one poet and of a hundred generations whose hands were never weary of the sword.

The Spider and the Wasp

ALEXANDER PETRUNKEVITCH

Alexander Petrunkevitch (1875–1964) was born in Russia. After receiving a good education, he became a renowned zoologist with an expertise in spiders. He moved to the United States to expand his research and, in 1911, published *Index Catalogue of Spiders of North, Central and South America*. He remained in the United States and taught at Yale University from 1910 to 1944. During this time, he published over one hundred books on spiders. Several insects are named after him.

"The Spider and the Wasp" appeared in *Scientific American* in 1952. It demonstrates not only his scientific, investigative mind, but also his ability with the language. He displays precision, attention to detail, classification of the issues, and careful comparison and contrast. The essay displays the results of his careful, scientific observation of the tarantula spider and the digger wasp. Yet the essay is not difficult for the layperson to read. Knowing that *Scientific American* went into homes, not laboratories, Petrunkevitch limited his scientific jargon. The result is a fascinating mystery story as the two insects confront one another, engage in mortal combat, and fight to the bitter end.

1 To hold its own in the struggle for existence, every species of animal must have a regular source of food, and if it happens to live

on other animals, its survival may be very delicately balanced. The hunter cannot exist without the hunted; if the latter should perish from the earth, the former would, too. When the hunted also prey on some of the hunters, the matter may become complicated.

2 This is nowhere better illustrated than in the insect world. Think of the complexity of a situation such as the following: There is a certain wasp, *Pimpla inquisitor*, whose larvae feed on the larvae of the tussock moth. *Pimpla* larvae in turn serve as food for the larvae of a second wasp, the latter in their turn nourish still a third wasp. What subtle balance between fertility and mortality must exist in the case of each of these four species to prevent the extinction of all of them! An excess of mortality over fertility in a single member of the group would ultimately wipe out all four.

3 This is not a unique case. The two great orders of insects, Hymenoptera and Diptera, are full of such examples of interrelationship. And the spiders (which are not insects but members of a separate order of arthropods) also are killers and victims of insects.

4 The picture is complicated by the fact that those species which are carnivorous in the larval stage have to be provided with animal food by a vegetarian mother. The survival of the young depends on the mother's correct choice of a food which she does not eat herself.

5 In the feeding and safeguarding of their progeny insects and spiders exhibit some interesting analogies to reasoning and some crass examples of blind instinct. The case I propose to describe here is that of the tarantula spiders and their arch-enemy, the digger wasps of the genus Pepsis. It is a classic example of what looks like intelligence pitted against instinct—a strange situation in which the victim, though fully able to defend itself, submits unwittingly to its destruction.

6 Most tarantulas live in the tropics, but several species occur in the temperate zone and a few are common in the southern U.S. Some varieties are large and have powerful fangs with which they can inflict a deep wound. These formidable looking spiders do not, however, attack man; you can hold one in your hand, if you are gentle, without being bitten. Their bite is dangerous only to insects and small mammals such as mice; for man it is no worse than a hornet's sting.

7 Tarantulas customarily live in deep cylindrical burrows, from which they emerge at dusk and into which they retire at dawn. Mature males wander about after dark in search of females and occasionally stray into houses. After mating, the male dies in a few weeks, but a female lives much longer and can mate several years in succession.

In a Paris museum is a tropical specimen which is said to have been living in captivity for 25 years.

8 A fertilized female tarantula lays from 200 to 400 eggs at a time; thus it is possible for a single tarantula to produce several thousand young. She takes no care of them beyond weaving a cocoon of silk to enclose the eggs. After they hatch, the young walk away, find convenient places in which to dig their burrows and spend the rest of their lives in solitude. Tarantulas feed mostly on insects and millepedes. Once their appetite is appeased, they digest the food for several days before eating again. Their sight is poor, being limited to a sensing of change in the intensity of light and to the perception of moving objects. They apparently have little or no sense of hearing, for a hungry tarantula will pay no attention to a loudly chirping cricket placed in its cage unless the insect happens to touch one of its legs.

9 But all spiders, and especially hairy ones, have an extremely delicate sense of touch. Laboratory experiments prove that tarantulas can distinguish three types of touch: pressure against the body wall, stroking of the body hair, and riffling of certain very fine hairs on the legs called trichobothria. Pressure against the body, by the finger or the end of a pencil, causes the tarantula to move off slowly for a short distance. The touch excites no defensive response unless the approach is from above where the spider can see the motion, in which case it rises on its hind legs, lifts its front legs, opens its fangs and holds this threatening posture as long as the object continues to move. When the motion stops, the spider drops back to the ground, remains quiet for a few seconds and then moves slowly away.

10 The entire body of a tarantula, especially its legs, is thickly clothed with hair. Some of it is short and wooly, some long and stiff. Touching this body hair produces one of two distinct reactions. When the spider is hungry, it responds with an immediate and swift attack. At the touch of a cricket's antennae the tarantula seizes the insect so swiftly that a motion picture taken at the rate of 64 frames per second shows only the result and not the process of capture. But when the spider is not hungry, the stimulation of its hairs merely causes it to shake the touched limb. An insect can walk under its hairy belly unharmed.

11 The trichobothria, very fine hairs growing from disklike membranes on the legs, were once thought to be the spider's hearing organs, but we now know that they have nothing to do with sound. They are sensitive only to air movement. A light breeze makes them

vibrate slowly, without disturbing the common hair. When one blows gently on the trichobothria, the tarantula reacts with a quick jerk of its four front legs. If the front and hind legs are stimulated at the same time, the spider makes a sudden jump. This reaction is quite independent of the state of its appetite.

12 These three tactile responses—to pressure on the body wall, to moving of the common hair, and to flexing of the trichobothria—are so different from one another that there is no possibility of confusing them. They serve the tarantula adequately for most of its needs and enable it to avoid most annoyances and dangers. But they fail the spider completely when it meets its deadly enemy, the digger wasp Pepsis.

13 These solitary wasps are beautiful and formidable creatures. Most species are either a deep shiny blue all over, or deep blue with rusty wings. The largest have a wing span of about four inches. They live on nectar. When excited, they give off a pungent odor—a warning that they are ready to attack. The sting is much worse than that of a bee or common wasp, and the pain and swelling last longer. In the adult stage the wasp lives only a few months. The female produces but a few eggs, one at a time at intervals of two or three days. For each egg the mother must provide one adult tarantula, alive but paralyzed. The tarantula must be of the correct species to nourish the larva. The mother wasp attaches the egg to the paralyzed spider's abdomen. Upon hatching from the egg, the larva is many hundreds of times smaller than its living but helpless victim. It eats no other food and drinks no water. By the time it has finished its single Gargantuan meal and become ready for wasphood, nothing remains of the tarantula but is indigestible chitinous skeleton.

14 The mother wasp goes tarantula-hunting when the egg in her ovary is almost ready to be laid. Flying low over the ground late on a sunny afternoon, the wasp looks for its victim or for the mouth of a tarantula burrow, a round hole edged by a bit of silk. The sex of the spider makes no difference, but the mother is highly discriminating as to species. Each species of Pepsis requires a certain species of tarantula, and the wasp will not attack the wrong species. In a cage with a tarantula which is not its normal prey, the wasp avoids the spider and is usually killed by it in the night.

15 Yet when a wasp finds the correct species, it is the other way about. To identify the species the wasp apparently must explore the spider with her antennae. The tarantula shows an amazing tolerance to this exploration. The wasp crawls under it and walks over it without

evoking any hostile response. The molestation is so great and so persistent that the tarantula often rises on all eight legs, as if it were on stilts. It may stand this way for several minutes. Meanwhile the wasp, having satisfied itself that the victim is of the right species, moves off a few inches to dig the spider's grave. Working vigorously with legs and jaws, it excavates a hole 8 to 10 inches deep with a diameter slightly larger than the spider's girth. Now and again the wasp pops out of the hole to make sure that the spider is still there.

16 When the grave is finished, the wasp returns to the tarantula to complete her ghastly enterprise. First she feels it all over once more with her antennae. Then her behavior becomes more aggressive. She bends her abdomen, protruding her sting, and searches for the soft membrane at the point where the spider's legs join its body—the only spot where she can penetrate the horny skeleton. From time to time, as the exasperated spider slowly shifts ground, the wasp turns on her back and slides along with the aid of her wings, trying to get under the tarantula for a shot at the vital spot. During all this maneuvering, which can last for several minutes, the tarantula makes no move to save itself. Finally the wasp corners it against some obstruction and grasps one of its legs in her powerful jaws. Now at last the harassed spider tries a desperate but vain defense. The two contestants roll over and over on the ground. It is a terrifying sight and the outcome is always the same. The wasp finally manages to thrust her sting into the soft spot and holds it there for a few seconds while she pumps in the poison. Almost immediately the tarantula falls paralyzed on its back. Its legs stop twitching; its heart stops beating. Yet it is not dead, as is shown by the fact that if taken from the wasp it can be restored to some sensitivity by being kept in a moist chamber for several months.

17 After paralyzing the tarantula, the wasp cleans herself by dragging her body along the ground and rubbing her feet, sucks the drop of blood oozing from the wound in the spider's abdomen, then grabs a leg of the flabby, helpless animal in her jaws and drags it down to the bottom of the grave. She stays there for many minutes, sometimes for several hours, and what she does all that time in the dark we do not know. Eventually she lays her egg and attaches it to the side of the spider's abdomen with a sticky secretion. Then she emerges, fills the grave with soil carried bit by bit in her jaws, and finally tramples the ground all around to hide any trace of the grave from prowlers. They she flies away, leaving her descendant safely started in life.

18 In all this the behavior of the wasp evidently is qualitatively different from that of the spider. The wasp acts like an intelligent animal. This is not to say that instinct plays no part or that she reasons as man does. But her actions are to the point; they are not automatic and can be modified to fit the situation. We do not know for certain how she identifies the tarantula—probably it is by some olfactory or chemo-tactile sense—but she does it purposefully and does not blindly tackle a wrong species.

19 On the other hand, the tarantula's behavior shows only confusion. Evidently the wasp's pawing gives it no pleasure, for it tries to move away. That the wasp is not simulating sexual stimulation is certain because male and female tarantulas react in the same way to its advances. That the spider is not anesthetized by some odorless secretion is easily shown by blowing lightly at the tarantula and making it jump suddenly. What, then, makes the tarantula behave as stupidly as it does?

20 No clear, simple answer is available. Possibly the stimulation by the wasp's antennae is masked by a heavier pressure on the spider's body, so that it reacts as when prodded by a pencil. But the explanation may be much more complex. Initiative in attack is not in the nature of tarantulas; most species fight only when cornered so that escape is impossible. Their inherited patterns of behavior apparently prompt them to avoid problems rather than attack them. For example, spiders always weave their webs in three dimensions, and when a spider finds that there is insufficient space to attach certain threads in the third dimension, it leaves the place and seeks another, instead of finishing the web in a single plane. This urge to escape seems to arise under all circumstances, in all phases of life, and to take the place of reasoning. For a spider to change the pattern of its web is as impossible as for an inexperienced man to build a bridge across a chasm obstructing his way.

21 In a way the instinctive urge to escape is not only easier but often more efficient than reasoning. The tarantula does exactly what is most efficient in all cases except in an encounter with a ruthless and determined attacker dependent for the existence of her own species on killing as many tarantulas as she can lay eggs. Perhaps in this case the spider follows its usual pattern of trying to escape, instead of seizing and killing the wasp, because it is not aware of its danger. In any case, the survival of the tarantula species as a whole is protected by the fact that the spider is much more fertile than the wasp.

What I Believe

E. M. FORSTER

E. M. Forster (1879–1970) was a British novelist, essayist, and college professor. After several unhappy years in the public schools, he came into his own at King's College, Cambridge, where he found good friends, intellectual debates, and scholarly pursuits. He was a member of the Bloomsbury Group, an informal association of people with avant-garde attitudes in revolt against Victorian restrictions on artistic, social, and sexual behavior. The Bloomsbury Group also included Virginia Woolf (see page 223). With an ample yearly stipend, Forster was able to travel widely and write freely. Among his novels are *Howard's End, A Room with a View, Maurice,* and *A Passage to India.*

In "What I Believe," we see the influence of the Bloomsbury Group, which followed the teachings of G. E. Moore, who taught Forster and his associates that "the most valuable things [are] the pleasures of human intercourse and the enjoyment of beautiful objects; . . . it is they that form the rational ultimate end of social progress." In his essay, Forster searches out his fundamental theories: the necessity of faith as a governing agent; the role of personal relationships to ward off cruelty and violence; the necessity of democracy that allows for criticism; the use of force to maintain control; and a rejection of hero worship because great men "produce a desert of uniformity around them and often a pool of blood, too." His is also a humanist theory; he argues that, in the face of totalitarian rage, "the individual remains firm and each of us must consent to be one, and to make the best of the difficult job."

1 I do not believe in belief. But this is an age of faith, in which one is surrounded by so many militant creeds that, in self-defense, one has to formulate a creed of one's own. Tolerance, good temper, and sympathy are no longer enough in a world which is rent by religious and racial persecution, in a world where ignorance rules, and science, which ought to have ruled, plays the subservient pimp. Tolerance, good temper, and sympathy—well, they are what matter really, and if the human race is not to collapse they must come to the front before long. But for the moment they don't seem enough; their action is no stronger than a flower battered beneath a military jack-boot. They want stiffening, even if the process coarsens them. Faith, to my mind, is a stiffening process, a sort of mental starch, which ought to be applied as sparingly as possible. I dislike the stuff. I do not believe in it, for its own sake, at all. My lawgivers are Erasmus and Montaigne, not Moses and St. Paul. My temple stands not upon Mount Moriah but in that Elysian Field where even the immoral are admitted.

2 I have, however, to live in an Age of Faith—the sort of thing I used to hear praised and recommended when I was a boy. It is damned unpleasant, really. It is bloody in every sense of the word. And I have to keep my end up in it. Where do I start?

3 With personal relationships. Here is something comparatively solid in a world full of violence and cruelty. Not absolutely solid, for psychology has split and shattered the idea of a "person" and has shown that there is something incalculable in each of us, which may at any moment rise to the surface and destroy our normal balance. We don't know what we're like. We can't know what we're like. We can't know what other people are like. How then can we put any trust in personal relationships, or cling to them in the gathering political storm? In theory we can't. But in practice we can and do. For the purpose of living one has to assume that the personality is solid, and the "self" is an entity, and to ignore all contrary evidence. And since to ignore evidence is one of the characteristics of faith, I certainly can proclaim that I believe in personal relationships.

4 Starting from them, I get a little order into the contemporary chaos. One must be fond of people and trust them if one isn't to make a mess of life, and it is therefore essential that they shouldn't let one down. They often do. The moral of which is that I must, myself, be as reliable as possible, and this I try to be. But reliability isn't a matter of contract. It is a matter for the heart, which signs no documents. In other words, reliability is impossible unless there is a natural warmth. Most men possess this warmth, though they often have bad luck and get chilled. Personal relationships are despised today. They are regarded as bourgeois luxuries, as products of a time of fair weather which has now passed, and we are urged to get rid of them, and to dedicate ourselves to some movement or cause instead. I hate the idea of dying for a cause, and if I had to choose between betraying my country and betraying my friend, I hope I should have the guts to betray my country. Such a choice may scandalize the modern reader, and he may stretch out his patriotic hand to the telephone at once, and ring up the police. It wouldn't have shocked Dante, though. Dante placed Brutus and Cassius in the lowest circle of Hell because they had chosen to betray their friend Julius Caesar, rather than their country, Rome.

5 This brings me along to democracy, "even Love, the Beloved Republic, which feeds upon Freedom and lives." Democracy isn't a beloved republic really, and never will be. But it is less hateful than other contemporary forms of government, and to that extent it deserves our support. It does start from the assumption that the individual is important, and that all types are needed to make a civilization. It doesn't divide its citizens into the bossers and the bossed, as an efficiency-regime tends to do. The people I admire most are those who are sensitive and want to create something or discover something, and don't see life in terms of power, and such people get more of a chance under a democracy than elsewhere. They found religions, great or small, or they produce literature and art, or they do disinterested scientific research, or they may be what are called "ordinary people," who are creative in their private lives, bring up their children decently, for instance, or help their neighbors. All these people need to express themselves, they can't do so unless society allows them liberty to do so, and the society which allows them most liberty is a democracy.

6 Democracy has another merit. It allows criticism, and if there isn't public criticism there are bound to be hushed-up scandals. That is why

I believe in the press, despite all its lies and vulgarity, and why I believe in Parliament. The British Parliament is often sneered at because it's a talking-shop. Well, I believe in it *because* it is a talking-shop. I believe in the Private Member who makes himself a nuisance. He gets snubbed and is told that he is cranky or ill-informed, but he exposes abuses which would otherwise never have been mentioned, and very often an abuse gets put right just by being mentioned. Occasionally, too, in my country, a well-meaning public official loses his head in the cause of efficiency, and thinks himself God Almighty. Such officials are particularly frequent in the Home Office. Well, there will be questions about them in Parliament sooner or later, and then they'll have to mend their ways. Whether Parliament is either a representative body or an efficient one is very doubtful, but I value it because it criticizes and talks, and because its chatter gets widely reported.

7 So two cheers for democracy: one because it admits variety and one because it permits criticism. Two cheers are quite enough: there is no occasion to give three. Only Love, the Beloved Republic, deserves that.

8 What about force, though? While we are trying to be sensitive and advanced and affectionate and tolerant, an unpleasant question pops up; doesn't all society rest upon force? If a government can't count upon the police and the army how can it hope to rule? And if an individual gets knocked on the head or sent to a labor camp, of what significance are his opinions?

9 This dilemma doesn't worry me as much as it does some. I realize that all society rests upon force. But all the great creative actions, all the decent human relations, occur during the intervals when force has not managed to come to the front. These intervals are what matter. I want them to be as frequent and as lengthy as possible and I call them "civilization." Some people idealize force and pull it into the foreground and worship it, instead of keeping it in the background as long as possible. I think they make a mistake, and I think that their opposites, the mystics, err even more when they declare that force doesn't exist. I believe that it does exist, and that one of our jobs is to prevent it from getting out of its box. It gets out sooner or later, and then it destroys us and all the lovely things which we have made. But it isn't out all the time, for the fortunate reason that the strong are so stupid. Consider their conduct for a moment in the Niebelungs' Ring. The giants there have the gold, or in other

words the guns; but they do nothing with it, they do not realize that they are all-powerful, with the result that the catastrophe is delayed and the castle of Valhalla, insecure but glorious, fronts the storms for generations. Fafnir, coiled round his hoard, grumbles and grunts; we can hear him under Europe today; the leaves of the wood already tremble, and the Bird calls its warnings uselessly. Fafnir will destroy us, but by a blessed dispensation he is stupid and slow, and creation goes on just outside the poisonous blast of his breath. The Nietzschean would hurry the monster up, the mystic would say he didn't exist, but Wotan, wiser than either, hastens to create warriors before doom declares itself. The Valkyries are symbols not only of courage but of intelligence; they represent the human spirit snatching its opportunity while the going is good, and one of them even finds time to love. Brunhilde's last song hymns the recurrence of love, and since it is the privilege of art to exaggerate, she goes even further and proclaims the love which is eternally triumphant and feeds upon Freedom, and lives.

10 So that is what I feel about force and violence. I look the other way until fate strikes me. Whether this is due to courage or to cowardice in my own case I cannot be sure. But I know that if men hadn't looked the other way in the past nothing of any value would survive. The people I respect most behave as if they were immortal and as if society were eternal. Both assumptions are false: both of them must be accepted as true if we are to go on eating and working and loving, and are to keep open a few breathing holes for the human spirit. No millennium seems likely to descend upon humanity; no better and stronger League of Nations will be instituted; no form of Christianity and no alternative to Christianity will bring peace to the world or integrity to the individual; no "change of heart" will occur. And yet we needn't despair, indeed we cannot despair; the evidence of history shows us that men have always insisted on behaving creatively under the shadow of the sword, and that we had better follow their example under the shadow of the airplanes.

11 There is of course hero worship, fervently recommended as a panacea in some quarters. But here we shall get no help. Hero worship is a dangerous vice, and one of the minor merits of a democracy is that it does not encourage it, or produce that unmanageable type of citizen known as the Great Man. It produces instead different kinds of small men, and that's a much finer achievement. But people who can't get interested in the variety of life and can't make up their

own minds get discontented over this, and they long for a hero to bow down before and to follow blindly. It's significant that a hero is an integral part of the authoritarian stock-in-trade today. An efficiency-regime can't be run without a few heroes stuck about to carry off the dullness—much as plums have to be put into a bad pudding to make it palatable. One hero at the top and a smaller one each side of him is a favorite arrangement, and the timid and the bored are comforted by such a trinity and, bowing down, feel exalted by it.

12 No, I distrust Great Men. They produce a desert of uniformity around them and often a pool of blood, too, and I always feel a little man's pleasure when they come a cropper. I believe in aristocracy though—if that's the right word, and if a democrat may use it. Not an aristocracy of power, based upon rank and influence, but an aristocracy of the sensitive, the considerate, and the plucky. Its members are to be found in all nations and classes, and all through the ages, and there is a secret understanding between them when they meet. They represent the true human tradition, the one permanent victory of our queer race over cruelty and chaos. Thousands of them perish in obscurity; a few are great names. They are sensitive for others as well as for themselves, they are considerate without being fussy, their pluck is not swankiness but the power to endure, and they can take a joke. I give no examples—it is risky to do that—but the reader may as well consider whether this is the type of person he would like to meet and to be, and whether (going further with me) he would prefer that the type should *not* be an ascetic one. I'm against asceticism myself. I'm with the old Scotchman who wanted less chastity and more delicacy. I don't feel that my aristocrats are a real aristocracy if they thwart their bodies, since bodies are the instruments through which we register and enjoy the world. Still, I don't insist here. This isn't a major point. It's clearly possible to be sensitive, considerate, and plucky and yet be an ascetic too, and if anyone possesses the first three qualities, I'll let him in! On they go—an invincible army, yet not a victorious one. The aristocrats, the elect, the chosen, the best people—all the words that describe them are false, and all attempts to organize them fail. Again and again authority, seeing their value, has tried to net them and to utilize them as the Egyptian priesthood or the Christian church or the Chinese civil service or the Group Movement, or some other worthy stunt. But they slip through the net and are gone; when the door is

shut they are no longer in the room; their temple, as one of them remarked, is the holiness of the heart's imagination, and their kingdom, though they never possess it, is the wide-open world.

13 With this type of person knocking about, and constantly crossing one's path if one has eyes to see or hands to feel, the experiment of earthly life cannot be dismissed as a failure. But it may well be hailed as a tragedy, the tragedy being that no device has been found by which these private decencies can be transferred to public affairs. As soon as people have power they go crooked and sometimes dotty, too, because the possession of power lifts them into a region where normal honesty never pays. For instance, the man who is selling newspapers outside the House of Parliament can safely leave his papers to go for a drink, and his cap beside them: anyone who takes a paper is sure to drop a copper into the cap. But the men who are inside the houses of Parliament—they can't trust one another like that; still less can the government they compose trust other governments. No caps upon the pavement here, but suspicion, treachery, and armaments. The more highly public life is organized the lower does its morality sink; the nations of today behave to each other worse than they ever did in the past; they cheat, rob, bully, and bluff, make war without notice, and kill as many women and children as possible; whereas primitive tribes were at all events restrained by taboos.

14 The Savior of the future—if ever he comes—will not preach a new gospel. He will merely utilize my aristocracy; he will make effective the good will and the good temper which are already existing. In other words he will introduce a new technique. In economics, we are told that if there was a new technique of distribution, there need be no poverty, and people would not starve in one place while crops were dug under in another. A similar change is needed in the sphere of morals and politics. The desire for it is by no means new; it was expressed, for example, in theological terms by Jacopone dà Todi over six hundred years ago. "Ordina questo amore, O tu che mi ami," he said. ("O thou who lovest me, set this love in order.") His prayer was not granted and I do not myself believe that it ever will be, but here, and not through a change of heart, is our probable route. Not by becoming better, but by ordering and distributing his native goodness, will man shut up force into its box, and so gain time to explore the universe and to set his mark upon it worthily.

15 Such a change, claim the orthodox, can only be made by Christian-

ity, and will be made by it in God's good time: man always has failed and always will fail to organize his own goodness, and it is presumptuous of him to try. This claim leaves me cold. I cannot believe that Christianity will ever cope with the present world-wide mess, and I think that such influence as it retains in modern society is due to its financial backing rather than to its spiritual appeal. It was a spiritual force once, but the indwelling spirit will have to be restated if it is to calm the waters again, and probably in a non-Christian form.

16 These are the reflections of an individualist and a liberal who has found his liberalism crumbling beneath him and at first felt ashamed. Then, looking around, he decided there was no special reason for shame, since other people, whatever they felt, were equally insecure. And as for individualism—there seems no way out of this, even if one wants to find one. The dictator-hero can grind down his citizens till they are all alike, but he can't melt them into a single man. He can order them to merge, he can incite them to mass-antics, but they are obliged to be born separately and to die separately and, owing to these unavoidable termini, will always be running off the totalitarian rails. The memory of birth and the expectation of death always lurk within the human being, making him separate from his fellows and consequently capable of intercourse with them. Naked I came into the world, naked I shall go out of it! And a very good thing, too, for it reminds me that I am naked under my shirt. Until psychologists and biologists have done much more tinkering than seems likely, the individual remains firm and each of us must consent to be one, and to make the best of the difficult job.

The Death of the Moth

VIRGINIA WOOLF

Virginia Woolf (1882–1941) was born in London, the daughter of Sir Leslie Stephen, who was renowned for his biographies of Alexander Pope, Samuel Johnson, and others. She received a good education and, in 1912, married the writer Leonard Woolf. They became one of the most celebrated literary couples in England. They were central figures in the Bloomsbury Group of literary figures and artists. The Woolfs also founded Hogarth Press, which published not only their own works but the works of many notable British writers.

Woolf wrote a number of innovative novels: *Mrs. Dalloway* (1925), *To the Lighthouse* (1927), *Orlando* (1928), *The Waves* (1931), and *Between the Acts* (1941). She also wrote many essays, both critical and meditative, which were collected, in part, in *The Common Reader* (1925), *The Second Common Reader* (1933), and *The Death of the Moth and Other Essays* (1942). The latter collection, published after her suicide in 1941, features her most popular essay.

"The Death of the Moth" displays Woolf's meditative style. With keen insight, she describes a moth fluttering on her window sill. As with her own life, the struggle against death by the little moth becomes a battle lost "against a power of such magnitude." It was a "minute wayside triumph of so great a force over so mean an antagonist." Yet the essay is not about death so much as about life: "Watching him, it seemed as if a fiber, very thin but pure, of the enormous energy of the world had been thrust into his frail and diminutive body." The essay is a classic because it captures in a few brief words the subjective, meditative mind of the writer as she contemplates her own future, and it features a finely chiseled style that combines rich, figurative language with careful, almost scientific observation.

1 Moths that fly by day are not properly to be called moths; they do not excite that pleasant sense of dark autumn nights and ivy-blossom which the commonest yellow-underwing asleep in the shadow of the curtain never fails to rouse in us. They are hybrid creatures, neither gay like butterflies nor somber like their own species. Nevertheless the present specimen, with his narrow hay-colored wings, fringed with a tassel of the same color, seemed to be content with life. It was a pleasant morning, mid-September, mild, benignant, yet with a keener breath than that of the summer months. The plough was already scoring the field opposite the window, and where the share had been, the earth was pressed flat and gleamed with moisture. Such vigor came rolling in from the fields and the down beyond that it was difficult to keep the eyes strictly turned upon the book. The rooks too were keeping one of their annual festivities; soaring around the tree tops until it looked as if a vast net with thousands of black knots in it had been cast up into the air; which, after a few moments sank slowly down upon the trees until every twig seemed to have a knot at the end of it. Then, suddenly, the net would be thrown into the air again in a wider circle this time, with the utmost clamor and vociferation, as though to be thrown into the air and settle slowly down upon the tree tops were a tremendously exciting experience.

2 The same energy which inspired the rooks, the ploughmen, the horses, and even, it seemed, the lean bare-backed downs, sent the moth fluttering from side to side of his square of the windowpane. One could not help watching him. One, was, indeed, conscious of a queer feeling of pity for him. The possibilities of pleasure seemed that morning so enormous and so various that to have only a moth's part in life, and a day moth's at that, appeared a hard fate, and his zest in enjoying his meager opportunities to the full, pathetic. He flew vigorously to one corner of his compartment, and, after waiting there a second, flew across to the other. What remained for him but

to fly to a third corner and then to a fourth? That was all he could do, in spite of the size of the downs, the width of the sky, the far-off smoke of houses, and the romantic voice, now and then, of a steamer out at sea. What he could do he did. Watching him, it seemed as if a fiber, very thin but pure, of the enormous energy of the world had been thrust into his frail and diminutive body. As often as he crossed the pane, I could fancy that a thread of vital light became visible. He was little or nothing but life.

3 Yet, because he was so small, and so simple a form of the energy that was rolling in at the open window and driving its way through so many narrow and intricate corridors in my own brain and in those of other human beings, there was something marvelous as well as pathetic about him. It was as if someone had taken a tiny bead of pure life and decking it as lightly as possible with down and feathers, had set it dancing and zigzagging to show us the true nature of life. Thus displayed one could not get over the strangeness of it. One is apt to forget all about life, seeing it humped and bossed and garnished and cumbered so that it has to move with the greatest circumspection and dignity. Again, the thought of all that life might have been had he been born in any other shape caused one to view his simple activities with a kind of pity.

4 After a time, tired by his dancing apparently, he settled on the window ledge in the sun, and, the queer spectacle being at an end, I forgot about him. Then, looking up, my eye was caught by him. He was trying to resume his dancing, but seemed either so stiff or so awkward that he could only flutter to the bottom of the window-pane; and when he tried to fly across it he failed. Being intent on other matters I watched these futile attempts for a time without thinking, unconsciously waiting for him to resume his flight, as one waits for a machine, that has stopped momentarily, to start again without considering the reason of its failure. After perhaps a seventh attempt he slipped from the wooden ledge and fell, fluttering his wings, on to his back on the windowsill. The helplessness of his attitude roused me. It flashed upon me that he was in difficulties; he could no longer raise himself; his legs struggled vainly. But, as I stretched out a pencil, meaning to help him to right himself, it came over me that the failure and awkwardness were the approach of death. I laid the pencil down again.

5 The legs agitated themselves once more. I looked as if for the enemy against which he struggled. I looked out of doors. What had

happened there? Presumably it was midday, and work in the fields had stopped. Stillness and quiet had replaced the previous animation. The birds had taken themselves off to feed in the brooks. The horses stood still. Yet the power was there all the same, massed outside, indifferent, impersonal, not attending to anything in particular. Somehow it was opposed to the little haycolored moth. It was useless to try to do anything. One could only watch the extraordinary efforts made by those tiny legs against an oncoming doom which could, had it chosen, have submerged an entire city, not merely a city, but masses of human beings; nothing, I knew had any chance against death. Nevertheless after a pause of exhaustion the legs fluttered again. It was superb this last protest, and so frantic that he succeeded at last in righting himself. One's sympathies, of course, were all on the side of life. Also, when there was nobody to care or to know, this gigantic effort on the part of an insignificant little moth, against a power of such magnitude, to retain what no one else valued or desired to keep, moved one strangely. Again, somehow, one saw life, a pure bead. I lifted the pencil again, useless though I knew it to be. But even as I did so, the unmistakable tokens of death showed themselves. The body relaxed, and instantly grew stiff. The struggle was over. The insignificant little creature now knew death. As I looked at the dead moth, this minute wayside triumph of so great a force over so mean an antagonist filled me with wonder. Just as life had been strange a few minutes before, so death was now as strange. The moth having righted himself now lay most decently and uncomplainingly composed. O yes, he seemed to say, death is stronger than I am.

Courtship Through the Ages

JAMES THURBER

James Thurber (1894–1961) was born in Columbus, Ohio. Like his friend E. B. White, he was drawn to journalism and joined the staff of *The New Yorker* in 1925. There he entertained several generations of Americans with his cartoon drawings, sketches, short stories, and essays. In 1929, he joined with White to produce the humorous work *Is Sex Necessary?* His book *My World—and Welcome to It* (1942) features the well-known story "The Secret Life of Walter Mitty," as well as the essay reprinted below. Thurber's critically acclaimed volumes included *The Thurber Carnival* (1945), *The Thurber Album* (1953), and *Thurber Country* (1953).

"Courtship Through the Ages" is a modern classic because it combines several of the best features of essay writing. First, it demonstrates the importance of humor, as shown by Thurber's lighthearted yet ironic view about males of differing species who have all sorts of problems attracting their females. Second, it demonstrates the value of detailed, perceptive examples to bring home a point. Third, it shows how personification can serve the cause of the humorist, for the various species take on decidedly human characteristics in every instance.

1 Surely nothing in the astonishing scheme of life can have nonplussed Nature so much as the fact that none of the females of any

of the species she created really cared very much for the male, as such. For the past ten million years Nature has been busily inventing ways to make the male attractive to the female, but the whole business of courtship, from the marine annelids up to man, still lumbers heavily along, like a complicated musical comedy. I have been reading the sad and absorbing story in Volume 6 (Cole to Dama) of the *Encyclopaedia Britannica*. In this volume you can learn all about cricket, cotton, costume designing, crocodiles, crown jewels, and Coleridge, but none of these subjects is so interesting as the Courtship of Animals, which recounts the sorrowful lengths to which all males must go to arouse the interest of a lady.

2 We all know, I think, that Nature gave man whiskers and a mustache with the quaint idea in mind that these would prove attractive to the female. We all know that, far from attracting her, whiskers and mustaches only made her nervous and gloomy, so that man had to go in for somersaults, tilting with lances, and performing feats of parlor magic to win her attention; he also had to bring her candy, flowers, and the furs of animals. It is common knowledge that in spite of all these "love displays" the male is constantly being turned down, insulted, or thrown out of the house. It is rather comforting, then, to discover that the peacock, for all his gorgeous plumage, does not have a particularly easy time in courtship; none of the males in the world do. The first peahen, it turned out, was only faintly stirred by her suitor's beautiful train. She would often go quietly to sleep while he was whisking it around. The *Britannica* tells us that the peacock actually had to learn a certain little trick to wake her up and revive her interest: he had to learn to vibrate his quills so as to make a rustling sound. In ancient times man himself, observing the ways of the peacock, probably tried vibrating his whiskers to make a rustling sound; if so, it didn't get him anywhere. He had to go in for something else; so, among other things, he went in for gifts. It is not unlikely that he got this idea from certain flies and birds who were making no headway at all with rustling sounds.

3 One of the flies of the family Empidae, who had tried everything, finally hit on something pretty special. He contrived to make a glistening transparent balloon which was even larger than himself. Into this he would put sweetmeats and tidbits and he would carry the whole elaborate envelope through the air to the lady of his choice. This amused her for a time, but she finally got bored with it. She demanded silly little colorful presents, something that you couldn't eat but that

would look nice around the house. So the male Empis had to go around gathering flower petals and pieces of bright paper to put into his balloon. On a courtship flight a male Empis cuts quite a figure now, but he can hardly be said to be happy. He never knows how soon the female will demand heavier presents, such as Roman coins and gold collar buttons. It seems probable that one day the courtship of the Empidae will fall down, as man's occasionally does, of its own weight.

4 The bowerbird is another creature that spends so much time courting the female that he never gets any work done. If all the male bowerbirds became nervous wrecks within the next ten or fifteen years, it would not surprise me. The female bowerbird insists that a playground be built for her with a specially constructed bower at the entrance. This bower is much more elaborate than an ordinary nest and is harder to build; it costs a lot more, too. The female will not come to the playground until the male has filled it up with a great many gifts: silvery leaves, red leaves, rose petals, shells, beads, berries, bones, dice, buttons, cigar bands, Christmas seals, and the Lord knows what else. When the female finally condescends to visit the playground, she is in a coy and silly mood and has to be chased in and out of the bower and up and down the playground before she will quit giggling and stand still long enough even to shake hands. The male bird is, of course, pretty well done in before the chase starts, because he has worn himself out hunting for eyeglass lenses and begonia blossoms. I imagine that many a bowerbird, after chasing a female for two or three hours, says the hell with it and goes home to bed. Next day, of course, he telephones someone else and the same trying ritual is gone through with again. A male bowerbird is as exhausted as a night-club habitué before he is out of his twenties.

5 The male fiddler crab has a somewhat easier time, but it can hardly be said that he is sitting pretty. He has one enormously large and powerful claw, usually brilliantly colored, and you might suppose that all he had to do was reach out and grab some passing cutie. The very earliest fiddler crabs may have tried this, but, if so, they got slapped for their pains. A female fiddler crab will not tolerate any caveman stuff; she never has and she doesn't intend to start now. To attract a female, a fiddler crab has to stand on tiptoe and brandish his claw in the air. If any female in the neighborhood is interested—and you'd be surprised how many are not—she comes over and engages him in light badinage, for which he is not in the mood.

As many as a hundred females may pass the time of day with him and go on about their business. By nightfall of an average courting day, a fiddler crab who has been standing on tiptoe for eight or ten hours waving a heavy claw in the air is in pretty sad shape. As in the case of the male of all species, however, he gets out of bed next morning, dashes some water on his face, and tries again.

6 The next time you encounter a male web-spinning spider, stop and reflect that he is too busy worrying about his love life to have any desire to bite you. Male web-spinning spiders have a tougher life than any other males in the animal kingdom. This is because the female web-spinning spiders have very poor eyesight. If a male lands on a female's web, she kills him before he has time to lay down his cane and gloves, mistaking him for a fly or a bumblebee who has tumbled into her trap. Before the species figured out what to do about this, millions of males were murdered by ladies they called on. It is the nature of spiders to perform a little dance in front of the female, but before a male spinner could get near enough for the female to see who he was and what he was up to, she would lash out at him with a flat-iron or a pair of garden shears. One night, nobody knows when, a very bright male spinner lay awake worrying about calling on a lady who had been killing suitors right and left. It came to him that this business of dancing as a love display wasn't getting anybody anywhere except the grave. He decided to go in for web-twitching, or strand-vibrating. The next day he tried it on one of the nearsighted girls. Instead of dropping in on her suddenly, he stayed outside the web and began monkeying with one of its strands. He twitched it up and down and in and out with such a lilting rhythm that the female was charmed. The serenade worked beautifully; the female let him live. The *Britannica*'s spider-watchers, however, report that this system is not always successful. Once in a while, even now, a female will fire three bullets into a suitor or run him through with a kitchen knife. She keeps threatening him from the moment he strikes the first low notes on the outside strings, but usually by the time he has got up to the high notes played around the center of the web, he is going to town and she spares his life.

7 Even the butterfly, as handsome a fellow as he is, can't always win a mate merely by fluttering around and showing off. Many butterflies have to have scent scales on their wings. Hepialus carries a powder puff in a perfumed pouch. He throws perfume at the ladies when they pass. The male tree cricket, Oecanthus, goes Hepialus one better

by carrying a tiny bottle of wine with him and giving drinks to such doxies as he has designs on. One of the male snails throws darts to entertain the girls. So it goes, through the long list of animals, from the bristle worm and his rudimentary dance steps to man and his gift of diamonds and sapphires. The golden-eye drake raises a jet of water with his feet as he flies over a lake; Hepialus has his powder puff, Oecanthus his wine bottle, man his etchings. It is a bright and melancholy story, the age-old desire of the male for the female, the age-old desire of the female to be amused and entertained. Of all the creatures on earth, the only males who could be figured as putting any irony into their courtship are the grebes and certain other diving birds. Every now and then a courting grebe slips quietly down to the bottom of a lake and then, with a mighty "Whoosh!" pops out suddenly a few feet from his girl friend, splashing water all over her. She seems to be persuaded that this is a purely loving display, but I like to think that the grebe always has a faint hope of drowning her or scaring her to death.

8 I will close this investigation into the mournful burdens of the male with *Britannica*'s story about a certain Argus pheasant. It appears that the Argus displays himself in front of a female who stands perfectly still without moving a feather. . . . The male Argus the *Britannica* tells about was confined in a cage with a female of another species, a female who kept moving around, emptying ashtrays and fussing with lampshades all the time the male was showing off his talents. Finally, in disgust, he stalked away and began displaying in front of his water trough. He reminds me of a certain male (*Homo sapiens*) of my acquaintance who one night after dinner asked his wife to put down her detective magazine so that he could read a poem of which he was very fond. She sat quietly enough until he was well into the middle of the thing, intoning with great ardor and intensity. Then suddenly there came a sharp, disconcerting *slap!* It turned out that all during the male's display, the female had been intent on a circling mosquito and had finally trapped it between the palms of her hands. The male in this case did not stalk away and display in front of a water trough; he went over to Tim's and had a flock of drinks and recited the poem to the fellas. I am sure they all told bitter stories of their own about how their displays had been interrupted by females. I am also sure that they all ended up singing "Honey, Honey, Bless Your Heart."

Grant and Lee: A Study in Contrasts

BRUCE CATTON

Bruce Catton (1899–1978) was born in Michigan where, as a young man, he worked at a newspaper. Later, he became one of the editors of *American Heritage* magazine. That experience instilled within him a deep, abiding love of history. His special talent enabled him to bring history to life with the style of a novelist. Indeed, his readers would await his next history in the manner that today's readers anticipate another novel by their favorite writer. Among his many historical accounts are *Mr. Lincoln's Army* (1951), *Glory Road* (1952), *A Stillness at Appomattox* (1953), *The Hallowed Ground* (1956), and *Gettysburg: The Final Fury* (1974).

"Grant and Lee: A Study in Contrasts" has become a classic example of comparison/contrast techniques. Lee represented the aristocratic patriarchy of a dying age, while Grant represented the rising age of democracy and its self-made individuals. Appomattox brought them together, so Catton wants to explain that the tenacity and fidelity of both men were ingredients that made America great. They fought with passion for their causes, and, after the battles were over, they expressed their dedication to peace for the whole nation. As Catton observes, "Two great

Americans, Grant and Lee—very different, yet under everything very much alike."

1 When Ulysses S. Grant and Robert E. Lee met in the parlor of a modest house at Appomattox Court House, Virginia, on April 9, 1865, to work out the terms for the surrender of Lee's Army of Northern Virginia, a great chapter in American life came to a close, and a great new chapter began.

2 These men were bringing the Civil War to its virtual finish. To be sure, other armies had yet to surrender, and for a few days the fugitive Confederate government would struggle desperately and vainly, trying to find some way to go on living now that its chief support was gone. But in effect it was all over when Grant and Lee signed the papers. And the little room where they wrote out the terms was the scene of one of the poignant, dramatic contrasts in American history.

3 They were two strong men these oddly different generals, and they represented the strengths of two conflicting currents that, through them, had come into final collision.

4 Back of Robert E. Lee was the notion that the old aristocratic concept might somehow survive and be dominant in American life.

5 Lee was tidewater Virginia, and in his background were family, culture, and tradition . . . the age of chivalry transplanted to a New World which was making its own legends and its own myths. He embodied a way of life that had come down through the age of knighthood and the English country squire. America was a land that was beginning all over again, dedicated to nothing much more complicated than the rather hazy belief that all men had equal rights and should have an equal chance in the world. In such a land Lee stood for the feeling that it was somehow of advantage to human society to have a pronounced inequality in the social structure. There should be a leisure class, backed by ownership of land; in turn, society itself should be keyed to the land as the chief source of wealth and influence. It would bring forth (according to this ideal) a class of men with a strong sense of obligation to the community; men who lived not to gain advantage for themselves, but to meet the solemn

obligations which had been laid on them by the very fact that they were privileged. From them the country would get its leadership; to them it could look for the higher values—of thought, of conduct, or personal deportment—to give it strength and virtue.

6 Lee embodied the noblest elements of this aristocratic ideal. Through him, the landed nobility justified itself. For four years, the Southern states had fought a desperate war to uphold the ideals for which Lee stood. In the end, it almost seemed as if the Confederacy fought for Lee; as if he himself was the Confederacy . . . the best thing that the way of life for which the Confederacy stood could ever have to offer. He had passed into legend before Appomattox. Thousands of tired, underfed, poorly clothed Confederate soldiers, long since past the simple enthusiasm of the early days of the struggle, somehow considered Lee the symbol of everything for which they had been willing to die. But they could not quite put this feeling into words. If the Lost Cause, sanctified by so much heroism and so many deaths, had a living justification, its justification was General Lee.

7 Grant, the son of a tanner on the Western frontier, was everything Lee was not. He had come up the hard way and embodied nothing in particular except the eternal toughness and sinewy fiber of the men who grew up beyond the mountains. He was one of a body of men who owed reverence and obeisance to no one, who were self-reliant to a fault, who cared hardly anything for the past but who had a sharp eye for the future.

8 These frontier men were the precise opposites of the tidewater aristocrats. Back of them, in the great surge that had taken people over the Alleghenies and into the opening Western country, there was a deep, implicit dissatisfaction with a past that had settled into grooves. They stood for democracy, not from any reasoned conclusion about the proper ordering of human society, but simply because they had grown up in the middle of democracy and knew how it worked. Their society might have privileges, but they would be privileges each man had won for himself. Forms and patterns meant nothing. No man was born to anything, except perhaps to a chance to show how far he could rise. Life was competition.

9 Yet along with this feeling had come a deep sense of belonging to a national community. The Westerner who developed a farm, opened a shop, or set up in business as a trader could hope to prosper only as his own community prospered—and his community ran from the Atlantic to the Pacific and from Canada down to Mexico. If the

land was settled, with towns and highways and accessible markets, he could better himself. He saw his fate in terms of the nation's own destiny. As its horizons expanded, so did his. He had, in other words, an acute dollars-and-cents stake in the continued growth and development of his country.

10 And that, perhaps, is where the contrast between Grant and Lee becomes most striking. The Virginia aristocrat, inevitably, saw himself in relation to his own region. He lived in a static society which could endure almost anything except change. Instinctively, his first loyalty would go to the locality in which that society existed. He would fight to the limit of endurance to defend it, because in defending it he was defending everything that gave his own life its deepest meaning.

11 The Westerner, on the other hand, would fight with an equal tenacity for the broader concept of society. He fought so because everything he lived by was tied to growth, expansion, and a constantly widening horizon. What he lived by would survive or fall with the nation itself. He could not possibly stand by unmoved in the face of an attempt to destroy the Union. He would combat it with everything he had, because he could only see it as an effort to cut the ground out from under his feet.

12 So Grant and Lee were in complete contrast, representing two diametrically opposed elements in American life. Grant was the modern man emerging; beyond him, ready to come on the stage, was the great age of steel and machinery, of crowded cities and a restless burgeoning vitality. Lee might have ridden down from the old age of chivalry, lance in hand, silken banner fluttering over his head. Each man was the perfect champion of his cause, drawing both his strengths and his weaknesses from the people he led.

13 Yet it was not all contrast, after all. Different as they were—in background, in personality, in underlying aspiration—these two great soldiers had much in common. Under everything else, they were marvelous fighters. Furthermore, their fighting qualities were really very much alike.

14 Each man had, to begin with, the great virtue of utter tenacity and fidelity. Grant fought his way down the Mississippi Valley in spite of acute personal discouragement and profound military handicaps. Lee hung on in the trenches at Petersburg after hope itself had died. In each man there was an indomitable quality . . . the born fighter's refusal to give up as long as he can still remain on his feet and lift his two fists.

15 Daring and resourcefulness they had, too: the ability to think faster and move faster than the enemy. These were the qualities which gave Lee the dazzling campaigns of Second Manassas and Chancellorsville and won Vicksburg for Grant.

16 Lastly, and perhaps greatest of all, there was the ability, at the end, to turn quickly from war to peace once the fighting was over. Out of the way these two men behaved at Appomattox came the possibility of a peace of reconciliation. It was a possibility not wholly realized, in the years to come, but which did, in the end, help the two sections to become one nation again . . . after a war whose bitterness might have seemed to make such a reunion wholly impossible. No part of either man's life became him more than the part he played in their brief meeting in the McLean house at Appomattox. Their behavior there put all succeeding generations of Americans in their debt. Two great Americans, Grant and Lee—very different, yet under everything very much alike. Their encounter at Appomattox was one of the great moments of American history.

Once More to the Lake

E. B. WHITE

E. B. White (1899–1985) was born in Mt. Vernon, New York. At Cornell University, he studied under William Strunk, Jr. Years later, after Strunk's death, White edited the textbook from Strunk's class, a small but extremely popular book, *The Elements of Style.* The Cornell experience stimulated his interest in writing, so in 1927 he joined the staff of *The New Yorker,* where he honed his skills as essayist, columnist, and novelist. His first book, *One Man's Meat* (1944), was a collection of columns he published in *Harper's* magazine from 1938 to 1943. He later published three more essay collections, *The Second Tree from the Corner* (1954), *The Points on My Compass* (1962), and *The Essays of E. B. White* (1976). White also gained a reputation as a writer of children's novels: *Stuart Little* (1945), *Charlotte's Web* (1952), and *The Trumpet of the Swan* (1970).

"Once More to the Lake" appeared in *The Essays of E. B. White,* and it provides an account of White's vacation with his son to an old, familiar campsite. The essay uses reminiscence, speculation, and exploration of a few almost insignificant moments in life to make a commentary on the human condition. White uses precise language, specific images, and a gentle tone to bring alive this place by the lake, a place that invites him to remember his youth but forces him to confront his own mortality.

August 1941

1 One summer, along about 1904, my father rented a camp on a lake in Maine and took us all there for the month of August. We all got ringworm from some kittens and had to rub Pond's Extract on our arms and legs night and morning, and my father rolled over in a canoe with all his clothes on; but outside of that the vacation was a success and from then on none of us ever thought there was any place in the world like that lake in Maine. We returned summer after summer—always on August 1 for one month. I have since become a salt-water man, but sometimes in summer there are days when the restlessness of the tides and the fearful cold of the sea water and the incessant wind that blows across the afternoon and into the evening make me wish for the placidity of a lake in the woods. A few weeks ago this feeling got so strong I bought myself a couple of bass hooks and a spinner and returned to the lake where we used to go, for a week's fishing and to revisit old haunts.

2 I took along my son, who had never had any fresh water up his nose and who had seen lily pads only from train windows. On the journey over to the lake I began to wonder what it would be like. I wondered how time would have marred this unique, this holy spot—the coves and streams, the hills that the sun set behind, the camps and the paths behind the camps. I was sure that the tarred road would have found it out, and I wondered in what other ways it would be desolated. It is strange how much you can remember about places like that once you allow your mind to return into the grooves that lead back. You remember one thing, and that suddenly reminds you of another thing. I guess I remembered clearest of all the early mornings, when the lake was cool and motionless, remembered how the bedroom smelled of the lumber it was made of and of the wet woods whose scent entered through the screen. The

partitions in the camp were thin and did not extend clear to the top of the rooms, and as I was always the first up I would dress softly so as not to wake the others, and sneak out into the sweet outdoors and start out in the canoe, keeping close along the shore in the long shadows of the pines. I remembered being very careful never to rub my paddle against the gunwale for fear of disturbing the stillness of the cathedral.

3 The lake had never been what you would call a wild lake. There were cottages sprinkled around the shores, and it was in farming country although the shores of the lake were quite heavily wooded. Some of the cottages were owned by nearby farmers, and you would live at the shore and eat your meals at the farmhouse. That's what our family did. But although it wasn't wild, it was a fairly large and undisturbed lake and there were places in it that, to a child at least, seemed infinitely remote and primeval.

4 I was right about the tar: It led to within half a mile of the shore. But when I got back there, with my boy, and we settled into a camp near a farmhouse and into the kind of summertime I had known, I could tell that it was going to be pretty much the same as it had been before—I knew it, lying in bed the first morning smelling the bedroom and hearing the boy sneak quietly out and go off along the shore in a boat. I began to sustain the illusion that he was I, and therefore, by simple transposition, that I was my father. This sensation persisted, kept cropping up all the time we were there. It was not an entirely new feeling, but in this setting it grew much stronger. I seemed to be living a dual existence. I would be in the middle of some simple act, I would be picking up a bait box or laying down a table fork, or I would be saying something and suddenly it would be not I but my father who was saying the words or making the gesture. It gave me a creepy sensation.

5 We went fishing the first morning. I felt the same damp moss covering the worms in the bait can, and saw the dragonfly alight on the tip of my rod as it hovered a few inches from the surface of the water. It was the arrival of this fly that convinced me beyond any doubt that everything was as it always had been, that the years were a mirage and that there had been no years. The small waves were the same, chucking the rowboat under the chin as we fished at anchor, and the boat was the same boat, the same color green and the ribs broken in the same places, and under the floorboards the same fresh water leavings and debris—the dead hellgrammite, the

wisps of moss, the rusty discarded fishhook, the dried blood from yesterday's catch. We stared silently at the tips of our rods, at the dragonflies that came and went. I lowered the tip of mine into the water, tentatively, pensively dislodging the fly, which darted two feet away, poised, darted two feet back, and came to rest again a little farther up the rod. There had been no years between the ducking of this dragonfly and the other one—the one that was part of memory. I looked at the boy, who was silently watching his fly, and it was my hands that held his rod, my eyes watching. I felt dizzy and didn't know which rod I was at the end of.

6 We caught two bass, hauling them in briskly as though they were mackerel, pulling them over the side of the boat in a businesslike manner without any landing net, and stunning them with a blow on the back of the head. When we got back for a swim before lunch, the lake was exactly where we had left it, the same number of inches from the dock, and there was only the merest suggestion of a breeze. This seemed an utterly enchanted sea, this lake you could leave to its own devices for a few hours and come back to, and find that it had not stirred, this constant and trustworthy body of water. In the shallows, the dark, water-soaked sticks and twigs, smooth and old, were undulating in clusters on the bottom against the clean ribbed sand, and the track of the mussel was plain. A school of minnows swam by, each minnow with its small individual shadow, doubling the attendance, so clear and sharp in the sunlight. Some of the other campers were in swimming, along the shore, one of them with a cake of soap, and the water felt thin and clear and unsubstantial. Over the years there had been this person with the cake of soap, this cultist, and here he was. There had been no years.

7 Up to the farmhouse to dinner through the teeming dusty field, the road under our sneakers was only a two-track road. The middle track was missing, the one with the marks of the hooves and the splotches of dried, flaky manure. There had always been three tracks to choose from in choosing which track to walk in; now the choice was narrowed down to two. For a moment I missed terribly the middle alternative. But the way led past the tennis court, and something about the way it lay there in the sun reassured me; the tape had loosened along the backline, the alleys were green with plantains and other weeds, and the net (installed in June and removed in September) sagged in the dry noon, and the whole place steamed with midday heat and hunger and emptiness. There was a choice of

pie for dessert, and one was blueberry and one was apple, and the waitresses were the same country girls, there having been no passage of time, only the illusion of it as in a dropped curtain—the waitresses were still fifteen; their hair had been washed, that was the only difference—they had been to the movies and seen the pretty girls with the clean hair.

8 Summertime, oh, summertime, pattern of life indelible with fade-proof lake, the wood unshatterable, the pasture with the sweetfern and the juniper forever and ever, summer without end; this was the background, and the life along the shore was the design, the cottages with their innocent and tranquil design, their tiny docks with the flagpole and the American flag floating against the white clouds in the blue sky, the little paths over the roots of the trees leading from camp to camp and the paths leading back to the outhouses and the can of lime for sprinkling, and at the souvenir counters at the store the miniature birchbark canoes and the postcards that showed things looking a little better than they looked. This was the American family at play, escaping the city heat, wondering whether the newcomers in the camp at the head of the cove were "common" or "nice," wondering whether it was true that the people who drove up for Sunday dinner at the farmhouse were turned away because there wasn't enough chicken.

9 It seemed to me, as I kept remembering all this, that those times and those summers had been infinitely precious and worth saving. There had been jollity and peace and goodness. The arriving (at the beginning of August) had been so big a business in itself, at the railway station the farm wagon drawn up, the first smell of the pine-laden air, the first glimpse of the smiling farmer, and the great importance of the trunks and your father's enormous authority in such matters, and the feel of the wagon under you for the long ten-mile haul, and at the top of the last long hill catching the first view of the lake after eleven months of not seeing this cherished body of water. The shouts and cries of the other campers when they saw you, and the trunks to be unpacked, to give up their rich burden. (Arriving was less exciting nowadays, when you sneaked up in your car and parked it under a tree near the camp and took out the bags and in five minutes it was all over, no fuss, no loud wonderful fuss about trunks.)

10 Peace and goodness and jollity. The only thing that was wrong now, really, was the sound of the place, an unfamiliar nervous sound

of the outboard motors. This was the note that jarred, the one thing that would sometimes break the illusion and set the years moving. In those other summertimes all motors were inboard; and when they were at a little distance, the noise they made was a sedative, an ingredient of summer sleep. They were one-cylinder and two-cylinder engines, and some were make-and-break and some were jump-spark, but they all made a sleepy sound across the lake. The one-lungers throbbed and fluttered, and the twin-cylinder ones purred and purred, and that was a quiet sound, too. But now the campers all had outboards. In the daytime, in the hot mornings, these motors made a petulant, irritable sound; at night in the still evening when the afterglow lit the water, they whined about one's ears like mosquitoes. My boy loved our rented outboard, and his great desire was to achieve single-handed mastery over it, and authority, and he soon learned the trick of choking it a little (but not too much), and the adjustment of the needle valve. Watching him I would remember the things you could do with the old one-cylinder engine with the heavy flywheel, how you could have it eating out of your hand if you got really close to it spiritually. Motorboats in those days didn't have clutches, and you would make a landing by shutting off the motor at the proper time and coasting in which a dead rudder. But there was a way of reversing them, if you learned the trick, by cutting the switch and putting it on again exactly on the final dying revolution of the flywheel, so that it would kick back against compression and begin reversing. Approaching a dock in a strong following breeze, it was difficult to slow up sufficiently by the ordinary coasting method, and if a boy felt he had complete mastery over his motor, he was tempted to keep it running beyond its time and then reverse it a few feet from the dock. It took a cool nerve, because if you threw the switch a twentieth of a second too soon you would catch the flywheel when it still had speed enough to go up past center, and the boat would leap ahead, charging bull-fashion at the dock.

11 We had a good week at the camp. The bass were biting well and the sun shone endlessly, day after day. We would be tired at night and lie down in the accumulated heat of the little bedrooms after the long hot day and the breeze would stir almost imperceptibly outside and the smell of the swamp drift in through the rusty screens. Sleep would come easily and in the morning the red squirrel would be on the roof, tapping out his gay routine. I kept remembering

everything, lying in bed in the mornings—the small steamboat that had a long rounded stern like the lip of a Ubangi, and how quietly she ran on the moonlight sails, when the older boys played their mandolins and the girls sang and we ate doughnuts dipped in sugar, and how sweet the music was on the water in the shining night, and what it had felt like to think about girls then. After breakfast we would go up to the store and the things were in the same place—the minnows in a bottle, the plugs and spinners disarranged and pawed over by the youngsters from the boys' camp, the Fig Newtons and the Beeman's gum. Outside, the road was tarred and cars stood in front of the store. Inside, all was just as it had always been, except there was more Coca-Cola and not so much Moxie and root beer and birch beer and sarsaparilla. We would walk out with the bottle of pop apiece and sometimes the pop would backfire up our noses and hurt. We explored the streams, quietly, where the turtles slid off the sunny logs and dug their way into the soft bottom; and we lay on the town wharf and fed worms to the tame bass. Everywhere we went I had trouble making out which was I, the one walking at my side, the one walking in my pants.

12 One afternoon while we were at that lake a thunderstorm came up. It was like the revival of an old melodrama that I had seen long ago with childish awe. The second-act climax of the drama of the electrical disturbance over a lake in America had not changed in any important respect. This was the big scene, still the big scene. The whole thing was so familiar, the first feeling of oppression and heat and a general air around camp of not wanting to go very far away. In midafternoon (it was all the same) a curious darkening of the sky, and a lull in everything that had made life tick; and then the way the boats suddenly swung the other way at their moorings with the coming of a breeze out of the new quarter, and the premonitory rumble. Then the kettle drum, then the snare, then the bass drum and cymbals, then crackling light against the dark, and the gods grinning and licking their chops in the hills. Afterward the calm, the rain steadily rustling in the calm lake, the return of light and hope and spirits, and the campers running out in joy and relief to go swimming in the rain, their bright cries perpetuating the deathless joke about how they were getting simply drenched, and the children, screaming with delight at the new sensation of bathing in the rain, and the joke about getting drenched linking the generations in a strong indestructible chain. And the comedian who waded in carrying an umbrella.

13 When the others went swimming my son said he was going in, too. He pulled his dripping trunks from the line where they had hung all through the shower and wrung them out. Languidly, and with no thought of going in, I watched him, his hard little body, skinny and bare, saw him wince slightly as he pulled up around his vitals the small, soggy, icy garment. As he buckled the swollen belt, suddenly my groin felt the chill of death.

The Real Secret of Piltdown

LOREN EISELEY

Loren Eiseley (1907–1977) was born in Lincoln, Nebraska. He attended the University of Nebraska, where he developed a deep and abiding interest in both anthropology and writing. He contributed essays to numerous magazines. His primary work, however, was in anthropology at the University of Pennsylvania, where he served as professor and provost for many years. A Guggenheim Foundation Fellow, he sponsored various anthropological expeditions for several universities and for the Smithsonian Institute.

He earned his reputation as a writer in 1957 with the publication of *The Immense Journey*, a collection of essays about evolution. He also wrote *Darwin's Century* (1958), *The Firmament of Time* (1960), *The Unexpected Universe* (1969), and *The Night Country* (1971).

Eiseley believed that animals comprehend their role in nature but that humans, "bereft of instinct, must search continually for meanings." In "The Real Secret of Piltdown," he explains in lucid fashion Darwin's theory balanced against the ideas of Alfred R. Wallace. Wallace, after all, had challenged Darwin's theory "by insisting that artistic, mathematical, and musical abilities could not be explained on the basis of natural selection and the struggle for existence." Eiseley points out that Wallace saw "some unknown spiritual element . . . at work in the elaboration of the human brain." The scientist and the humanist come together in Eiseley's summation: "Those who would revile us by pointing to an ape at the foot of our family tree grasp little of the awe with which the modern scientist now puzzles over man's lonely and supreme ascent."

1 How did man get his brain? Many years ago Charles Darwin's great contemporary, and co-discoverer with him of the principle of natural selection, Alfred Russel Wallace, propounded that simple question. It is a question which has bothered evolutionists ever since, and when Darwin received his copy of an article Wallace had written on this subject he was obviously shaken. It is recorded that he wrote in anguish across the paper, "No!" and underlined the "No" three times heavily in a rising fervor of objection.

2 Today the question asked by Wallace and never satisfactorily answered by Darwin has returned to haunt us. A skull, a supposedly very ancient skull, long used as one of the most powerful pieces of evidence documenting the Darwinian position upon human evolution, has been proven to be a forgery, a hoax perpetrated by an unscrupulous but learned amateur. In the fall of 1953 the famous Piltdown cranium, known in scientific circles all over the world since its discovery in a gravel pit on the Sussex Downs in 1911, was jocularly dismissed by the world's press as the skull that had "made monkeys out of the anthropologists." Nobody remembered in 1953 that Wallace, the great evolutionist, had protested to a friend in 1913, "The Piltdown skull does not prove much, if anything!"

3 Why had Wallace made that remark? Why, almost alone among the English scientists of his time, had he chosen to regard with a dubious eye a fossil specimen that seemed to substantiate the theory to which he and Darwin had devoted their lives? He did so for one reason: he did not believe what the Piltdown skull appeared to reveal as to the nature of the process by which the human brain had been evolved. He did not believe in a skull which had a modern brain box attached to an apparently primitive face and given, in the original estimates, an antiquity of something over a million years.

4 Today we know that the elimination of the Piltdown skull from the growing list of valid human fossils in no way affects the scientific

acceptance of the theory of evolution. In fact, only the circumstance that Piltdown had been discovered early, before we had a clear knowledge of the nature of human fossils and the techniques of dating them, made the long survival of this extraordinary hoax possible. Yet in the end it has been the press, absorbed in a piece of clever scientific detection, which has missed the real secret of Piltdown. Darwin saw in the rise of man, with his unique, time-spanning brain, only the undirected play of such natural forces as had created the rest of the living world of plants and animals. Wallace, by contrast, in the case of man, totally abandoned this point of view and turned instead toward a theory of a divinely directed control of the evolutionary process. The issue can be made clear only by a rapid comparison of the views of both men.

5 As everyone who has studied evolution knows, Darwin propounded the theory that since the reproductive powers of plants and animals potentially far outpace the available food supply, there is in nature a constant struggle for existence on the part of every living thing. Since animals vary individually, the most cleverly adapted will survive and leave offspring which will inherit, and in their turn enhance, the genetic endowment they have received from their ancestors. Because the struggle for life is incessant, this unceasing process promotes endless slow changes in bodily form, as living creatures are subjected to different natural environments, different enemies, and all the vicissitudes against which life has struggled down the ages.

6 Darwin, however, laid just one stricture on his theory: it could, he maintained, "render each organized being only as perfect or a little more perfect than other inhabitants of the same country." It could allow any animal only a relative superiority, never an absolute perfection—otherwise selection and the struggle for existence would cease to operate. To explain the rise of man through the slow, incremental gains of natural selection, Darwin had to assume a long struggle of man with man and tribe with tribe.

7 He had to make this assumption because man had far outpaced his animal associates. Since Darwin's theory of the evolutionary process is based upon the practical value of all physical and mental characters in the life struggle, to ignore the human struggle of man with man would have left no explanation as to how humanity by natural selection alone managed to attain an intellectual status so far beyond that of any of the animals with which it had begun its competition for survival.

8 To most of the thinkers of Darwin's day this seemed a reasonable

explanation. It was a time of colonial expansion and ruthless business competition. Peoples of primitive cultures, small societies lost on the world's margins, seemed destined to be destroyed. It was thought that Victorian civilization was the apex of human achievement and that other races with different customs and ways of life must be biologically inferior to Western man. Some of them were even described as only slightly superior to apes. The Darwinians, in a time when there were no satisfactory fossils by which to demonstrate human evolution, were unconsciously minimizing the abyss which yawned between man and ape. In their anxiety to demonstrate our lowly origins they were throwing modern natives into the gap as representing living "missing links" in the chain of human ascent.

9 It was just at this time that Wallace lifted a voice of lonely protest. The episode is a strange one in the history of science, for Wallace had, independently of Darwin, originally arrived at the same general conclusion as to the nature of the evolutionary process. Nevertheless, only a few years after the publication of Darwin's work, *The Origin of Species*, Wallace had come to entertain a point of view which astounded and troubled Darwin. Wallace, who had had years of experience with natives of the tropical archipelagoes, abandoned the idea that they were of mentally inferior cast. He did more. He committed the Darwinian heresy of maintaining that their mental powers were far in excess of what they really needed to carry on the simple food-gathering techniques by which they survived.

10 "How, then," Wallace insisted, "was an organ developed so far beyond the needs of its possessor? Natural selection could only have endowed the savage with a brain a little superior to that of an ape, whereas he actually possesses one but little inferior to that of the average member of our learned societies."

11 At a time when many primitive people were erroneously assumed to speak only in grunts or to chatter like monkeys, Wallace maintained his view of the high intellectual powers of natives by insisting that "the capacity of uttering a variety of distinct articulate sounds and of applying to them an almost infinite amount of modulation . . . is not in any way inferior to that of the higher races. An instrument has been developed in advance of the needs of its possessor."

12 Finally, Wallace challenged the whole Darwinian position on man by insisting that artistic, mathematical, and musical abilities could not be explained on the basis of natural selection and the struggle for existence. Something else, he contended, some unknown spiritual

element, must have been at work in the elaboration of the human brain. Why else would men of simple cultures possess the same basic intellectual powers which the Darwinists maintained could be elaborated only by competitive struggle?

13 "If you had not told me you had made these remarks," Darwin said, "I should have thought they had been added by someone else. I differ grievously from you and am very sorry for it." He did not, however, supply a valid answer to Wallace's queries. Outside of murmuring about the inherited effects of habit—a contention without scientific validity today—Darwin clung to his original position. Slowly Wallace's challenge was forgotten and a great complacency settled down upon the scientific world.

14 For seventy years after the publication of *The Origin of Species* in 1859, there were only two finds of fossil human skulls which seemed to throw any light upon the Darwin-Wallace controversy. One was the discovery of the small-brained Java Ape Man, the other was the famous Piltdown or "dawn man." Both were originally dated as lying at the very beginning of the Ice Age, and, though these dates were later to be modified, the skulls, for a very long time, were regarded as roughly contemporaneous and very old.

15 Two more unlike "missing links" could hardly be imagined. Though they were supposed to share a million-year antiquity, the one was indeed quite primitive and small-brained; the other, Piltdown, in spite of what seemed a primitive lower face, was surprisingly modern in brain. Which of these forms told the true story of human development? Was a large brain old? Had ages upon ages of slow, incremental, Darwinian increase produced it? The Piltdown skull seemed to suggest such a development.

16 Many were flattered to find their anthropoid ancestry seemingly removed to an increasingly remote past. If one looked at the Java Ape Man, one was forced to contemplate an ancestor, not terribly remote in time, who still had a face and a brain which hinted strongly of the ape. Yet, when by geological evidence this "erect walking ape-man" was finally assigned to a middle Ice Age antiquity, there arose the immediate possibility that Wallace could be right in his suspicion that the human brain might have had a surprisingly rapid development. By contrast, the Piltdown remains seemed to suggest a far more ancient and slow-paced evolution of man. The Piltdown hoaxer, in attaching an ape jaw to a human skull fragment, had, perhaps unwittingly, created a creature which supported the Darwinian idea

of man, not too unlike the man of today, extending far back into pre-Ice Age times.

17 Which story was the right one? Until the exposé of Piltdown in 1953, both theories had to be considered possible and the two hopelessly unlike fossils had to be solemnly weighed in the same balance. Today Piltdown is gone. In its place we are confronted with the blunt statement of two modern scientists, M. R. A. Chance and A. P. Mead.

18 "No adequate explanation," they confess over eighty years after Darwin scrawled his vigorous "No!" upon Wallace's paper, "has been put forward to account for so large a cerebrum as that found in man."

19 We have been so busy tracing the tangible aspects of evolution in the *forms of animals* that our heads, the little globes which hold the midnight sky and the shining, invisible universes of thought, have been taken about as much for granted as the growth of a yellow pumpkin in the fall.

20 Now a part of this mystery as it is seen by the anthropologists of today lies in the relation of the brain to time. "If," Wallace had said, "researches in all parts of Europe and Asia fail to bring to light any proofs of man's presence far back in the Age of Mammals, *it will be at least a presumption that he came into existence at a much later date and by a more rapid process of development.*" If human evolution should prove to be comparatively rapid, "explosive" in other words, Wallace felt that his position would be vindicated, because such a rapid development of the brain would, he thought, imply a divinely directed force at work in man. In the 1870's when he wrote, however, human prehistory was largely an unknown blank. Today we can make a partial answer to Wallace's question. Since the exposure of the Piltdown hoax all of the evidence at our command—and it is considerable—points to man, in his present form, as being one of the youngest and newest of all earth's swarming inhabitants.

21 The Ice Age extends behind us in time for, at most, a million years. Though this may seem long to one who confines his studies to the written history of man, it is, in reality, a very short period as the student of evolution measures time. It is a period marked more by the extinction of some of the last huge land animals, like the hairy mammoth and the saber-toothed tiger, than it is by the appearance of new forms of life. To this there is only one apparent exception: the rise and spread of man over the Old World land mass.

22 Most of our knowledge of him—even in his massive-faced, beetle-browed stage—is now confined, since the loss of Piltdown, to the last half of the Ice Age. If we pass backward beyond this point we can find traces of crude tools, stone implements which hint that some earlier form of man was present here and there in Europe, Asia, and particularly Africa in the earlier half of Ice Age time, but to the scientist it is like peering into the mists floating over an unknown landscape. Here and there through the swirling vapor one catches a glimpse of a shambling figure, or a half-wild primordial face stares back at one from some momentary opening in the fog. Then, just as one grasps at a clue, the long gray twilight settles in and the wraiths and the half-heard voices pass away.

23 Nevertheless, particularly in Africa, a remarkable group of human-like apes have been discovered: creatures with small brains and teeth of a remarkably human cast. Prominent scientists are still debating whether they are on the direct line of ascent to man or are merely near relatives of ours. Some, it is now obvious, existed too late in time to be our true ancestors, though this does not mean that their bodily characters may not tell us what the earliest anthropoids who took the human turn of the road were like.

24 These apes are not all similar in type or appearance. They are men and yet not men. Some are frailer-bodied, some have great, bone-cracking jaws and massive gorilloid crests atop their skulls. This fact leads us to another of Wallace's remarkable perceptions of long ago. With the rise of the truly human brain, Wallace saw that man had transferred to his machines and tools many of the alterations of parts that in animals take place through evolution of the body. Unwittingly, man had assigned to his machines the selective evolution which in the animal changes the nature of its bodily structure through the ages. Man of today, the atomic manipulator, the aeronaut who flies faster than sound, has precisely the same brain and body as his ancestors of twenty thousand years ago who painted the last Ice Age mammoths on the walls of caves in France.

25 To put it another way, it is man's ideas that have evolved and changed the world about him. Now, confronted by the lethal radiations of open space and the fantastic speeds of his machines, he has to invent new electronic controls that operate faster than his nerves, and he must shield his naked body against atomic radiation by the use of protective metals. Already he is physically antique in this robot world he has created. All that sustains him is that small globe of gray

matter through which spin his ever-changing conceptions of the universe.

26 Yet, as Wallace, almost a hundred years ago, glimpsed this timeless element in man, he uttered one more prophecy. When we come to trace our history into the past, he contended, sooner or later we will come to a time when the body of man begins to differ and diverge more extravagantly in its appearance. Then, he wrote, we shall know that we stand close to the starting point of the human family. In the twilight before the dawn of the human mind, man will not have been able to protect his body from change and his remains will bear the marks of all the forces that play upon the rest of life. He will be different in his form. He will be, in other words, as variable in body as we know the South African man-apes to be.

27 Today, with the solution of the Piltdown enigma, we must settle the question of the time involved in human evolution in favor of Wallace, not Darwin; we need not, however, pursue the mystical aspects of Wallace's thought—since other factors yet to be examined may well account for the rise of man. The rapid fading out of archaeological evidence of tools in lower Ice Age times—along with the discovery of man-apes of human aspect but with ape-sized brains, yet possessing a diverse array of bodily characters—suggests that the evolution of the human brain was far more rapid than that conceived of in early Darwinian circles. At that time it was possible to hear the Eskimos spoken of as possible survivals of Miocene men of several million years ago. By contrast to this point of view, man and his rise now appear short in time—explosively short. There is every reason to believe that whatever the nature of the forces involved in the production of the human brain, a long slow competition of human group with human group or race with race would not have resulted in such similar mental potentialities among all peoples everywhere. Something—some other factor—has escaped our scientific attention.

28 There are certain strange bodily characters which mark man as being more than the product of a dog-eat-dog competition with his fellows. He possesses a peculiar larval nakedness, difficult to explain on survival principles; his periods of helpless infancy and childhood are prolonged; he has aesthetic impulses which, though they vary in intensity from individual to individual, appear in varying manifestations among all peoples. He is totally dependent, in the achievement of human status, upon the careful training he receives in human society.

29 Unlike a solitary species of animal, he cannot develop alone. He has suffered a major loss of precise instinctive controls of behavior. To make up for this biological lack, society and parents condition the infant, supply his motivations, and promote his long-drawn training at the difficult task of becoming a normal human being. Even today some individuals fail to make this adjustment and have to be excluded from society.

30 We are now in a position to see the wonder and terror of the human predicament: man is totally dependent on society. Creature of dream, he has created an invisible world of ideas, beliefs, habits, and customs which buttress him about and replace for him the precise instincts of the lower creatures. In this invisible universe he takes refuge, but just as instinct may fail an animal under some shift of environmental conditions, so man's cultural beliefs may prove inadequate to meet a new situation, or, on an individual level, the confused mind may substitute, by some terrible alchemy, cruelty for love.

31 The profound shock of the leap from animal to human status is echoing still in the depths of our subconscious minds. It is a transition which would seem to have demanded considerable rapidity of adjustment in order for human beings to have survived, and it also involved the growth of prolonged bonds of affection in the subhuman family, because otherwise its naked, helpless offspring would have perished.

32 It is not beyond the range of possibility that this strange reduction of instincts in man in some manner forced a precipitous brain growth as a compensation—something that had to be hurried for survival purposes. Man's competition, it would thus appear, may have been much less with his own kind than with the dire necessity of building about him a world of ideas to replace his lost animal environment. As we will show later, he is a pedomorph, a creature with an extended childhood.

33 Modern science would go on to add that many of the characters of man, such as his lack of fur, thin skull, and globular head, suggest mysterious changes in growth rates which preserve, far into human maturity, foetal or infantile characters which hint that the forces creating man drew him fantastically out of the very childhood of his brutal forerunners. Once more the words of Wallace come back to haunt us: "We may safely infer that the savage possesses a brain capable, if cultivated and developed, of performing work of a kind and degree far beyond what he ever requires it to do."

34 As a modern man, I have sat in concert halls and watched huge

audiences floating dazed on the voice of a great singer. Alone in the dark box I have heard far off as if ascending out of some black stairwell the guttural whisperings and bestial coughings out of which the voice arose. Again, I have sat under the slit dome of a mountain observatory and marveled, as the great wheel of the galaxy turned in all its midnight splendor, that the mind in the course of three centuries has been capable of drawing into its strange, nonspatial interior that world of infinite distance and multitudinous dimensions.

35 Ironically enough, science, which can show us the flints and the broken skulls of our dead fathers, has yet to explain how we have come so far so fast, nor has it any completely satisfactory answer to the question asked by Wallace long ago. Those who would revile us by pointing to an ape at the foot of our family tree grasp little of the awe with which the modern scientist now puzzles over man's lonely and supreme ascent. As one great student of paleoneurology, Dr. Tilly Edinger, recently remarked, "If man has passed through a Pithecanthropus phase, the evolution of his brain has been unique, not only in its result but also in its tempo. . . . Enlargement of the cerebral hemispheres by 50 percent seems to have taken place, speaking geologically, within an instant, and without having been accompanied by any major increase in body size."

36 The true secret of Piltdown, though thought by the public to be merely the revelation of an unscrupulous forgery, lies in the fact that it has forced science to reëxamine carefully the history of the most remarkable creation in the world—the human brain.

The Myth of Sisyphus

ALBERT CAMUS

Albert Camus (1913–1960) was a French novelist, playwright, essayist, and journalist. He was born in Algeria of French parents, but he did not go to France until 1939. Alarmed by the advance of Nazism, he joined the French resistance in 1942 and served as editor of the rebellion's underground newspaper, *Combat.* In 1957, he won the Nobel Prize for literature.

Known as an existentialist, he believed that existence was a given fact, one that preceded any knowledge of God or an afterlife. For Camus, the individual person, honest with himself or herself, must face life without the religious wrappings of belief in God. These ideas are explored in his major works—*The Stranger* (1942), *The Plague* (1947), and *The Fall* (1957).

Camus published "The Myth of Sisyphus" in 1942, the same year he joined the underground forces to fight the Nazi regime. In it, he argues that human beings tend to cling desperately to life even when their lives have no significant meanings or purposes. Thus their lives are absurd. Sisyphus, of course, was the mortal who had to repeatedly roll a rock to the mountaintop only to watch it tumble back down the hill. His was thought to be a "futile and hopeless labor." Yet Camus examines those moments when Sisyphus rested from his labor as he trudged back down the hill. He finds in those moments "the recipe for the absurd victory" as enunciated by Oedipus: "Despite so many ordeals, my advanced age and the nobility of my soul make me conclude that all is well." For Camus, "Happiness and the absurd are two sons of the same earth." Camus argues that the human struggle should be enough to charge the human soul and bring a smile. After all, "One must imagine Sisyphus happy."

1 The gods had condemned Sisyphus to ceaselessly rolling a rock to the top of a mountain, whence the stone would fall back of its own weight. They had thought with some reason that there is no more dreadful punishment than futile and hopeless labor.

2 If one believes Homer, Sisyphus was the wisest and most prudent of mortals. According to another tradition, however, he was disposed to practice the profession of highwayman. I see no contradiction in this. Opinions differ as to the reasons why he became the futile laborer of the underworld. To begin with, he is accused of a certain levity in regard to the gods. He stole their secrets. Aegina, the daughter of Aesopus, was carried off by Jupiter. The father was shocked by that disappearance and complained to Sisyphus. He, who knew of the abduction, offered to tell about it on condition that Aesopus would give water to the citadel of Corinth. To the celestial thunderbolts he preferred the benediction of water. He was punished for this in the underworld. Homer tells us also that Sisyphus had put Death in chains. Pluto could not endure the sight of his deserted, silent empire. He dispatched the god of war, who liberated Death from the hands of her conqueror.

3 It is said also that Sisyphus, being near to death, rashly wanted to test his wife's love. He ordered her to cast his unburied body into the middle of the public square. Sisyphus woke up in the underworld. And there, annoyed by an obedience so contrary to human love, he obtained from Pluto permission to return to earth in order to chastise his wife. But when he had seen again the face of this world, enjoyed water and sun, warm stones and the sea, he no longer wanted to go back to the infernal darkness. Recalls, signs of anger, warnings were of no avail. Many years more he lived facing the curve of the gulf, the sparkling sea, and the smiles of earth. A decree of the gods was necessary. Mercury came and seized the impudent man by the collar and, snatching him from his joys, led him forcibly back to the underworld, where his rock was ready for him.

4 You have already grasped that Sisyphus is the absurd hero. He *is*, as much through his passions as through his torture. His scorn of the gods, his hatred of death, and his passion for life won him that unspeakable penalty in which the whole being is exerted toward accomplishing nothing. This is the price that must be paid for the passions of this earth. Nothing is told us about Sisyphus in the underworld. Myths are made for the imagination to breathe life into them. As for this myth, one sees merely the whole effort of a body straining to raise the huge stone, to roll it and push it up a slope a hundred times over; one sees the face screwed up, the cheek tight against the stone, the shoulder bracing the clay-covered mass, the foot wedging it, the fresh start with arms outstretched, the wholly human security of two earth-clotted hands. At the very end of his long effort measured by skyless space and time without depth, the purpose is achieved. Then Sisyphus watches the stone rush down in a few moments toward that lower world whence he will have to push it up again toward the summit. He goes back down to the plain.

5 It is during that return, that pause, that Sisyphus interests me. A face that toils so close to stones is already stone itself! I see that man going back down with a heavy yet measured step toward the torment of which he will never know the end. That hour like a breathing-space which returns as surely as his suffering, that is the hour of consciousness. At each of those moments when he leaves the heights and gradually sinks toward the lairs of the gods, he is superior to his fate. He is stronger than his rock.

6 If this myth is tragic, that is because its hero is conscious. Where would his torture be, indeed, if at every step the hope of succeeding upheld him? The workman of today works every day in his life at the same tasks, and this fate is no less absurd. But it is tragic only at the rare moments when it becomes conscious. Sisyphus, proletarian of the gods, powerless and rebellious, knows the whole extent of his wretched condition: it is what he thinks of during his descent. The lucidity that was to constitute his torture at the same time crowns his victory. There is no fate that cannot be surmounted by scorn.

7 If the descent is thus sometimes performed in sorrow, it can also take place in joy. This word is not too much. Again I fancy Sisyphus returning toward his rock, and the sorrow was in the beginning. When the images of earth cling too tightly to memory, when the call of happiness becomes too insistent, it happens that melancholy

rises in man's heart: this is the rock's victory, this is the rock itself. The boundless grief is too heavy to bear. These are our nights of Gethsemane. But crushing truths perish from being acknowledged. Thus, Oedipus at the outset obeys fate without knowing it. But from the moment he knows, his tragedy begins. Yet at the same moment, blind and desperate, he realizes that the only bond linking him to the world is the cool hand of a girl. Then a tremendous remark rings out: "Despite so many ordeals, my advanced age and the nobility of my soul make me conclude that all is well." Sophocles' Oedipus, like Dostoevsky's Kirilov, thus gives the recipe for the absurd victory. Ancient wisdom confirms modern heroism.

8 One does not discover the absurd without being tempted to write a manual of happiness. "What! by such narrow ways—?" There is but one world, however. Happiness and the absurd are two sons of the same earth. They are inseparable. It would be a mistake to say that happiness necessarily springs from the absurd discovery. It happens as well that the feeling of the absurd springs from happiness. "I conclude that all is well," says Oedipus, and that remark is sacred. It echoes in the wild and limited universe of man. It teaches that all is not, has not been, exhausted. It drives out of this world a god who had come into it with dissatisfaction and a preference for futile sufferings. It makes of fate a human matter, which must be settled among men.

9 All Sisyphus' silent joy is contained therein. His fate belongs to him. His rock is his thing. Likewise, the absurd man, when he contemplates his torment, silences all the idols. In the universe suddenly restored to its silence, the myriad wondering little voices of the earth rise up. Unconscious, secret calls, invitations from all the faces, they are the necessary reverse and price of victory. There is no sun without shadow, and it is essential to know the night. The absurd man says yes and his effort will henceforth be unceasing. If there is a personal fate, there is no higher destiny, or at least there is but one which he concludes is inevitable and despicable. For the rest, he knows himself to be the master of his days. At that subtle moment when man glances backward over his life, Sisyphus returning toward his rock, in that slight pivoting he contemplates that series of unrelated actions which becomes his fate, created by him, combined under his memory's eye and soon sealed by his death. Thus, convinced of the wholly human origin of all that is human, a blind man eager to see who knows that the night has no end, he is still on the go. The rock is still rolling.

I leave Sisyphus at the foot of the mountain! One always finds one's burden again. But Sisyphus teaches the higher fidelity that negates the gods and raises rocks. He too concludes that all is well. This universe henceforth without a master seems to him neither sterile nor futile. Each atom of that stone, each mineral flake of that night-filled mountain, in itself forms a world. The struggle itself toward the heights is enough to fill a man's heart. One must imagine Sisyphus happy.

Notes of a Native Son

JAMES BALDWIN

James Baldwin (1924–1987) was a native of New York's Harlem and labeled himself a native son of the black ghetto. He fought his way into the literary world after abandoning an interest in the ministry. Several scholarships and fellowships allowed him to work in Paris during his early career so that he could produce the novels *Go Tell It on the Mountain* (1953) and *Giovanni's Room* (1956). During that time, he also developed a set of essays, *Notes of a Native Son* (1955). Additional fiction and essays followed, such as *Nobody Knows My Name* (essays, in 1961), *Another Country* (a novel, in 1962), and *Going to Meet the Man* (a set of stories, in 1965).

In the following essay, "Notes of a Native Son," which won critical acclaim, Baldwin works to identify himself. He examines his role as an American, as a writer, and as an African American. He assumes a specific role—spokesperson on race relations. He writes, "The color of my skin makes me, automatically, an expert." Also affecting Baldwin's sense of alienation was his homosexuality, which, during his life, remained covert.

In this essay, he reminisces about his love/hate relationship with his father, who has died. Returning for the funeral, he encounters prejudice and must confront again his own deep rage toward white people. One incident with a white waitress who refused to serve him provoked him into action that later shocked him: "I saw nothing very clearly but I did see this: that my life, my *real* life, was in danger, and not from anything other people might do but from the hatred I carried in my own heart."

I

1 On the 29th of July, in 1943, my father died. On the same day, a few hours later, his last child was born. Over a month before this, while all our energies were concentrated in waiting for these events, there had been, in Detroit, one of the bloodiest race riots of the century. A few hours after my father's funeral, while he lay in state in the undertaker's chapel, a race riot broke out in Harlem. On the morning of the 3rd of August, we drove my father to the graveyard through a wilderness of smashed plate glass.

2 The day of my father's funeral had also been my nineteenth birthday. As we drove him to the graveyard, the spoils of injustice, anarchy, discontent, and hatred were all around us. It seemed to me that God himself had devised, to mark my father's end, the most sustained and brutally dissonant of codas. And it seemed to me, too, that the violence which rose all about us as my father left the world had been devised as a corrective for the pride of his eldest son. I had declined to believe in that apocalypse which had been central to my father's vision; very well, life seemed to be saying, here is something that will certainly pass for an apocalypse until the real thing comes along. I had inclined to be contemptuous of my father for the conditions of his life, for the conditions of our lives. When his life had ended I began to wonder about that life and also, in a new way, to be apprehensive about my own.

3 I had not known my father very well. We had got on badly, partly because we shared, in our different fashions, the vice of stubborn pride. When he was dead I realized that I had hardly ever spoken to him. When he had been dead a long time I began to wish I had. It seems to be typical of life in America where opportunities, real and fancied, are thicker than anywhere else on the globe, that the second

generation has no time to talk to the first. No one, including my father, seems to have known exactly how old he was, but his mother had been born during slavery. He was of the first generation of free men. He, along with thousands of other Negroes, came North after 1919 and I was part of that generation which had never seen the landscape of what Negroes sometimes call the Old Country.

4 He had been born in New Orleans and had been a quite young man there during the time that Louis Armstrong, a boy, was running errands for the dives and honky-tonks of what was always presented to me as one of the most wicked of cities—to this day, whenever I think of New Orleans, I also helplessly think of Sodom and Gomorrah. My father never mentioned Louis Armstrong, except to forbid us to play his records; but there was a picture of him on our wall for a long time. One of my father's strong-willed female relatives had placed it there and forbade my father to take it down. He never did, but he eventually maneuvered her out of the house and when, some years later, she was in trouble and near death, he refused to do anything to help her.

5 He was, I think, very handsome. I gather this from photographs and from my own memories of him, dressed in his Sunday best and on his way to preach a sermon somewhere, when I was little. Handsome, proud, and ingrown, "like a toe-nail," somebody said. But he looked to me, as I grew older, like pictures I had seen of African tribal chieftains: he really should have been naked, with war-paint on and barbaric mementos, standing among spears. He could be chilling in the pulpit and indescribably cruel in his personal life and he was certainly the most bitter man I have ever met; yet it must be said that there was something else in him, buried in him, which lent him his tremendous power and, even, a rather crushing charm. It had something to do with his blackness, I think—he was very black—with his blackness and his beauty, and with the fact that he knew that he was black but did not know that he was beautiful. He claimed to be proud of his blackness but it had also been the cause of much humiliation and it had fixed bleak boundaries to his life. He was not a young man when we were growing up and he had already suffered many kinds of ruin; in his outrageously demanding and protective way he loved his children, who were black like him and menaced, like him; and all these things sometimes showed in his face when he tried, never to my knowledge with any success, to establish contact with any of us. When he took one of his children

on his knee to play, the child always became fretful and began to cry; when he tried to help one of us with our homework the absolutely unabating tension which emanated from him caused our minds and our tongues to become paralyzed, so that he, scarcely knowing why flew into a rage and the child, not knowing why, was punished. If it ever entered his head to bring a surprise home for his children, it was, almost unfailingly, the wrong surprise and even the big watermelons he often brought home on his back in the summertime led to the most appalling scenes. I do not remember in all those years, that one of children was ever glad to see him come home. From what I was able to gather of his early life, it seemed that this inability to establish contact with other people had always marked him and had been one of the things which had driven him out of New Orleans. There was something in him therefore, groping and tentative, which was never expressed and which was buried with him. One saw it most clearly when he was facing new people and hoping to impress them. But he never did, not for long. We went from church to smaller and more improbable church, he found himself in less and less demand as a minister, and by the time he died none of his friends had come to see him for a long time. He had lived and died in an intolerable bitterness of spirit and it frightened me, as we drove him to the graveyard through those unquiet, ruined streets, to see how powerful and overflowing his bitterness could be and to realize that this bitterness now was mine.

6 When he died I had been away from home for a little over a year. In that year I had had time to become aware of the meaning of all my father's bitter warnings, had discovered the secret of his proudly pursed lips and rigid carriage: I had discovered the weight of white people in the world. I saw that this had been for my ancestors and now would be for me an awful thing to live with and that the bitterness which had helped to kill my father could also kill me.

7 He had been ill a long time—in the mind, as we now realized, reliving instances of his fantastic intransigence in the new light of his affliction and endeavoring to feel a sorrow for him which never, quite, came true. We had not known that he was being eaten up by paranoia, and the discovery that his cruelty, to our bodies and our minds, had been one of the symptoms of his illness was not, then, enough to enable us to forgive him. The younger children felt, quite simply, relief that he would not be coming home anymore. My mother's observation that it was he, after all, who had kept them

alive all these years meant nothing because the problems of keeping children alive are not real for children. The older children felt, with my father gone, that they could invite their friends to the house without fear that their friends would be insulted or, as had sometimes happened with me, being told that there friends were in league with the devil and intended to rob our family of everything we owned. (I didn't fail to wonder, and it made me hate him, what on earth we owned that anybody else would want.)

8 His illness was beyond all hope of healing before anyone realized that he was ill. He had always been so strange and had lived, like a prophet, in such unimaginably close communion with the Lord that his long silences which were punctuated by moans and hallelujahs and snatches of old songs while he sat at the living-room window never seemed odd to us. It was not until he refused to eat because, he said, his family was trying to poison him that my mother was forced to accept as a fact what had, until then, been only an unwilling suspicion. When he was committed, it was discovered that he had tuberculosis and, as it turned out, the disease of his mind allowed the disease of his body to destroy him. For the doctors could not force him to eat, either, and, though he was fed intravenously, it was clear from the beginning that there was no hope for him.

9 In my mind's eye I could see him, sitting at the window, locked up in his terrors; hating and fearing every living soul including his children who had betrayed him, too, by reaching towards the world which had despised him. There were nine of us. I began to wonder what it could have felt like for such a man to have had nine children whom he could barely feed. He used to make little jokes about our poverty, which never, of course, seemed very funny to us; they could not have seemed very funny to him, either, or else our all too feeble response to them would never have caused such rages. He spent great energy and achieved, to our chagrin, no small amount of success in keeping us away from the people who surrounded us, people who had all-night rent parties to which we listened when we should have been sleeping, people who cursed and drank and flashed razor blades on Lenox Avenue. He could not understand why, if they had so much energy to spare, they could not use it to make their lives better. He treated almost everybody on our block with a most uncharitable asperity and neither they, nor of course, their children were slow to reciprocate.

10 The only white people who came to our house were welfare

workers and bill collectors. It was almost always my mother who dealt with them, for my father's temper, which was at the mercy of his pride, was never to be trusted. It was clear that he felt their very presence in his home to be a violation: this was conveyed by his carriage almost ludicrously stiff, and by his voice, harsh and vindictively polite. When I was around nine or ten I wrote a play which was directed by a young, white schoolteacher, a woman, who then took an interest in me, and gave me books to read and, in order to corroborate my theatrical bent, decided to take me to what she somewhat tactlessly referred to as "real" plays. Theatergoing was forbidden in our house, but, with the really cruel intuitiveness of a child, I suspected that the color of this woman's skin would carry the day for me. When, at school, she suggested taking me to the theater, I did not, as I might have done if she had been a Negro, find a way of discouraging her, but agreed that she should pick me up at my house one evening. I then, very cleverly, left all the rest to my mother, who suggested to my father, as I knew she would, that it would not be very nice to let such a kind woman make the trip for nothing. Also, since it was a schoolteacher, I imagine that my mother countered the idea of sin with the idea of "education," which word, even with my father, carried a kind of bitter weight.

11 Before the teacher came my father took me aside to ask *why* she was coming, what *interest* she could possibly have in our house, in a boy like me. I said I didn't know but I, too, suggested that it had something to do with education. And I understood that my father was waiting for me to say something—I didn't quite know what; perhaps that I wanted his protection against this teacher and her "education." I said none of these things and the teacher came and we went out. It was clear, during the brief interview in our living room, that my father was agreeing very much against his will and that he would have refused permission if he had dared. The fact that he did not dare caused me to despise him: I had no way of knowing that he was facing in that living room a wholly unprecedented and frightening situation.

12 Later, when my father had been laid off from his job, this woman became very important to us. She was really a very sweet and generous woman and went to a great deal of trouble to be of help to us, particularly during one awful winter. My mother called her by the highest name she knew: she said she was a "christian." My father could scarcely disagree but during the four or five years of our relatively close associa-

tion he never trusted her and was always trying to surprise in her open, Midwestern face the genuine, cunningly hidden, and hideous motivation. In later years, particularly when it began to be clear that this "education" of mine was going to lead me to perdition, he became more explicit and warned me that my white friends in high school were not really my friends and that I would see, when I was older, how white people would do anything to keep a Negro down. Some of them could be nice, he admitted, but none of them were to be trusted and most of them were not even nice. The best thing was to have as little to do with them as possible. I did not feel this way and I was certain, in my innocence, that I never would.

13 But the year which preceded my father's death had made a great change in my life. I had been living in New Jersey, working in defense plants, working and living among southerners, white and black. I knew about the south, of course, and about how southerners treated Negroes and how they expected them to behave, but it had never entered my mind that anyone would look at me and expect *me* to behave that way. I learned in New Jersey that to be a Negro meant, precisely, that one was never looked at but was simply at the mercy of the reflexes the color of one's skin caused in other people. I acted in New Jersey as I had always acted, that is as though I thought a great deal of myself—I had to *act* that way—with results that were, simply, unbelievable. I had scarcely arrived before I had earned the enmity, which was extraordinarily ingenious, of all my superiors and nearly all my co-workers. In the beginning, to make matters worse, I simply did not know what was happening. I did not know what I had done, and I shortly began to wonder what *anyone* could possibly do, to bring about such unanimous, active, and unbearably vocal hostility. I knew about jim-crow but I had never experienced it. I went to the same self-service restaurant three times and stood with all the Princeton boys before the counter, waiting for a hamburger and coffee; it was always an extraordinarily long time before anything was set before me; but it was not until the fourth visit that I learned that, in fact, nothing had ever been set before me: I had simply picked something up. Negroes were not served there, I was told, and they had been waiting for me to realize that I was always the only Negro present. Once I was told this, I determined to go there all the time. But now they were ready for me and, though some dreadful scenes were subsequently enacted in that restaurant, I never ate there again.

14 It was the same story all over New Jersey, in bars, bowling alleys, diners, places to live. I was always being forced to leave, silently, or with mutual imprecations. I very shortly became notorious and children giggled behind me when I passed and their elders whispered or shouted—they really believed that I was mad. And it did begin to work on my mind, of course; I began to be afraid to go anywhere and to compensate for this I went places to which I really should not have gone and where, God knows, I had no desire to be. My reputation in town naturally enhanced my reputation at work and my working day became one long series of acrobatics designed to keep me out of trouble. I cannot say that these acrobatics succeeded. It began to seem that the machinery of the organization I worked for was turning over, day and night, with but one aim: to eject me. I was fired once, and contrived, with the aid of a friend from New York, to get back on the payroll; was fired again, and bounced back again. It took a while to fire me for the third time, but the third time took. There were no loopholes anywhere. There was not even any way of getting back inside the gates.

15 That year in New Jersey lives in my mind as though it were the year during which, having an unsuspected predilection for it, I first contracted some dread, chronic disease, the unfailing symptom of which is a kind of blind fever, a pounding in the skull and fire in the bowels. Once this disease is contracted, one can never be really carefree again, for the fever, without an instant's warning, can recur at any moment. It can wreck more important things than race relations. There is not a Negro alive who does not have this rage in his blood—one has the choice, merely, of living with it consciously or surrendering to it. As for me, this fever has recurred in me, and does, and will until the day I die.

16 My last night in New Jersey, a white friend from New York took me to the nearest big town, Trenton, to go to the movies and have a few drinks. As it turned out, he also saved me from, at the very least, a violent whipping. Almost every detail of that night stands out very clearly in my memory. I even remember the name of the movie we saw because its title impressed me as being so patly ironical. It was a movie about the German occupation of France, starring Maureen O'Hara and Charles Laughton and called *This Land Is Mine*. I remember the name of the diner we walked into when the movie ended: it was the "American Diner." When we walked in the counterman asked what we wanted and I remember answering with

the casual sharpness which had become my habit: "We want a hamburger and a cup of coffee, what do you think we want?" I do not know why, after a year of such rebuffs, I so completely failed to anticipate his answer, which was, of course, "We don't serve Negroes here." This reply failed to discompose me, at least for the moment. I made some sardonic comment about the name of the diner and we walked out into the streets.

17 This was the time of what was called the "brown-out," when the lights in all American cities were very dim. When we re-entered the streets something happened to me which had the force of an optical illusion, or a nightmare. The streets were very crowded and I was facing north. People were moving in every direction but it seemed to me, in that instance, that all of the people I could see, and many more than that, were moving toward me, against me, and that everyone was white. I remember how their faces gleamed. And I felt, like a physical sensation, a *click* at the nape of my neck as though some interior string connecting my head to my body had been cut. I began to walk. I heard my friend call after me, but I ignored him. Heaven only knows what was going on in his mind, but he had the good sense not to touch me—I don't know what would have happened if he had—and to keep me in sight. I don't know what was going on in my mind, either; I certainly had no conscious plan. I wanted to do something to crush these white faces, which were crushing me. I walked for perhaps a block or two until I came to an enormous, glittering, and fashionable restaurant in which I knew not even the intercession of the Virgin would cause me to be served. I pushed through the doors and took the first vacant seat I saw, at a table for two, and waited.

18 I do not know how long I waited and I rather wonder, until today, what I could possibly have looked like. Whatever I looked like, I frightened the waitress who shortly appeared, and the moment she appeared all of my fury flowed towards her. I hated her for her white face, and for her great, astounded, frightened eyes. I felt that if she found a black man so frightening I would make her fright worthwhile.

19 She did not ask me what I wanted, but repeated, as though she had learned it somewhere, "We don't serve Negroes here." She did not say it with the blunt, derisive hostility to which I had grown so accustomed, but, rather, with a note of apology in her voice, and fear. This made me colder and more murderous than ever. I felt I

had to do something with my hands. I wanted her to come close enough for me to get her neck between my hands.

20 So I pretended not to have understood her, hoping to draw her closer. And she did step a very short step closer, with her pencil poised incongruously over her pad, and repeated the formula: ". . . don't serve Negroes here."

21 Somehow, with the repetition of that phrase, which was already ringing in my head like a thousand bells of a nightmare, I realized that she would never come any closer and that I would have to strike from a distance. There was nothing on the table but an ordinary watermug half full of water, and I picked this up and hurled it with all my strength at her. She ducked and it missed her and shattered against the mirror behind the bar. And, with that sound, my frozen blood abruptly thawed, I returned from wherever I had been, I *saw*, for the first time, the restaurant, the people with their mouths open, already, as it seemed to me, rising as one man, and I realized what I had done, and where I was, and I was frightened. I rose and began running for the door. A round, potbellied man grabbed me by the nape of the neck just as I reached the doors and began to beat me about the face. I kicked him and got loose and ran into the streets. My friend whispered, "*Run!*" and I ran.

22 My friend stayed outside the restaurant long enough to misdirect my pursuers and the police, who arrived, he told me, at once. I do not know what I said to him when he came to my room that night. I could not have said much. I felt, in the oddest, most awful way, that I had somehow betrayed him. I lived it over and over and over again, the way one relives an automobile accident after it has happened and one finds oneself alone and safe. I could not get over two facts, both equally difficult for the imagination to grasp, and one was that I could have been murdered. But the other was that I had been ready to commit murder. I saw nothing very clearly but I did see this: that my life, my *real* life, was in danger, and not from anything other people might do but from the hatred I carried in my own heart.

2

23 I had returned home around the second week in June—in great haste because it seemed that my father's death and my mother's

confinement were both but a matter of hours. In the case of my mother, it soon became clear that she had simply made a miscalculation. This had always been her tendency and I don't believe that a single one of us arrived in the world, or has since arrived anywhere else, on time. But none of us dawdled so intolerably about the business of being born as did my baby sister. We sometimes amused ourselves, during those endless, stifling weeks, by picturing the baby sitting within in the safe, warm dark, bitterly regretting the necessity of becoming a part of our chaos and stubbornly putting it off as long as possible. I understood her perfectly and congratulated her on showing such good sense so soon. Death, however, sat as purposefully at my father's bedside as life stirred within my mother's womb and it was harder to understand why he so lingered in that long shadow. It seemed that he had bent, and for a long time, too, all of his energies towards dying. Now death was ready for him but my father held back.

24 All of Harlem, indeed, seemed to be infected by waiting. I had never before known it to be so violently still. Racial tensions throughout this country were exacerbated during the early years of the war, partly because the labor market brought together hundreds of thousands of ill-prepared people and partly because Negro soldiers, regardless of where they were born, received their military training in the south. What happened in defense plants and army camps had repercussions, naturally, in every Negro ghetto. The situation in Harlem had grown bad enough for clergymen, policemen, educators, politicians, and social workers to assert in one breath that there was no "crime wave" and to offer, in the very next breath, suggestions as to how to combat it. These suggestions always seemed to involve playgrounds, despite the fact that racial skirmishes were occurring in the playgrounds, too. Playground or not, crime wave or not, the Harlem police force had been augmented in March, and the unrest grew—perhaps, in fact, partly as a result of the ghetto's hatred of policemen. Perhaps the most revealing news item, out of the steady parade of reports of muggings, stabbings, shootings, assaults, gang wars, and accusations of police brutality, is the item concerning six Negro girls who set upon a white girl in the subway because, as they all too accurately put it, she was stepping on their toes. Indeed she was, all over the nation.

25 I had never before been so aware of policemen, on foot, on horseback, on corners, everywhere, always two by two. Nor had I

ever been so aware of small knots of people. They were on stoops and on corners and in doorways, and what was striking about them, I think, was that they did not seem to be talking. Never, when I passed these groups, did the usual sound of a curse or a laugh ring out and neither did there seem to be any hum of gossip. There was certainly, on the other hand, occurring between them communication extraordinarily intense. Another thing that was striking was the unexpected diversity of the people who made up these groups. Usually, for example, one would see a group of sharpies standing on the street corner, jiving the passing chicks; or a group of older men, usually, for some reason, in the vicinity of a barber shop, discussing baseball scores, or the numbers, or making rather chilling observations about women they had known. Women, in a general way, tended to be seen less often together—unless they were church women, or very young girls, or prostitutes met together for an unprofessional instant. But that summer I saw the strangest combinations: large, respectable, churchly matrons standing on the stoops or the corners with their hair tied up, together with a girl in sleazy satin whose face bore the marks of gin and the razor, or heavyset, abrupt, non-nonsense older men, in company with the most disreputable and fanatical "race" men, or these same "race" men with the sharpies, or these sharpies with the churchly women. Seventh Day Adventists and Methodists and Spiritualists seemed to be hobnobbing with Holyrollers and they were all, alike, entangled with the most flagrant disbelievers; something heavy in their stance seemed to indicate that they had all, incredibly, seen a common vision, and on each face there seemed to be the same strange, bitter shadow.

26 The churchly women and the matter-of-fact, no-nonsense men had children in the Army. The sleazy girls they talked to had lovers there, the sharpies and the "race" men had friends and brothers there. It would have demanded an unquestioning patriotism, happily as uncommon in this country as it is undesirable, for these people not to have been disturbed by the bitter letters they received, by the newspaper stories they read, not to have been enraged by the posters, then to be found all over New York, which described the Japanese as "yellow-bellied Japs." It was only the "race" men, to be sure, who spoke ceaselessly of being revenged—how this vengeance was to be exacted was not clear—for the indignities and dangers suffered by Negro boys in uniform; but everybody felt a directionless, hopeless bitterness, as well as that panic which can scarcely be suppressed

when one knows that a human being one loves is beyond one's reach, and in danger. This helplessness and this gnawing uneasiness does something, at length, to even the toughest mind. Perhaps the best way to sum all this up is to say that the people I knew felt, mainly, a peculiar kind of relief when they knew that their boys were being shipped out of the south, to do battle overseas. It was, perhaps, like feeling the most dangerous part of a dangerous journey had been passed and that now, even if death should come, it would come with honor and without the complicity of their countrymen. Such a death would be, in short, a fact with which one could hope to live.

27 It was on the 28th of July, which I believe was a Wednesday, that I visited my father for the first time during his illness and for the last time in his life. The moment I saw him I knew why I had put off this visit so long. I had told my mother that I did not want to see him because I hated him. But this was not true. It was only that I *had* hated him and I wanted to hold on to this hatred. I did not want to look on him as a ruin: it was not a ruin I had hated. I imagine that one of the reasons people cling to their hates so stubbornly is because they sense, once hate is gone, that they will be forced to deal with pain.

28 We traveled out to him, his older sister and myself, to what seemed to be the very end of a very Long Island. It was hot and dusty and we wrangled, my aunt and I, all the way out, over the fact that I had recently begun to smoke and, as she said, to give myself airs. But I knew that she wrangled with me because she could not bear to face the fact of her brother's dying. Neither could I endure the reality of her despair, her unstated bafflement as to what had happened to her brother's life, and her own. So we wrangled and I smoked and from time to time she fell into a heavy reverie. Covertly, I watched her face, which was the face of an old woman; it had fallen in, the eyes were sunken and lightless; soon she would be dying, too.

29 In my childhood—it had not been so long ago—I had thought her beautiful. She had been quick-witted and quick-moving and very generous with all the children and each of her visits had been an event. At one time one of my brothers and myself had thought of running away to live with her. Now she could no longer produce out of her handbag some unexpected and yet familiar delight. She made me feel pity and revulsion and fear. It was awful to realize that she no longer caused me to feel affection. The closer we came to

the hospital the more querulous she became and at the same time, naturally, grew more dependent on me. Between pity and guilt and fear I began to feel that there was another me trapped in my skull like a jack-in-the-box who might escape my control at any moment and fill the air with screaming.

30 She began to cry the moment we entered the room and she saw him lying there, all shriveled and still, like a little black monkey. The great, gleaming apparatus which fed him and would have compelled him to be still even if he had been able to move brought to mind, not beneficence, but torture; the tubes entering his arm made me think of pictures I had seen when a child, of Gulliver, tied down by the pygmies on that island. My aunt wept and wept, there was a whistling sound in my father's throat; nothing was said; he could not speak. I wanted to take his hand, to say something. But I do not know what I could have said, even if he could have heard me. He was not really in that room with us, he had at last really embarked on his journey; and though my aunt told me that he said he was going to meet Jesus, I did not hear anything except that whistling in his throat. The doctor came back and we left, into that unbearable train again, and home. In the morning came the telegram saying that he was dead. Then the house was suddenly full of relatives, friends, hysteria, and confusion and I quickly left my mother and the children to the care of those impressive women, who, in Negro communities at least, automatically appear at times of bereavement armed with lotions, proverbs, and patience, and an ability to cook. I went downtown. By the time I returned, later the same day, my mother had been carried to the hospital and the baby had been born.

3

31 For my father's funeral I had nothing black to wear and this posed a nagging problem all day long. It was one of those problems, simple, or impossible of solution, to which the mind insanely clings in order to avoid the mind's real trouble. I spent most of that day at the downtown apartment of a girl I knew, celebrating my birthday with whiskey and wondering what to wear that night. When planning a birthday celebration one naturally does not expect that it will be up against competition from a funeral and this girl had anticipated taking

me out that night, for a big dinner and a night club afterwards. Sometime during the course of that long day we decided that we would go out anyway, when my father's funeral service was over. I imagine *I* decided it, since, as the funeral hour approached, it became clearer and clearer to me that I would not know what to do with myself when it was over. The girl, stifling her very lively concern as to the possible effects of the whiskey on one of my father's chief mourners, concentrated on being conciliatory and practically helpful. She found a black shirt for me somewhere and ironed it and, dressed in the darkest pants and jacket I owned, and slightly drunk, I made my way to my father's funeral.

32 The chapel was full, but not packed, and very quiet. There were, mainly, my father's relatives, and his children, and here and there I saw faces I had not seen since childhood, the faces of my father's one-time friends. They were very dark and solemn now, seeming somehow to suggest that they had known all along that something like this would happen. Chief among the mourners was my aunt, who had quarreled with my father all his life; by which I do not mean to suggest that her mourning was insincere or that she had not loved him. I suppose that she was one of the few people in the world who had, and their incessant quarreling proved precisely the strength of the tie that bound them. The only other person in the world, as far as I knew, whose relationship to my father rivaled my aunt's in depth was my mother, who was not there.

33 It seemed to me, of course, that it was a very long funeral. But it was, if anything, a rather shorter funeral than most, nor, since there were no overwhelming, uncontrollable expressions of grief, could it be called—if I dare use the word—successful. The minister who preached my father's funeral sermon was one of the few my father had still been seeing as he neared his end. He presented to us in his sermon a man whom none of us had ever seen—a man thoughtful, patient, and forbearing, a Christian inspiration to all who knew him, and a model for his children. And no doubt the children, in their disturbed and guilty state, were almost ready to believe this; he had been remote enough to be anything and, anyway, the shock of the incontrovertible, that it was really our father lying up there in that casket, prepared the mind for anything. His sister moaned and this grief-stricken moaning was taken as corroboration. The other faces held a dark, non-commital thoughtfulness. This was not the man they had known, but they had scarcely expected to be confronted

with *him*; this was, in a sense deeper than questions of fact, the man they had not known, and the man they had not known may have been the real one. The real man, whoever he had been, had suffered and now he was dead: this was all that was sure and all that mattered now. Every man in the chapel hoped that when his hour came he, too, would be eulogized, which is to say forgiven, and that all of his lapses, greeds, errors, and strayings from the truth would be invested with coherence and looked upon with charity. This was perhaps the last thing human beings could give each other and it was what they demanded, after all, of the Lord. Only the Lord saw the midnight tears, only He was present when one of His children, moaning and wringing hands, paced up and down the room. When one slapped one's child in anger the recoil in the heart reverberated through heaven and became part of the pain of the universe. And when the children were hungry and sullen and distrustful and one watched them, daily, growing wilder, and further away, and running headlong into danger, it was the Lord who knew what the charged heart endured as the strap was laid to the backside; the Lord alone who knew what one *would* have said if one had had, like the Lord, the gift of the living word. It was the Lord who knew of the impossibility every parent in that room faced: how to prepare the child for the day when the child would be despised and how to *create* in the child—by what means?—a stronger antidote to this poison than one had found for oneself. The avenues, side streets, bars, billiard halls, hospitals, police stations, and even the playgrounds of Harlem—not to mention the houses of correction, the jails, and the morgue—testified to the potency of the poison while remaining silent as to the efficacy of whatever antidote, irresistably raising the question of whether or not such an antidote existed; raising, which was worse, the question of whether or not an antidote was desirable; perhaps poison should be fought with poison. With these several schisms in the mind and with more terrors in the heart than could be named, it was better not to judge the man who had gone down under an impossible burden. It was better to remember: *Thou knowest this man's fall; but thou knowest not his wrassling.*

34 While the preacher talked and I watched the children—years of changing their diapers, scrubbing them, slapping them, taking them to school, and scolding them had had the perhaps inevitable result of making me love them, though I am not sure I knew this then—my mind was busily breaking out with a rash of disconnected impressions.

Snatches of popular songs, indecent jokes, bits of books I had read, movie sequences, faces, voices, political issues—I thought I was going mad; all these impressions suspended, as it were, in the solution of the faint nausea produced in me by the heat and liquor. For a moment I had the impression that my alcoholic breath, inefficiently disguised with chewing gum, filled the entire chapel. Then someone began singing one of my father's favorite songs and, abruptly, I was with him, sitting on his knee, in the hot, enormous, crowded church which was the first church we attended. It was the Abyssinia Baptist Church on 138th Street. We had not gone there long. With this image, a host of others came. I had forgotten, in the rage of my growing up, how proud my father had been of me when I was little. Apparently, I had had a voice and my father had liked to show me off before the members of the church. I had forgotten what he had looked like when he was pleased but now I remembered that he had always been grinning with pleasure when my solos ended. I even remembered certain expressions on his face when he teased my mother—had he loved her? I would never know. And when had it all begun to change? For now it seemed that he had not always been cruel. I remembered being taken for a haircut and scraping my knee on the footrest of the barber's chair and I remembered my father's face as he soothed my crying and applied the stinging iodine. Then I remembered our fights, fights which had been of the worst possible kind because my technique had been silence.

35 I remembered the one time in all our life together when we had really spoken to each other.

36 It was on a Sunday and it must have been shortly before I left home. We were walking, just the two of us, in our usual silence, to or from church. I was in high school and had been doing a lot of writing and I was, at about this time, the editor of the high school magazine. But I had also been a Young Minister and had been preaching from the pulpit. Lately, I had been taking fewer engagements and preached as rarely as possible. It was said in the church, quite truthfully, that I was "cooling off."

37 My father asked me abruptly, "You'd rather write than preach, wouldn't you?"

38 I was astonished at his question—because it was a real question. I answered, "Yes."

39 That was all we said. It was awful to remember that that was all we had *ever* said.

40 The casket now was opened and the mourners were being led up the aisle to look for the last time on the deceased. The assumption was that the family was too overcome with grief to be allowed to make this journey alone and I watched while my aunt was led to the casket and, muffled in black, and shaking, led back to her seat. I disapproved of forcing the children to look on their dead father, considering that the shock of his death, or, more truthfully, the shock of death as a reality, was already a little more than a child could bear, but my judgment in this matter had been overruled and there they were, bewildered and frightened and very small, being led, one by one, to the casket. But there is also something very gallant about children at such moments. It has something to do with their silence and gravity and with the fact that one cannot help them. Their legs, somehow, seemed *exposed*, so that it is at once incredible and terribly clear that their legs are all they have to hold them up.

41 I had not wanted to go to the casket myself and I certainly had not wished to be led there, but there was no way of avoiding either of these forms. One of the deacons led me up and I looked on my father's face. I cannot say that it looked like him at all. His blackness had been equivocated by powder and there was no suggestion in that casket of what his power had or could have been. He was simply an old man dead, and it was hard to believe that he had ever given anyone either joy or pain. Yet, his life filled that room. Further up the avenue his wife was holding his newborn child. Life and death so close together, and love and hatred, and right and wrong, said something to me which I did not want to hear concerning man, concerning the life of man.

42 After the funeral, while I was downtown desperately celebrating my birthday, a Negro soldier, in the lobby of the Hotel Braddock, got into a fight with a white policeman over a Negro girl. Negro girls, white policemen, in or out of uniform, and Negro males—in or out of uniform—were part of the furniture of the lobby of the Hotel Braddock and this was certainly not the first time such an incident had occurred. It was destined, however, to receive unprecedented publicity, for the fight between the policeman and the soldier ended with the shooting of the soldier. Rumor, flowing immediately to the streets outside, stated that the soldier had been shot in the back, an instantaneous and revealing invention, and that the soldier had died protecting a Negro woman. The facts were somewhat different—for example, the soldier had not been shot in the back, and

was not dead, and the girl seems to have been as dubious a symbol of womanhood as her white counterpart in Georgia usually is, but no one was interested in the facts. They preferred the invention because this invention expressed and corroborated their hates and fears so perfectly. It is just as well to remember that people are always doing this. Perhaps many of those legends, including Christianity, to which the world clings began their conquest of the world with just some such concerted surrender to distortion. The effect, in Harlem, of this particular legend was like the effect of a lit match in a tin of gasoline. The mob gathered before the doors of the Hotel Braddock simply began to swell and to spread in every direction, and Harlem exploded.

43 The mob did not cross the ghetto lines. It would have been easy, for example, to have gone over Morningside Park on the west side or to have crossed the Grand Central railroad tracks at 125th Street on the east side, to wreak havoc in white neighborhoods. The mob seems to have been mainly interested in something more potent and real than the white face, that is, in white power, and the principal damage done during the riot of the summer of 1943 was to white business establishments in Harlem. It might have been a far bloodier story, of course, if, at the hour the riot began, these establishments had still been open. From the Hotel Braddock the mob fanned out, east and west along 125th Street, and for the entire length of Lenox, Seventh, and Eighth avenues. Along each of these avenues, and along each major side street—116th, 125th, 135th, and so on—bars, stores, pawnshops, restaurants, even little luncheonettes had been smashed open and entered and looted—looted, it might be added, with more haste than efficiency. The shelves really looked as though a bomb had struck them. Cans of beans and soup and dog food, along with toilet paper, corn flakes, sardines, and milk tumbled every which way, and abandoned cash registers and cases of beer leaned crazily out of the splintered windows and were strewn along the avenues. Sheets, blankets, and clothing of every description formed a kind of path, as though people had dropped them while running. I truly had not realized that Harlem *had* so many stores until I saw them all smashed open; the first time the word *wealth* ever entered my mind in relation to Harlem was when I saw it scattered in the streets. But one's first, incongruous impression of plenty was countered immediately by an impression of waste. None of this was doing anybody any good. It would have been better to have left the plate glass as it had been and the goods lying in the stores.

44 It would have been better, but it would also have been intolerable, for Harlem had needed something to smash. To smash something is the ghetto's chronic need. Most of the time it is the members of the ghetto who smash each other, and themselves. But as long as the ghetto walls are standing there will always come a moment when these outlets do not work. That summer, for example, it was not enough to get into a fight on Lenox Avenue, or curse out one's cronies in the barber shops. If ever, indeed, the violence which fills Harlem's churches, pool halls, and bars erupts outward in a more direct fashion, Harlem and its citizens are likely to vanish in an apocalyptic flood. That this is not likely to happen is due to a great many reasons, most hidden and powerful among them the Negro's real relation to the white American. This relation prohibits, simply, anything as uncomplicated and satisfactory as pure hatred. In order really to hate white people, one has to blot so much out of the mind—and the heart—that this hatred itself becomes an exhausting the self-destructive pose. But this does not mean, on the other hand, that love comes easily: the white world is too powerful, too complacent, too ready with gratuitous humiliation, and, above all, too ignorant and too innocent for that. One is absolutely forced to make perpetual qualifications and one's own reactions are always canceling each other out. It is this, really, which has driven so many people mad, both white and black. One is always in the position of having to decide between amputation and gangrene. Amputation is swift but time may prove that the amputation was not necessary—or one may delay the amputation too long. Gangrene is slow, but it is impossible to be sure that one is reading one's symptoms right. The idea of going through life as a cripple is more than one can bear, and equally unbearable is the risk of swelling up slowly, in agony, with poison. And the trouble, finally, is that the risks are real even if the choices do not exist.

45 "But as for me and my house," my father had said, "we will serve the Lord." I wondered, as we drove him to his resting place, what this line had meant for him. I had heard him preach it many times. I had preached it once myself, proudly giving it an interpretation different from my father's. Now the whole thing came back to me, as though my father and I were on our way to Sunday school and I were memorizing the golden text: *And if it seem evil unto you to serve the Lord, choose you this day whom you will serve; whether the gods which your fathers served that were on the other side of the flood,*

or the gods of the Amorites, in which land ye dwell: but as for me and my house, we will serve the Lord. I suspected in these familiar lines a meaning which had never been there for me before. All of my father's texts and songs, which I had decided were meaningless, were arranged before me at his death like empty bottles, waiting to hold the meaning which life would give them for me. This was his legacy: nothing is ever escaped. That bleakly memorable morning I hated the unbelievable streets and the Negroes and whites who had, equally, made them that way. But I knew that it was folly, as my father would have said, this bitterness was folly. It was necessary to hold on to the things that mattered. The dead man mattered, the new life mattered; blackness and whiteness did not matter; to believe that they did was to acquiesce in one's own destruction. Hatred, which could destroy so much, never failed to destroy the man who hated and this was an immutable law.

46 It began to seem that one would have to hold in the mind forever two ideas which seemed to be in opposition. The first idea was acceptance, the acceptance, totally without rancor, of life as it is, and men as they are: in the light of this idea, it goes without saying that injustice is a commonplace. But this did not mean that one could be complacent, for the second idea was of equal power: that one must never, in one's own life, accept these injustices as commonplace but must fight them with all one's strength. This fight begins, however, in the heart and it now had been laid to my charge to keep my own heart free of hatred and despair. This intimation made my heart heavy and, now that my father was irrecoverable, I wished that he had been beside me so that I could have searched his face for the answers which only the future would give me now.

Marrying Absurd

JOAN DIDION

Joan Didion (b. 1934) was born in Sacramento, California. Didion says that she found comfort in books during her childhood, for she moved with her family constantly from one Army base to another during World War II. She gained some of her writing skills by copying passages from Joseph Conrad and Ernest Hemingway. At the University of California at Berkeley, she first published in the campus magazine *Occident*. Later, in New York, she wrote for *Vogue*. She returned to California in 1964 to write a series of columns on social issues for *The Saturday Evening Post*. She gained critical acclaim when these essays were published in 1968 under the title *Slouching towards Bethlehem*, which makes an allusion to "The Second Coming" by William Butler Yeats, a poem that predicts the future as a frightening, amoral beast slouching toward Bethlehem to be born.

A novelist, essayist, and screenwriter, Didion has lived and worked primarily in California, which provides the setting for her satiric and ironic commentary on the American scene. She collaborated on the movies *A Star Is Born* (1976) and *True Confessions* (1981). Her novels include *Play It as It Lays* (1971) and *A Book of Common Prayer* (1976).

"Marrying Absurd" combines Didion's penetrating social observations with the precision of her ironic style. John Leonard of the *New York Times* has written, "Nobody writes better English prose than Joan Didion. Try to rearrange one of her sentences, and you've realized that the sentence was inevitable, a hologram." This essay shows Didion's search for something better than the false aura of an artificial city.

1 To be married in Las Vegas, Clark County, Nevada, a bride must swear that she is eighteen or has parental permission and a bridegroom that he is twenty-one or has parental permission. Someone must put up five dollars for the license. (On Sundays and holidays, fifteen dollars. The Clark County Courthouse issues marriage licenses at any time of the day or night except between noon and one in the afternoon, between eight and nine in the evening, and between four and five in the morning.) Nothing else is required. The State of Nevada, alone among these United States, demands neither a premarital blood test nor a waiting period before or after the issuance of a marriage license. Driving in across the Mojave from Los Angeles, one sees the signs way out on the desert, looming up from that moonscape of rattlesnakes and mesquite, even before the Las Vegas lights appear like a mirage on the horizon: "GETTING MARRIED? Free License Information First Strip Exit." Perhaps the Las Vegas wedding industry achieved its peak operational efficiency between 9:00 p.m. and midnight of August 26, 1965, an otherwise unremarkable Thursday which happened to be, by Presidential order, the last day on which anyone could improve his draft status merely by getting married. One hundred and seventy-one couples were pronounced man and wife in the name of Clark County and the State of Nevada that night, sixty-seven of them by a single justice of the peace, Mr. James A. Brennan. Mr. Brennan did one wedding at the Dunes and the other sixty-six in his office, and charged each couple eight dollars. One bride lent her veil to six others. "I got it down from five to three minutes," Mr. Brennan said later of his feat. "I could've married them *en masse*, but they're people, not cattle. People expect more when they get married."

2 What people who get married in Las Vegas actually do expect—what, in the largest sense, their "expectations" are—strikes one as a curious and self-contradictory business. Las Vegas is the most extreme and allegorical of American settlements, bizarre and beautiful in its venality and in its devotion to immediate gratification,

a place the tone of which is set by mobsters and call girls and ladies' room attendants with amyl nitrite poppers in their uniform pockets. Almost everyone notes that there is no "time" in Las Vegas, no night and no day and no past and no future (no Las Vegas casino, however, has taken the obliteration of the ordinary time sense quite so far as Harold's Club in Reno, which for a while issued, at odd intervals in the day and night, mimeographed "bulletins" carrying news from the world outside); neither is there any logical sense of where one is. One is standing on a highway in the middle of a vast hostile desert looking at an eighty-foot sign which blinks "STARDUST" or "CAESAR'S PALACE." Yes, but what does that explain? This geographical implausibility reinforces the sense that what happens there has no connection with "real" life; Nevada cities like Reno and Carson are ranch towns, Western towns, places behind which there is some historical imperative. But Las Vegas seems to exist only in the eye of the beholder. All of which makes it an extraordinarily stimulating and interesting place, but an odd one in which to want to wear a candlelight satin Priscilla of Boston wedding dress with Chantilly lace insets, tapered sleeves and a detachable modified train.

3 And yet the Las Vegas wedding business seems to appeal to precisely that impulse. "Sincere and Dignified Since 1954," one wedding chapel advertises. There are nineteen such wedding chapels in Las Vegas, intensely competitive, each offering better, faster, and, by implication, more sincere services than the next: Our Photos Best Anywhere, Your Wedding on A Phonograph Record, Candlelight with Your Ceremony, Honeymoon Accommodations, Free Transportation from Your Motel to Courthouse to Chapel and Return to Motel, Religious or Civil Ceremonies, Dressing Rooms, Flowers, Rings, Announcements, Witnesses Available, and Ample Parking. All of these services, like most others in Las Vegas (sauna baths, payroll-check cashing, chinchilla coats for sale or rent) are offered twenty-four hours a day, seven days a week, presumably on the premise that marriage, like craps, is a game to be played when the table seems hot.

4 But what strikes one most about the Strip chapels, with their wishing wells and stained-glass paper windows and their artificial bouvardia, is that so much of their business is by no means a matter of simple convenience, of late-night liaisons between show girls and baby Crosbys. Of course there is some of that. (One night about

eleven o'clock in Las Vegas I watched a bride in an orange minidress and masses of flame-colored hair stumble from a Strip chapel on the arm of her bridegroom, who looked the part of the expendable nephew in movies like *Miami Syndicate.* "I gotta get the kids," the bride whimpered. "I gotta pick up the sitter, I gotta get to the midnight show." "What you gotta get," the bridegroom said, opening the door of a Cadillac Coupe de Ville and watching her crumple on the seat, "is sober.") But Las Vegas seems to offer something other than "convenience"; it is merchandising "niceness," the facsimile of proper ritual, to children who do not know how else to find it, how to make the arrangements, how to do it "right." All day and evening long on the Strip, one sees actual wedding parties, waiting under the harsh lights at a crosswalk, standing uneasily in the parking lot of the Frontier while the photographer hired by The Little Church of the West ("Wedding Place of the Stars") certifies the occasion, takes the picture: the bride in a veil and white satin pumps, the bridegroom usually in a white dinner jacket, and even an attendant or two, a sister or a best friend in hot-pink *peau de soie,* a flirtation veil, a carnation nosegay. "When I Fall in Love It Will Be Forever," the organist plays, and then a few bars of Lohengrin. The mother cries; the stepfather, awkward in his role, invites the chapel hostess to join them for a drink at the Sands. The hostess declines with a professional smile; she has already transferred her interest to the group waiting outside. One bride out, another in, and again the sign goes up on the chapel door: "One moment please—Wedding."

5 I sat next to one such wedding party in a Strip restaurant the last time I was in Las Vegas. The marriage had just taken place; the bride still wore her dress, the mother her corsage. A bored waiter poured out a few swallows of pink champagne ("on the house") for everyone but the bride, who was too young to be served. "You'll need something with more kick than that," the bride's father said with heavy jocularity to his new son-in-law; the ritual jokes about the wedding night had a certain Panglossian character, since the bride was clearly several months pregnant. Another round of pink champagne, this time not on the house, and the bride began to cry. "It was just as nice," she sobbed, "as I hoped and dreamed it would be."

The Nuclear Winter

CARL SAGAN

Carl Sagan (b. 1934) was born in New York City and educated at the University of Chicago. Since then, he has maintained two careers, one as an eminent astronomer and another as a successful writer. He launched his writing career in 1963 by contributing several chapters to *Intelligent Life in the Universe,* a book so popular that it has been reprinted fourteen times. In 1977, Sagan published *Dragons of Eden,* a study of human intelligence. In 1980, his television program, *Cosmos,* brought him immediate, worldwide fame.

In the 1970s, Sagan and several colleagues at NASA's Ames Research Center applied theories about a global dust storm to Earth's atmosphere, basing the research on the Mariner 9 landing on Mars in late 1971. Their scientific article, "Global Atmospheric Consequences of Nuclear War," applied the theories to nuclear war. Using that article as a springboard, Sagan wrote "The Nuclear Winter" and published it in *Parade Magazine* on October 30, 1983. His Halloween message into the living rooms of Sunday morning newspaper readers sent a chill over the nation. He had reached a massive audience rather than a narrow group of scientists.

Sagan's essay combines scientific analysis with persuasive discourse to show how a nuclear war might affect the earth and its population. Although he does not openly make a plea, Sagan issues an implicit call to action: he urges readers to support nuclear control that would set stringent limits on stockpiled weapons.

Into the eternal darkness, into fire, into ice.
—Dante, *The Inferno*

1 Except for fools and madmen, everyone knows that nuclear war would be an unprecedented human catastrophe. A more or less typical strategic warhead has a yield of 2 megatons, the explosive equivalent of 2 million tons of TNT. But 2 million tons of TNT is about the same as all the bombs exploded in World War II—a single bomb with the explosive power of the entire Second World War but compressed into a few seconds of time and an area 30 or 40 miles across. . . .

2 In a 2-megaton explosion over a fairly large city, buildings would be vaporized, people reduced to atoms and shadows, outlying structures blown down like matchsticks and raging fires ignited. And if the bomb were exploded on the ground, an enormous crater, like those that can be seen through a telescope on the surface of the Moon, would be all that remained where midtown once had been. There are now more than 50,000 nuclear weapons, more than 13,000 megatons of yield, deployed in the arsenals of the United States and the Soviet Union—enough to obliterate a million Hiroshimas.

3 But there are fewer than 3000 cities on the Earth with populations of 100,000 or more. You cannot find anything like a million Hiroshimas to obliterate. Prime military and industrial targets that are far from cities are comparatively rare. Thus, there are vastly more nuclear weapons than are needed for any plausible deterrence of a potential adversary.

4 Nobody knows, of course, how many megatons would be exploded in a real nuclear war. There are some who think that a nuclear war can be "contained," bottled up before it runs away to involve much of the world's arsenals. But a number of detailed analyses, war games run by the U.S. Department of Defense, and official Soviet pronouncements all indicate that this containment may be too much to hope for: Once the bombs begin exploding, communications failures, disorganization, fear, the necessity of mak-

ing in minutes decisions affecting the fates of millions, and the immense psychological burden of knowing that your own loved ones may already have been destroyed are likely to result in a nuclear paroxysm. Many investigations, including a number of studies for the U.S. government, envision the explosion of 5000 to 10,000 megatons—the detonation of tens of thousands of nuclear weapons that now sit quietly, inconspicuously, in missile silos, submarines and long-range bombers, faithful servants awaiting orders.

5 The World Health Organization, in a recent detailed study chaired by Sune K. Bergstrom (the 1982 Nobel laureate in physiology and medicine), concludes that 1.1 billion people would be killed outright in such a nuclear war, mainly in the United States, the Soviet Union, Europe, China and Japan. An additional 1.1 billion people would suffer serious injuries and radiation sickness, for which medical help would be unavailable. It thus seems possible that more than 2 billion people—almost half of all the humans on Earth—would be destroyed in the immediate aftermath of a global thermonuclear war. This would represent by far the greatest disaster in the history of the human species and, with no other adverse effects, would probably be enough to reduce at least the Northern Hemisphere to a state of prolonged agony and barbarism. Unfortunately, the real situation would be much worse.

6 In technical studies of the consequences of nuclear weapons explosions, there has been a dangerous tendency to underestimate the results. This is partly due to a tradition of conservatism which generally works well in science but which is of more dubious applicability when the lives of billions of people are at stake. In the Bravo test of March 1, 1954, a 15-megaton thermonuclear bomb was exploded on Bikini Atoll. It had about double the yield expected, and there was an unanticipated last-minute shift in the wind direction. As a result, deadly radioactive fallout came down on Rongelap in the Marshall Islands, more than 200 kilometers away. Almost all the children on Rongelap subsequently developed thyroid nodules and lesions, and other long-term medical problems, due to the radioactive fallout.

7 Likewise, in 1973, it was discovered that high-yield airbursts will chemically burn the nitrogen in the upper air, converting it into oxides of nitrogen; these, in turn, combine with and destroy the protective ozone in the Earth's atmosphere. The surface of the Earth is shielded from deadly solar ultraviolet radiation by a layer of ozone

so tenuous that, were it brought down to sea level, it would be only 3 millimeters thick. Partial destruction of this ozone layer can have serious consequences for the biology of the entire planet.

8 These discoveries, and others like them, were made by chance. They were largely unexpected. And now another consequence—by far the most dire—has been uncovered, again more or less by accident.

9 The U.S. Mariner 9 spacecraft, the first vehicle to orbit another planet, arrived at Mars in late 1971. The planet was enveloped in a global dust storm. As the fine particles slowly fell out, we were able to measure temperature changes in the atmosphere and on the surface. Soon it became clear what had happened:

10 The dust, lofted by high winds off the desert into the upper Martian atmosphere, had absorbed the incoming sunlight and prevented much of it from reaching the ground. Heated by the sunlight, the dust warmed the adjacent air. But the surface, enveloped in partial darkness, became much chillier than usual. Months later, after the dust fell out of the atmosphere, the upper air cooled and the surface warmed, both returning to their normal conditions. We were able to calculate accurately, from how much dust there was in the atmosphere, how cool the Martian surface ought to have been.

11 Afterwards, I and my colleagues, James B. Pollack and Brian Toon of NASA's Ames Research Center, were eager to apply these insights to Earth. In a volcanic explosion, dust aerosols are lofted into the high atmosphere. We calculated by how much the Earth's global temperature should decline after a major volcanic explosion and found that our results (generally a fraction of a degree) were in good accord with actual measurements. Joining forces with Richard Turco, who has studied the effects of nuclear weapons for many years, we then began to turn our attention to the climatic implications of nuclear war. [The scientific paper, "Global Atmospheric Consequences of Nuclear War," is written by R. P. Turco, O. B. Toon, T. P. Ackerman, J. B. Pollack and Carl Sagan. From the last names of the authors, this work is generally referred to as "TTAPS."]

12 We knew that nuclear explosions, particularly ground-bursts, would lift an enormous quantity of fine soil particles into the atmosphere (more than 100,000 tons of fine dust for every megaton exploded in a surface burst). Our work was further spurred by Paul Crutzen of the Max Planck Institute for Chemistry in Mainz, West Germany, and by John Birks of the University of Colorado, who

pointed out that huge quantities of smoke would be generated in the burning of cities and forests following a nuclear war.

13 Groundbursts—at hardened missile silos, for example—generate fine dust. Airbursts—over cities and unhardened military installations—make fires and therefore smoke. The amount of dust and soot generated depends on the conduct of the war, the yields of the weapons employed and the ratio of groundbursts to airbursts. So we ran computer models for several dozen different nuclear war scenarios. Our baseline case, as in many other studies, was a 5000-megaton war with only a modest fraction of the yield (20 percent) expended on urban or industrial targets. Our job, for each case, was to follow the dust and smoke generated, see how much sunlight was absorbed and by how much the temperatures changed, figure out how the particles spread in longitude and latitude, and calculate how long before it all fell out of the air back onto the surface. Since the radioactivity would be attached to these same fine particles, our calculations also revealed the extent and timing of the subsequent radioactive fallout.

14 Some of what I am about to describe is horrifying. I know, because it horrifies me. There is a tendency—psychiatrists call it "denial"—to put it out of our minds, not to think about it. But if we are to deal intelligently, wisely, with the nuclear arms race, then we must steel ourselves to contemplate the horrors of nuclear war.

15 The results of our calculations astonished us. In the baseline case, the amount of sunlight at the ground was reduced to a few percent of normal—much darker, in daylight, than in a heavy overcast and too dark for plants to make a living from photosynthesis. At least in the Northern Hemisphere, where the great preponderance of strategic targets lies, a deadly gloom would persist for months.

16 Even more unexpected were the temperatures calculated. In the baseline case, land temperatures, except for narrow strips of coastline, dropped to minus 25° Celsius (minus 13° Fahrenheit) and stayed below freezing for months—even for a summer war. (Because the atmospheric structure becomes much more stable as the upper atmosphere is heated and the lower air is cooled, we may have severely *under*estimated how long the cold and the dark would last.) The oceans, a significant heat reservoir, would not freeze, however, and a major ice age would probably not be triggered. But because the temperatures would drop so catastrophically, virtually all crops and farm animals, at least in the Northern Hemisphere, would be

destroyed, as would most varieties of uncultivated or undomesticated food supplies. Most of the human survivors would starve.

17 In addition, the amount of radioactive fallout is much more than expected. Many previous calculations simply ignored the intermediate timescale fallout. That is, calculations were made for the prompt fallout—the plumes of radioactive debris blown downwind from each target—and for the long-term fallout, the fine radioactive particles lofted into the stratosphere that would descend about a year later, after most of the radioactivity had decayed. However, the radioactivity carried into the upper atmosphere (but not as high as the stratosphere) seems to have been largely forgotten. We found for the baseline case that roughly 30 percent of the land at northern midlatitudes could receive a radioactive dose greater than 250 rads, and that about 50 percent of northern midlatitudes could receive a dose greater than 100 rads. A 100-rad dose is the equivalent of about 1000 medical X-rays. A 400-rad dose will, more likely than not, kill you.

18 The cold, the dark and the intense radioactivity, together lasting for months, represent a severe assault on our civilization and our species. Civil and sanitary services would be wiped out. Medical facilities, drugs, the most rudimentary means for relieving the vast human suffering, would be unavailable. Any but the most elaborate shelters would be useless, quite apart from the question of what good it might be to emerge a few months later. Synthetics burned in the destruction of the cities would produce a wide variety of toxic gases, including carbon monoxide, cyanides, dioxins and furans. After the dust and soot settled out, the solar ultraviolet flux would be much larger than its present value. Immunity to disease would decline. Epidemics and pandemics would be rampant, especially after the billion or so unburied bodies began to thaw. Moreover, the combined influence of these severe and simultaneous stresses on life are likely to produce even more adverse consequences—biologists call them synergisms—that we are not yet wise enough to foresee.

19 So far, we have talked only of the Northern Hemisphere. But it now seems—unlike the case of a single nuclear weapons test—that in a real nuclear war, the heating of the vast quantities of atmospheric dust and soot in northern midlatitudes will transport these fine particles toward and across the Equator. We see just this happening in Martian dust storms. The Southern Hemisphere would experience effects that, while less severe than in the Northern Hemisphere, are nevertheless extremely ominous. The illusion with which some people

in the Northern Hemisphere reassure themselves—catching an Air New Zealand flight in a time of serious international crisis, or the like—is now much less tenable, even on the narrow issue of personal survival for those with the price of a ticket.

20 But what if nuclear wars *can* be contained, and much less than 5,000 megatons is detonated? Perhaps the greatest surprise in our work was that even small nuclear wars can have devastating climatic effects. We considered a war in which a mere 100 megatons were exploded, less than one percent of the world arsenals, and only in low-yield airbursts over cities. This scenario, we found, would ignite thousands of fires, and the smoke from these fires alone would be enough to generate an epoch of cold and dark almost as severe as in the 5000-megaton case. The threshold for what Richard Turco has called The Nuclear Winter is very low.

21 Could we have overlooked some important effect? The carrying of dust and soot from the Northern to the Southern Hemisphere (as well as more local atmospheric circulation) will certainly thin the clouds out over the Northern Hemisphere. But, in many cases, this thinning would be insufficient to render the climatic consequences tolerable—and every time it got better in the Northern Hemisphere, it would get worse in the Southern.

22 Our results have been carefully scrutinized by more than 100 scientists in the United States, Europe and the Soviet Union. There are still arguments on points of detail. But the overall conclusion seems to be agreed upon: There are severe and previously unanticipated global consequences of nuclear war—subfreezing temperatures in a twilit radioactive gloom lasting for months or longer.

23 Scientists initially underestimated the effects of fallout, were amazed that nuclear explosions in space disabled distant satellites, had no idea that the fireballs from high-yield thermonuclear explosions could deplete the ozone layer and missed altogether the possible climatic effects of nuclear dust and smoke. What else have we overlooked?

24 Nuclear war is a problem that can be treated only theoretically. It is not amenable to experimentation. Conceivably, we have left something important out of our analysis, and the effects are more modest than we calculate. On the other hand, it is also possible—and, from previous experience, even likely—that there are further adverse effects that no one has yet been wise enough to recognize. With billions of lives at stake, where does conservatism lie—in assuming that the results will be better than we calculate, or worse?

25 Many biologists, considering the nuclear winter that these calculations describe, believe they carry somber implications for life on Earth. Many species of plants and animals would become extinct. Vast numbers of surviving humans would starve to death. The delicate ecological relations that bind together organisms on Earth in a fabric of mutual dependency would be torn, perhaps irreparably. There is little question that our global civilization would be destroyed. The human population would be reduced to prehistoric levels, or less. Life for any survivors would be extremely hard. And there seems to be a real possibility of the extinction of the human species.

26 It is now almost 40 years since the invention of nuclear weapons. We have not yet experienced a global thermonuclear war—although on more than one occasion we have come tremulously close. I do not think our luck can hold forever. Men and machines are fallible, as recent events remind us. Fools and madmen do exist, and sometimes rise to power. Concentrating always on the near future, we have ignored the long-term consequences of our actions. We have placed our civilization and our species in jeopardy.

27 Fortunately, it is not yet too late. We can safeguard the planetary civilization and the human family if we so choose. There is no more important or more urgent issue.

Acknowledgments

Aristotle, "The Aim of Man." Reprinted with the permission of Simon & Schuster from the Macmillan College text NICOMACHEAN ETHICS by Aristotle, translated by Martin Ostwald. Copyright © 1962, 1986 by Macmillan Publishing Company, Inc.

Baldwin, James, "Notes of a Native Son" from NOTES OF A NATIVE SON by James Baldwin. Copyright © 1955, renewed 1983 by James Baldwin. Reprinted by permission of Beacon Press.

Camus, Albert, "The Myth of Sisyphus." From THE MYTH OF SISYPHUS AND OTHER ESSAYS, by Albert Camus, trans., Justin O'Brien. Copyright © 1955 by Alfred A. Knopf Inc. Reprinted by permission of the publisher.

Catton, Bruce, "Grant and Lee: A Study in Contrasts" from THE AMERICAN STORY, edited by Earl Schenck Miers. Copyright U.S. Capitol Historical Society, all rights reserved. Reprinted by permission.

Didion, Joan, "Marrying Absurd" from SLOUCHING TOWARDS BETHLEHEM by Joan Didion. Copyright © 1961, 1967, 1968 by Joan Didion. Reprinted by permission of Farrar, Straus & Giroux, Inc.

Eiseley, Loren, "The Real Secret of Piltdown" from THE IMMENSE JOURNEY by Loren Eiseley. Copyright © 1955 by Loren Eiseley. Reprinted by permission of Random House, Inc.

Forster, E. M., "What I Believe" from WHAT I BELIEVE by E. M. Forster. Reprinted by permission of King's College, Cambridge and The Society of Authors as the literary representatives of the E. M. Forster Estate.

Machiavelli, Niccolo. From PORTABLE MACHIAVELLI by Peter Bondanella and Mark Musa. Copyright © 1979 by Viking Penguin, Inc. Used by permission of Viking Penguin, a division of Penguin Books USA Inc.

Montaigne, Michel de, "Of Drunkenness." Reprinted from THE COMPLETE ESSAYS OF MONTAIGNE, translated by Donald M. Frame with the permission of the publishers, Stanford University Press. © 1958 by the Board of Trustees of the Leland Stanford Junior University.

Nietzsche, Friedrich, "Apollonianism and Dionysianism," from THE BIRTH OF TRAGEDY AND THE GENEALOGY OF MORALS by Friedrich Nietzsche. Copyright © 1956 by Doubleday, a division of Bantam, Doubleday, Dell Publishing Group, Inc. Used by permission of Doubleday, a division of Bantam Doubleday Dell Publishing Group, Inc.

Petrunkevitch, Alexander, "The Spider and the Wasp" in SCIENTIFIC AMERICAN, August 1952. Copyright 1952 by Scientific American, Inc. All rights reserved. Reprinted with permission.

Sagan, Carl, "The Nuclear Winter." Copyright © 1983 by Carl Sagan. Originally published in PARADE. Reprinted by permission of the author.

Thurber, James, "Courtship Through the Ages." Copr. © 1942 James Thurber. Copr. © 1970 Helen Thurber and Rosemary A. Thurber. From MY WORLD—AND WELCOME TO IT published by Harcourt Brace & Co.

White, E. B., "Once More To the Lake" from ONE MAN'S MEAT by E. B. White. Copyright 1941 by E. B. White. Reprinted by permission of HarperCollins Publishers, Inc.

Woolf, Virginia, "The Death of the Moth" from THE DEATH OF THE MOTH AND OTHER ESSAYS by Virginia Woolf, copyright 1942 by Harcourt Brace & Company and renewed 1970 by Marjorie T. Parsons, Executrix, reprinted by permission of the publisher.

Yeats, W. B., "The Symbolism of Poetry." Reprinted with permission of Simon & Schuster from ESSAYS AND INTRODUCTIONS by W. B. Yeats. © Mrs. W. B. Yeats 1961.

Index of Authors and Titles

Instructor's Manual

Plato's Heirs

Classic Essays

James D. Lester
Austin Peay State University

NTC Publishing Group
NTC Lincolnwood, Illinois USA

Contents

Preface

NTC's Library of Classic Essays was developed to provide students with in-depth yet inexpensive collections of classic essays. While the scope of each book is necessarily limited (by design and by practicalities), we hope that, individually and as a whole, this series illuminates this diverse genre for your students.

This Instructor's Manual is intended to help you introduce the essays in the student text to your students. For each essay, there is a brief paragraph outlining possible approaches to classroom discussion, along with suggested discussion questions and writing assignments. While these materials are no replacement for your insight into the essays, we hope that they might help you to arouse your students' interest in and responsiveness to these classic essays.

CLASSIC ESSAYS: THE ORIGINS OF THE FORM

The Allegory of the Cave

PLATO

You might begin by explaining Plato's use of the dialogue form as the method for his discourse. He used this form primarily because he could explore opposing ideas through the voices of two people. If necessary, explain the term *allegory* and discuss its role in Plato's essay (see paragraph 35). Plato argues that the enlightened person, having attained a vision of the good, must descend to the cave and help others. Motivate the students by asking them to compare Plato's ideas with the current argument for term limits on political service.

Discussion Questions

1. Who are the people lost within the cave?
2. Who are the people who find their way out into the bright sunlight?
3. What is the role of the true statesman?
4. Why does Plato say that the best statesman will be one who is reluctant to rule?
5. Would Plato embrace the concept of term limits for political service? Why or why not?

Writing Assignments

1. Incorporate Plato's style in an essay arguing the virtues of term limits.
2. Write an essay defining the word *statesman*. How does a statesman differ from a career politician?
3. Write an essay in dialogue form arguing the opposing sides of an issue.

The Aim of Man

ARISTOTLE

If you have already read the Plato essay, you might start by discussing Plato's influence on Aristotle, who was his most famous student. Both men comment on the discovery of the *good* and the manner in which it affects the enlightened person. You might also discuss what is meant by the *good*—"that at which all things aim"—whether this be an activity or a product. Students should examine the role of statecraft, as Aristotle argues that "the aim of statecraft is man's proper good because it enfolds all others." Your discussion might also examine Aristotle's careful structure, his use of definition, his defense of each assertion, and his genial, conversational tone. Ask the students to examine paragraph 10, in which Aristotle lists three types of human life—the vulgarians, the political, and the contemplative. Ask your students to examine "happiness" as the ultimate aim of one's life (paragraph 14). Discuss with the students the sources of happiness.

Discussion Questions

1. What are Aristotle's three types of life? (See paragraph 10.)
2. How does Aristotle view a life of money-making? (See paragraph 11.)

3. What is the role of happiness in Aristotle's scheme?
4. What are the sources of happiness?
5. Why does he say a child cannot be happy? (See paragraph 25.)
6. How does he define a happy person? (See paragraph 31.)
7. Do contemporary politicians practice statecraft with an eye on the *good?*

Writing Assignments

1. In an essay, elaborate on your definition of happiness in terms of today's society.
2. Write an essay defending Aristotle's emphasis on *virtue* as a key ingredient of happiness.
3. Write an essay exploring the role of *statecraft* in modern politics.

The Qualities of the Prince

NICCOLÒ MACHIAVELLI

This essay, like the ones by Plato and Aristotle, offers you and your students an opportunity to examine the role of government in the lives of the people. Discuss Machiavelli's admonition for a strong military, as well as his opinion that the United States, because of its armed forces, has won the begrudging respect of the world. Discuss paragraph 10 with the students and ask them if the U.S. government's generosity has damaged its credibility and the safety of its people. Ask the students to discuss the idea of *authority*, relating it perhaps to the quelling of an uprising—the American Civil War, Russia's attack on Chechnya, and others. Ask the students if, according to Machiavelli, *misstatements* by those who govern can or should be forgiven.

Discussion Questions

1. Why should a prince (government) maintain a strong army?
2. Why should a prince (government) be miserly?
3. How much authority should a governor exercise in quelling revolutionary actions?
4. From a governor's standpoint, is it better to be feared or loved?
5. How do Machiavelli's principles apply to today's society? Could our government leaders learn something from Machiavelli? If so, would it be harmful or beneficial to the nation?

Writing Assignments

1. Write an essay examining the economic stability that might occur if the federal government balanced the budget and reduced or significantly lowered the deficit.
2. Write an essay exploring the lives of politicians who did not heed Machiavelli's advice about meddling with the property or with the women of their citizens.
3. Write an essay examining *authority* in government. Do our governors, police, and others in positions of power have sufficient authority? Do the courts use their authority to act fairly?

Of Drunkenness

MICHEL DE MONTAIGNE

This essay gives you the opportunity to examine the informal, conversational style of the personal essay, which Montaigne originated in the sixteenth century. In particular, look at Montaigne's personal, expressive voice, his jovial and conversational tone, his ability to inform without lecturing, and his display of a vast reading knowledge. The personal essay is known for these features: self-revelation, a confidential approach, humor, graceful style, a somewhat rambling structure (compare Montaigne's structure with the formal one of Aristotle), a tentative and incomplete treatment of the subject, and unusual themes and topics taken from everyday life. Engage the students in a discussion of "binge drinking" as it occurs among college students and others. Ask them what Montaigne thinks about the consumption of alcohol, and how he might respond to "binge drinking."

Discussion Questions

1. What elements of the personal essay does Montaigne incorporate into his writing?
2. Is it necessary to be a statesman (as Montaigne was) before others will listen with respect to an essay's content?
3. Does Montaigne advise total abstinence from alcohol?
4. What does he say is the worst aspect of drunkenness? (See paragraph 4.)

Writing Assignments

1. Write an essay exploring the nature of binge drinking and how it differs from or is similar to others types of overindulgence.
2. Write an essay defending, as Montaigne does, drinking in moderation. Does medical science support Montaigne's views?
3. Write an essay exploring the various ways in which people lose control of their senses and, as a result, possibly of their virtues.

The Four Idols

FRANCIS BACON

In the seventeenth century, many writers continued the style of Montaigne's personal essay; however, Francis Bacon added another dimension—aphorism. Bacon's essays featured maxims and adages for what he deemed proper behavior; for example, "The errors of young men are the ruin of business." He speaks not in speculation but in certitude, and he willingly shares his solutions. This essay gives you the opportunity to discuss scientific reasoning with your students—in particular, the *empirical* method and the use of deduction and induction to arrive at conclusions. Because he wrote during the Renaissance, it is natural that Bacon would advance scientific inquiry as a valid tool to replace, in part, the philosophical logic of Aristotle and Plato. Discuss with your students the dangers of relying on personal perceptions, personal experience, language, and a misplaced trust in the earlier teachings of scientists. Explore each of the four idols in your discussion.

Discussion Questions

1. Explain what Bacon means by Idols of the Tribe.
2. Explain what Bacon means by Idols of the Cave.
3. Explain what Bacon means by Idols of the Marketplace.
4. Explain what Bacon means by Idols of the Theater.
5. Why was Bacon suspicious of philosophy? (See paragraph 33.)

Writing Assignments

1. Write an essay exposing and denouncing four idols of modern thinking that distort and/or ignore scientific reason.
2. Using modern terminology, write an essay explaining the Idols of the Tribe.
3. Write an essay using evidence from inductive thinking to arrive at a conclusion. In other words, state a generalization and then try to prove it by collecting evidence. You might begin with a generalization such as: "huge trucks are making our highways a killing field" or "banning handguns will not stop the senseless drive-by shootings that affect our neighborhoods."

CLASSIC ESSAYS OF THE 18TH AND 19TH CENTURIES: THE FORM REFINED

A Modest Proposal

JONATHAN SWIFT

With this essay, you have an opportunity to examine with your students the concepts of irony and satire, as handled by a master in the field. With this essay, Swift demonstrates the power of the ironic essay to alter public opinion. To reinforce the idea of the ironic essay, you might bring to class examples of contemporary satire and irony, such as a Dave Barry column. You might also give the students a summary overview of *Gulliver's Travels*, Swift's most famous satire on society. The essay gives you the opportunity to open a debate on America's welfare situation that Congress would like to amend.

Discussion Questions

1. What radical plan does Swift advance for the relief of the poor and starving Irish people? What is his underlying message?
2. Is Swift being ironic in paragraph 29? How does he suspend irony to make his point?
3. Compare Swift's advice in paragraph 29 to our government's stance on welfare. How are the two situations similar? How do they differ?

4. What is Swift's opinion of the Irish citizens?
5. Does Swift appeal more to emotion or to reason?

Writing Assignments

1. Using a fictitious persona, write an essay that, like Swift's, offers an absurd solution to a campus-wide problem. Include a paragraph that suspends irony to state your true feelings.
2. Write an essay examining the role of the speaker in nonfiction prose, particularly the ability of an essayist to speak in a voice other than his or her personal voice.
3. Research your topic, then write an essay analyzing Swift's attitude toward the people of Ireland.

Humour

JOSEPH ADDISON AND RICHARD STEELE

These two writers made famous the periodical essay, a form of writing that will open up a discussion of the role of newspaper columnists in shaping the ideas and behavior of a community or nation. Point out that, like Swift, Addison and Steele used satire, but with a straightforward emphasis on advice about political and social issues. In addition, they examined in the Renaissance tradition the emerging theories of the scientific community as well as the philosophical suppositions of the day. Remind your students that Addison and Steele, like contemporary reporters such as Tom Brokaw, Sam Donaldson, or Rush Limbaugh, made efforts to challenge attitudes, affect public thought, and provoke discussion. With regard to this particular essay, discuss with the students the differences between a truly humorous person and a writer of false humor.

Discussion Questions

1. What is the role of newspapers in observing and criticizing the social and political programs of a community or country?
2. Newt Gingrich argues that newspersons have a "gottcha" consciousness and always look for the negative, not the positive. Do reporters have an obligation to be fair?
3. What makes a person truly humorous? What qualities do you associate with such a person?
4. What is meant by false humor?
5. What allegory is used in paragraph 2 to define humor?
6. Explain how Good Sense is the father of wit, who in turn is the father of humor.
7. Describe the genealogy of False Humour. (See paragraph 4.)

Writing Assignments

1. Using the allegorical method of Addison and Steele, write an essay distinguishing between the various elements of a topic, such as *friend, honor, public service, scholar*, and so forth.
2. Write an essay examining the humor of contemporary writers such as Dave Barry, the late Lewis Gizzard, and others.
3. Write a biographical essay describing in detail a truly humorous person that you know well. What makes this person funny? Does he or she have a serious side and a meaningful message?

The Crisis

THOMAS PAINE

This essay by Paine gives you a chance to continue your discussion of the role of journalists in affecting public opinion. You might explain how Paine used periodical publications and pamphlets to wave the banner of his feelings. Ask your students to identify contemporary figures who use a public forum to state their private agendas. Discuss with your students the contrast between today's journalistic freedom and the fact that Paine was once tried for treason for speaking his mind. You might also discuss with your students the role of propaganda in promoting national causes and in arousing the support of the populace.

Discussion Questions

1. What is a "summer soldier"? a "sunshine patriot"?
2. Why does Paine denounce England as guilty of tyranny?
3. Describe Paine's participation in the revolutionary conflict. (See paragraph 5.)
4. What reason does Paine give for the British decision to fight the war in the middle colonies and not in New England?
5. According to Paine, what was a Tory?
6. Why were the Tories a disappointment both to General Howe and to the patriots?

Writing Assignments

1. Write an essay exploring the implications of the line "If there must be trouble, let it be in my day, that my child may have peace."
2. Write a paper on the second amendment right to bear arms. Are we well protected by this law? If America was invaded, would privately owned weapons become a valuable resource?
3. Write a paper tracing the full historical facts that Paine describes only briefly.

from A Vindication of the Rights of Woman

MARY WOLLSTONECRAFT

This essay introduces feminism as a subject for the personal essay, giving you a chance to discuss the role of the essay in advancing women's rights. Wollstonecraft laid the groundwork for all feminists to follow, from Elizabeth Cady Stanton to Gloria Steinem, from Eleanor Roosevelt to Hillary Rodham Clinton. You might examine with the students the logic of Wollstonecraft's argument. Also, examine how her argument reflects current thinking.

Discussion Questions

1. In what sense is Wollstonecraft's first paragraph a Marxist argument?
2. How do laws make an "absurd unit of a man and his wife"? (See paragraph 3.)
3. Read paragraph 21 aloud and then paraphrase Wollstonecraft's argument.
4. How might Wollstonecraft respond to the current status of women in the military?

Writing Assignments

1. Write a paraphrase of Wollstonecraft's essay using contemporary ideas, issues, and language.
2. Write an essay that examines in depth the attempt by women to achieve their economic independence from men.
3. Write an essay comparing women who marry for support to women who marry to be a companion to a man economically, socially, sexually, and in every other way.

Grace before Meat

CHARLES LAMB

The romantic movement of the nineteenth century brought a revival of interest in the personal essay with an emphasis on autobiographical details, sentiment, light-hearted humor, literary taste, and a confidential style. You might discuss with your students the fickle nature of periodical publications which shift and change with the demands of the reading public. In the early decades of the nineteenth century, the personality of the writer became a staple of the essays that appeared in *Blackwood's Magazine* and the *London Magazine.* Explain to your students that Lamb refined the periodical essay and published most of his successful essays in the *London Magazine.* Ask your students to respond to Lamb's ideas about prayers before meals, keeping the focus on the wit rather than the irreverence. This dialogue might launch a discussion on the current role of public prayers before games, at graduations, or—now banned in most states—in public schools. Ask the students to discuss the personality of the speaker and how that personality colors the content of the essay.

Discussion Questions

1. Why does Lamb question the role of prayers before meals?
2. Why is he especially uncomfortable with a prayer before a sumptuous feast?

3. Why does Lamb quote from *Paradise Regained?* (See paragraph 7.)
4. How does Lamb mix literary allusions into his prose? What effect does this have?
5. How successful is Lamb in taking a minor issue, an everyday occasion, and transforming it into an essay?
6. How important is Lamb's voice and personality to the success of his essay?

Writing Assignments

1. Write an essay that takes a humorous approach to mundane activity, such as commuting to school or work, writing with a computer, preparing a meal, and so forth.
2. Write an essay exploring the issues of public prayers in today's society.
3. Write an essay in which you make references to various literary works that support the issue you wish to examine. If necessary, use a dictionary of quotations to supplement your knowledge.

On the Feeling of Immortality in Youth

WILLIAM HAZLITT

This writer gives you a chance to discuss with your students the role of the essayist as critic. Hazlitt was intense, passionate, and opinionated—qualities shared by many critics and news reporters today. Talk with the students about columnists and commentators with different styles—those who are quietly moderate, loquacious, or bellicose. Invite the students into a discussion on a young person's exuberance for life compared with the depression experienced by some elderly people. Ask your students to analyze Hazlitt's line at the end of paragraph 3: "The young are prodigal of life from a superabundance of it; the old are tenacious on the same score, because they have little left, and cannot enjoy even what remains of it." Have your students study paragraph 4, in which Hazlitt's third-person point of view shifts to a personal one.

Discussion Questions

1. Comment on the line "No young man believes he shall ever die."
2. In what sense does Hazlitt criticize young people?
3. Do you agree with Hazlitt that "the mind contrives for a long time to reject [death] with disdain and loathing as a monstrous and improbable fiction . . ."?
4. Comment on Hazlitt's line "Art we know is long; life, we feel, should be so too."
5. In what sense is death a long, continuing process, rather than a sudden termination?

Writing Assignments

1. Write an essay examining the ways in which some young people plunge recklessly through life as though death were only a figment of the imagination.
2. Write an essay researching the process of dying and the complications facing today's healthcare workers who must deal with death.
3. Write an essay in the style of Hazlitt titled "On the Feeling of Superiority of the Elderly" or "On the Conservative Nature of the Elderly."

Nature

RALPH WALDO EMERSON

This essay provides you with an opportunity to discuss with your students the didactic nature of some essays—that is, the writer's desire to pontificate and moralize for the reader. Explain to your students that during the nineteenth century, many writers felt obligated to provide not only social and political theories but also moral enlightenment. Emerson adds to this his theory of transcendentalism. Discuss with your students the sources of didactic messages today such as television, billboards, bumper stickers, and magazine articles. Ask the students, in evaluating Emerson's essay, to explain how he can say, "I am part or particle of God." You might also invite the students into a discussion of idealism and how the age of romanticism replaced the rational thought of neoclassicists like Jefferson. You might also discuss in depth the role of nature for Emerson and the other writers of the romantic period. You might combine your discussion of Emerson with an examination of Thoreau and his essay *Walden*, in which Thoreau put into practice the life advocated by Emerson.

Discussion Questions

1. Can a personal, expressive essay be religious in nature? Does moralizing enhance or lessen the enjoyment of an essay?
2. What is the theory of transcendentalism?
3. Where do you find messages today that moralize?
4. What is idealism? How can you contrast it with pessimism? With realism? With neoclassicism? With a sense of the absurd?

Writing Assignments

1. Like Emerson, contemplate the glory and grandeur of nature, then write an essay expressing your relationship with nature and

its many wonders. Do you feel part of nature or do you feel isolated from it?

2. Write a didactic essay prescribing a program of moral progress for yourself and, perhaps, for your reader as well.
3. Research your topic, then write an essay examining the hippie movement in the 1960s and its motivating philosophy—in particular, the manner in which the hippies were idealists in the Emersonian sense.

Genius and Originality

JOHN STUART MILL

This essay gives you the opportunity to discuss in some depth the role of the essayist as social critic. Mill advanced his theory of Utilitarianism, which proposed that moral, social, and political activities should be directed toward achieving the greatest good for the greatest number of people. Discuss with your students the content of his essay "Genius and Originality"—in particular, his theory that genius needs breathing room. Ask your students to respond to Mill's argument that people of genius cannot fit well "into any of the small number of moulds which society provides in order to save its members the trouble of forming their own character."

Discussion Questions

1. Why do bright people need the freedom that Mill proposes?
2. Why does Mill fear the "mediocrity of the masses"?
3. According to Mill, what happens to the person who dares to be eccentric?
4. Do any of your acquaintances fit neatly into one of "the small number of moulds which society provides in order to save its members the trouble of forming their own character"?

5. How do you answer Mill's charge that "No government by a democracy . . . ever did or could rise above mediocrity . . ."?

Writing Assignments

1. Write an essay addressing the role of eccentric or bright people in our society. Does the government put the needs of special interest groups before the needs of the majority?
2. Write an essay addressing Mill's contention that a true democracy will allow the mediocrity of the masses to become "the ascendant power among mankind."
3. Write an essay that classifies and examines in depth the various molds into which people situate themselves in order to avoid originality.

from Civil Disobedience

HENRY DAVID THOREAU

If you have already discussed John Stuart Mill with your students, Thoreau's essay is a logical progression. Point out that Mill asks for individuals to step boldly forward and to act in response to their genius. Thoreau also asks the individual to assert independence by acting on his or her conscience. Stress to them Thoreau's concept that the state must "recognize the individual as a higher and independent power." Ask your students to discuss the positive and the negative results of civil disobedience. Allow them free reign to examine freedom from government restraint, unnecessary taxation, the idea of a standing army, and unjust regulations.

Discussion Questions

1. What is "civil disobedience"?
2. What can happen to someone who purposely disobeys a government regulation?
3. Is the government the people, or has it gained autonomy from the people?
4. How do you respond to Thoreau's idea "That government is best which governs not at all"?
5. What would happen today if, as Thoreau suggests, "a thousand men were not to pay their tax bills this year"? (See paragraph 17.)

Writing Assignments

1. Write an essay examining the influence of Thoreau on the thinking of Martin Luther King, Jr., and Mahatma Gandhi.
2. Write an essay examining how Rosa Parks put into action the words of Thoreau.
3. Write an essay exploring Thoreau's argument (paragraph 10) that "All voting is a sort of gaming, like checkers or backgammon, with a slight moral tinge to it, a playing with right and wrong, with moral questions; and betting naturally accompanies it."

from The Narrative of the Life of Frederick Douglass, an American Slave

FREDERICK DOUGLASS

Your discussion of Frederick Douglass, following the study of Thoreau, should focus on the life of one man—an African-American—who lived the principle advocated by Thoreau. Douglass uses the narrative essay to explore historical and autobiographic details. Explain to your students the biographical details of Douglass's life, especially the role that education played in his rise to intellectual freedom. The portion of the narrative reproduced in the text gives you the opportunity to examine several aspects of Douglass's life—his sense of slavery, his emergence as a frustrated freeman, his emotions upon his escape to New York, his marriage, his journey to New Bedford, and ultimately, his emergence as a spokesman for the anti-slavery union.

Discussion Questions

1. Why does Douglass chastise those people operating the underground railroad to free the slaves?
2. Why did his master's payment represent a greater injustice to Douglass than if he had received no payment?
3. What severe limitations were placed on Douglass as a freeman? (See paragraph 4.)

4. What significant events occurred on the 11th of August, 1841? (See paragraph 16.)
5. What role did education play in Douglass's rise from slavery?

Writing Assignments

1. Write a brief biography of Douglass's life, showing his determination not only to escape bondage but to speak out on behalf of those still in bondage.
2. Write an autobiography to show the key events and significant people that molded and shaped the person you are today.
3. Write an essay comparing Douglass's account of slavery with that of Booker T. Washington.

Sweetness and Light

MATTHEW ARNOLD

Like Hazlitt and Mill, Arnold was a social critic, and so this essay offers another chance to discuss social and political matters in England. The Victorian compromise allowed the middle class to gain power at the expense of the aristocracy and the proletariat. Explain to your students that Arnold, in *Culture and Anarchy,* is addressing the strength of Victorian England—the rising middle class that had money, power, and the ability to make things happen. It was the middle class, he thought, that could help England avoid the revolution of anarchy. He preached the message of culture to these people in the hope that they would spend their money and energy raising England to another golden age of art, culture, reason, control, and fidelity to beauty.

Discussion Questions

1. What is culture?
2. What is anarchy?

3. How can culture help prevent the anarchy that Arnold seems to fear?
4. Why does he use the title "Sweetness and Light" for this section of *Culture and Anarchy*?
5. Why is *curiosity* a key word for Arnold? (See paragraph 3.)
6. What is the role of religion in Arnold's scheme? (See paragraph 7.)
7. What is Arnold's attitude toward the industrial revolution and its reliance on machinery? (See paragraph 8.)
8. How did the Puritans demonstrate "sweetness and light" to Arnold? (See paragraphs 14–15.)
9. Why is the atmosphere of Oxford vital to Arnold's philosophy? (See paragraph 18.)

Writing Assignments

1. Carry the banner of Matthew Arnold by writing an updated version of "Sweetness and Light." Write an essay advancing the idea of culture in order to bring America to a higher level.
2. Research your topic, then write an essay explaining the cultural advantages of your college campus and the city where it is located.
3. Write an essay studying the dangers of anarchy in today's society. What might trigger a riot? What might cause a revolution? What might cause a state's secession?

A Liberal Education

THOMAS HENRY HUXLEY

Huxley's essay gives you the opportunity to explore two important issues—the use of anology and the role of education—and reinforces

Douglass's view on the importance of education for one who wishes to advance. Huxley also urges that education enables a civilization to move forward. Discuss with your students the importance of learning a craft, learning the rules of the game, learning how to perform within a given environment. Ask them to respond to Huxley's admonition that the "player on the other side never overlooks a mistake, or makes the smallest allowance for ignorance" and that this player will checkmate us "without remorse." Ask them to discuss in depth Huxley's definition of education as explained in paragraph 4. Although this essay does not examine the issue in depth, ask the students to discuss their ideas of a "liberal education."

Discussion Questions

1. If life is a game of chess that each of us must play, who is our opponent and how wise is this opponent?
2. What is Huxley's definition of education? (See paragraph 4.)
3. Do you agree with Huxley—who argues this point elsewhere in his writings—that schools should require less rote memory work? Why or why not?

Writing Assignments

1. Using analogy, write an essay describing how well your education has prepared you for life. For example, if life is like a game of chess, how well did you learn the rules through your education?
2. Write an essay that depends on a metaphor or simile for its structure. Choose a subject and compare it to something else—for example, love is a vegetable garden, deciding on a major is like a trip to the supermarket, choosing a spouse is like pulling the lever of a slot machine.
3. Write an essay defining your concept of a "liberal education."

Shadow Lake

JOHN MUIR

Muir's essay gives you an introduction to the environmental essay, a popular style continued by such writers as Annie Dillard, John McPhee, Rachel Carson, Wendell Barry, and many others. Discuss with your students the didactic tone of this essay, and how that tone helps deliver Muir's message. It might be helpful to give some details of John Muir's life, especially his dedicated efforts to preserve the natural resources of the country. In particular, discuss with your students the conflict over these resources—the release of wolves into the hills, the limits on deer hunting, the protection of the spotted owl, as well as issues peculiar to your region of the country.

Discussion Questions

1. What environmental issues does Muir raise that continue to be controversial even today?
2. What is the Sierra Club? Why did Muir found it?
3. Why is Muir known as the "Father of the National Park System"?
4. Can you identify environmental issues that affect your region of the country? Which side would you take in a debate?

Writing Assignments

1. Select an environmental problem in your area and write an essay defending or condemning the practices of any group associated with this issue.
2. Research the National Park System and write an essay either defending its preservation efforts or criticizing its submission to the demands of special interest groups.

3. Write an essay offering a solution to landfills and the dilemma over how to deal with our mounting piles of garbage.

Apollonianism and Dionysianism

FRIEDRICH NIETZSCHE

Nietzsche's essay introduces your students to the type of modern essay that examines the human psyche and its diversity. This type of essay grows out of the traditions established by Plato and Aristotle, who also examined human emotions and motivations. You might begin by asking your students to explain, in their terms, *psychology*. Lead them into an examination of *behavior*, and then ask them to discuss Apollonian control and Dionysian passion. It might be necessary to explain that Apollo was the sun god who symbolized reason and intellectual mastery and that Dionysius was a vegetation god who delighted in wine, gluttony, and sexual indulgence. Allow the students to discuss how these two forces affect us throughout our lives, particularly during the college years.

Discussion Questions

1. Who was Apollo? Who was Dionysius?
2. When do the forces of Apollonianism and Dionysianism seem balanced, and when do they seem out of balance?
3. How do the *dream* and *intoxication* relate to Nietzsche's theories?
4. What do the ideas of Schopenhauer contribute to the essay? (See paragraphs 3 and 4.)

5. What is the principle of individuation?
6. How does music reflect the two sides of human nature?

Writing Assignments

1. Write an essay that explains in depth the advantages of an Apollonian spirit.
2. Write an essay that explains in depth the advantages of a Dionysian spirit.
3. Write an essay explaining the role of *individuation* in modern society.

A Slave among Slaves

BOOKER T. WASHINGTON

With Washington's essay, as with Douglass's, you have an opportunity to explore various features of the autobiographical essay—its historical perspective, the intimate first-person voice, the commitment to a set of values, and the role of social forces in shaping and determining life's journey. Both Douglass and Washington base their writings on the qualities of courage, determination, and endurance. You might discuss several aspects of *Up from Slavery* with your students: the tribulations of plantation life, the communication network among the slaves, how the slaves felt toward the white masters and mistresses, and their hesitation and uncertainty once their freedom was announced.

Discussion Questions

1. What does Washington know about his heritage and family roots?
2. How important were he and his mother to plantation life?
3. Was Washington as a child given relatively easy tasks to perform? Was he allowed to play?
4. How did most slaves feel toward their masters?
5. What was the state of mind of most slaves after their freedom was announced?

Writing Assignments

1. Write an essay examining the historical concept raised by Washington that, for most slaves, "freedom was a more serious thing than they had expected to find it."
2. Research your topic, then write an essay examining in detail the hierarchy of the class system on a typical plantation.
3. Research your topic, then write an essay exploring the dispute between Booker T. Washington and W. E. B. DuBois.
4. Write an essay chronicling the history of the Tuskegee Institute.

The Symbolism of Poetry

WILLIAM BUTLER YEATS

This essay enables you to explore the nature of the essay in literature. Most successful writers and many critics have coined their own definitions for what constitutes good writing. Discuss with your students the role of the writer who criticizes his or her craft. Are these people objective judges? Next, ask the students to analyze Yeats's determination to examine his own philosophy as a writer and, consequently, his own use of symbolism in his drama and poetry. Where does Yeats demonstrate his bias—that is, his comments on the "buried reality" or his own "divine life"? You might need to explain to your students the general nature of archetypal symbolism. Ask your students to comment on the role of symbols in creating emotions in color, in sound, in image.

Discussion Questions

1. What is symbolism? How does Yeats define it?
2. What, in your terms, is a "buried reality"?
3. Explain what Yeats means when he says that a sound, a color, or a form can evoke an emotion?
4. What role does rhythm play in complementing the symbolism of poetry? (See paragraph 6.)
5. Why does Yeats spend so much time explaining the role of color in symbolism? (See paragraph 7.)
6. What is Yeats's criticism of Tennyson? (See paragraph 8.)

Writing Assignments

1. Write an essay exploring Yeats's comments in paragraph 8: "you cannot give a body to something that moves beyond the senses, unless your words are as subtle, as complex, as full of mysterious life, as the body of a flower or of a woman."
2. Write an essay defining *symbolism*.
3. Write an essay explaining the symbolism in one of Yeats's poems. In particular, explain how the symbolism reveals the underlying emotion of the poet.

The Spider and the Wasp

ALEXANDER PETRUNKEVITCH

This essay gives you the opportunity to explain to your students how the essay form provides a venue for the scientist to reach the general public. This venue has enabled modern scientists such as Carl Sagan to touch the minds and hearts of millions of people. Explain to your students that Petrunkevitch—a world-renowned expert on spiders—wrote both for his peers in the scientific community and for the public. Challenge your students to analyze the language used by Petrunkevitch—in particular, the way its scientific flavor is mellowed by "public" language in order to appeal to a general audience. Ask the students to discuss the special talents of a particular species and how one small and seemingly weaker species might overpower its opponent.

Discussion Questions

1. Does Petrunkevitch speak in scientific jargon? Explain.
2. In what way does the author develop this essay as a mystery story? Does this technique bring scientific inquiry from the lab into the living room?
3. Who wins the battle? Why?
4. What role, according to the author, do intelligence and instinct play in this drama? (See paragraph 18.)
5. What advantage does the spider have over the wasp? (See paragraph 21.)

Writing Assignments

1. Write an essay in the style of Petrunkevitch describing the conflict of one species with another.
2. Develop an allegory in which the spider and wasp assume a gender, then write an essay exploring the implications of such an allegory. Which gender is represented by the spider and which by the wasp? Why did you make the choice that you did? What are the implications of your choice?
3. In paragraph 21, Petrunkevitch suggests that the victor of the battle may not always be the winner of the war. Write an environmental essay examining the give-and-take of nature and its creatures.

What I Believe

E. M. FORSTER

This essay provides you with an opportunity to explore fully the *expressive* essay, which reveals the writer's private beliefs in a first-person point of view. Forster held firm beliefs on many topics and expressed them freely in his writings. Ask your students to respond to his elevation of "tolerance, good temper, and sympathy" as the core of his religious creed. Ask them to comment on Forster's views on friendship, democracy, the necessity of police and an army, hero worship, and the importance of individualism.

Discussion Questions

1. What is the core of Forster's religious creed?
2. What does he mean when he says, "My lawgivers are Erasmus and Montaigne, not Moses and St. Paul"?
3. What is his attitude toward personal relationships? (See paragraphs 3–4.)
4. Given the choice of betraying his country or betraying his friend, what choice would Forster make?
5. According to Forster, what are the two primary merits of a democracy? (See paragraphs 5–6.)
6. What special twist does Forster give on the use of force by the police and the army?
7. What is hero worship? How does Forster view hero worship?
8. How does Forster define the "Savior of the future"?

Writing Assignments

1. Using the Forster essay as your model, write an essay exploring some of your personal theories and ideas on contemporary life in America.

2. After carefully reading paragraphs 5–6, write an essay describing democracy in our times. Does it still encourage variety and permit criticism?
3. Forster creates an interesting dilemma for anybody who has ever defended or protected a friend, by saying that he would betray his country before he would betray a friend. Write an essay examining the contemporary roles of friendship and allegiance to one's country.

The Death of the Moth

VIRGINIA WOOLF

If you have already read Forster's essay, you might tell the students that Woolf and Forster were both members of the Bloomsbury group, and point out their influence on each other, as demonstrated by their personal, meditative styles. Explain that Woolf was a master of the *interior monologue*, a narrative style built on the stream-of-consciousness technique which features the uninterrupted, uneven, and seemingly endless flow of the narrator's thoughts on the subject. Discuss with your students Woolf's blend of scientific observation and subjective deliberations. Ask them to consider the use of personification as an element of the essay—that is, the way the moth comes to represent a human being. Ask students to name the subject of the essay—is it life, death, or perhaps the strength of death as a worthy opponent?

Discussion Questions

1. Is the essay about death?
2. How scientific is Woolf's description?

3. Although Woolf's reflective meditation remains private, does it convey universal values? If so, how? What are the values?
4. Explain the central analogy on which the essay is built.
5. In what sense does the moth represent Woolf and other human beings?

Writing Assignments

1. Find a topic for which you can use analogy in the pattern of Woolf, then develop an essay using the analogy either to begin the essay or to serve as its central core.
2. In an essay, describe a physical scene using your private voice and feelings in the manner of Woolf.
3. Research the life of Virginia Woolf, then write an interpretation of her essay using a biographical approach. Is Woolf contemplating her own death by suicide?

Courtship Through The Ages

JAMES THURBER

This essay allows you to discuss the essay as a vehicle for humor. Let your students discuss Thurber's methods for achieving humor, especially his irony and hyperbole. Ask them to examine Thurber's thesis that the females of a species really do not care much for the male. You might have students discuss the various creatures and their antics in attracting the opposite sex. Ask students to identify elements of personification that Thurber uses in order to relate each creature to human beings.

Discussion Questions

1. Thurber argues that females have a universal attitude toward males. What is that attitude?
2. How does Thurber use irony to achieve his humor?
3. How does Thurber use hyperbole (exaggeration) to achieve his humor?
4. Discuss Thurber's use of personification to amplify his thesis.

Writing Assignments

1. Write an essay in the manner of Thurber that uses some behavior of animals to depict similar behavior in humans.
2. Write an essay that uses hyperbole (exaggeration) to build its argument. Try to satirize an institution or organization, not an individual. Direct your attack, for example, at drug law enforcement, IRS tax forms, government deductions from your paycheck, and so forth.
3. After doing some research, write an essay on the humor of James Thurber.

Grant and Lee: A Study in Contrasts

BRUCE CATTON

This essay enables you to examine in fine detail the rhetorical device of comparison and contrast. This essay also opens the door to a discussion of the historical essay and its place in historical magazines like *American Heritage*. You might provoke a discussion about the social structure of the South by asking the students if that system could exist today in any effective manner. You might also discuss modern history by mentioning countries that are currently embroiled in internal disputes and armed hostilities.

Discussion Questions

1. What did General Lee represent, according to Catton?
2. What did General Grant represent?
3. Although they had radical differences, what did the two men have in common?
4. Could the social structure of the South exist today in any form for America or any other country?
5. What countries in our time have been torn apart by internal war?

Writing Assignments

1. In the manner of Catton, write an essay that compares two historic figures, such as Booker T. Washington and W. E. B. DuBois, Alexander Hamilton and Thomas Jefferson, Elizabeth Cady Stanton and Susan B. Anthony, Eleanor Roosevelt and Hillary Clinton, or Newt Gingrich and Bill Clinton.
2. Write an essay that describes what course the nation might have taken if Grant had signed surrender papers instead of Lee.
3. Write a biographical essay on either Grant or Lee.

Once More to the Lake

E. B. WHITE

This essay will demonstrate for your students a modern application of essay techniques developed by Montaigne, Lamb, and others—the expressive essay of reminiscence that explores a few precious moments and examines their importance not only to the author but to all people. A moment in life gains symbolic implications. Ask your students to explore the significance of White's revelation at the end of the essay. Ask them to examine their own past lives to see if any one event carries significance today. White is also a good essayist for demonstrating the use of precise imagery to carry connotative messages.

Discussion Questions

1. What happens in this reminiscence that causes White to feel "the chill of death"?
2. How does White make an otherwise trivial trip to a campsite interesting? That is, how does his language and his use of imagery bring to life the visit to the lake?
3. How do distortions of time invade the author's sense of time?

Writing Assignments

1. In the manner of White, write an essay of reminiscence. Remember to give the essay universal appeal so that your readers can share the moment.
2. Write an essay of description. Select a time and place, one that carries emotional significance to you, and describe it with detailed, explicit imagery.
3. White was a coauthor of the bestselling book *The Elements of Style*. Locate a copy of the book and write an essay that explores the style of "Once More to the Lake" with the rules advanced in *The Elements of Style*.

The Real Secret of Piltdown

LOREN EISELEY

This essay enables you to discuss with your students the role of the essay for the anthropologist who wishes to explore human history with his or her readers. In the tradition of Charles Darwin, Thomas Huxley, Margaret Mead, and many others, Eiseley probes the deepest recesses of the human memory and existence. Allow your students to explore their thoughts about the contributions of the anthropologists. Ask them to discuss the differences between animals and nature in contrast to human beings and nature. A comparison of Alfred Wallace and Charles Darwin, as drawn by Eiseley, will probably be necessary, especially if students are to appreciate Eiseley's summation.

Discussion Questions

1. What is the role of an anthropologist?
2. Do you agree with Eiseley that animals seem to comprehend their role in nature but that humans, "bereft of instinct, must search continually for meanings"?
3. Why would a scientist attempt to deceive the scientific community? Do you know of any recent deceptions by scientists?
4. Who was Alfred R. Wallace? How did he disagree with Darwin?
5. Why does Eiseley say that Wallace, not Darwin, had made the correct reading of human development?
6. What makes Eiseley so sure that human beings are "one of the youngest and newest of all earth's swarming inhabitants"?

Writing Assignments

1. Write an essay that explores fully Eiseley's summation: "Those who would revile us by pointing to an ape at the foot of our

family tree grasp little of the awe with which the modern scientists now puzzles over man's lonely and supreme ascent."

2. After doing some research, write a detailed essay about the hoax of Piltdown.

The Myth of Sisyphus

ALBERT CAMUS

This essay offers a slightly different viewpoint—the literary essay, based on a myth, story, or piece of literature. It is a cousin to literary criticism, but differs in that it remains an essay in the Montaigne sense of introspective meditation, not only on the work in question but on some aspect of human life. Discuss first with your students the story of Sisyphus and its traditional interpretation. Then examine Camus's apparent use of the myth to explain the *absurd*. Finally, let the students discuss Camus's ability to put a positive twist on this ancient tale of agony.

Discussion Questions

1. What is the myth of Sisyphus? Why did the gods punish him?
2. How does Sisyphus represent "the passion for life"?
3. Why does Sisyphus represent the *absurd*?
4. Which moment of Sisyphus's ordeal fascinates Camus?
5. How does Camus interpret the tale in order to arrive at a "recipe for the absurd victory"?
6. In what sense is this essay a piece of literary interpretation? In what sense is it a meditation on the human condition? (See Montaigne, Forster, or Woolf.)

Writing Assignments

1. Select a mythic figure such as King Arthur, Moses, Faust, or Osiris. Research your subject carefully, then write an essay in

the fashion of Camus, that not only examines the story and the mythic figure but also makes a comment about the human condition.

2. Research Albert Camus, then write an essay exploring his sense of the absurd.
3. Write an essay examining existentialism and Camus's connection with the philosophy.

Notes of a Native Son

JAMES BALDWIN

This essay gives you the opportunity to extend your discussion of issues raised in the essays by Douglass and Washington. Like other essayists, Baldwin writes to identify himself, so you should focus your discussion on his role as an American, as an African-American, as a writer, and as a spokesperson for the civil rights movement of the 1960s and 1970s. Explain that the title alludes to the novel *Native Son* by Richard Wright, a story that depicts a black man who turns to violence to voice his anger. You might also cite Baldwin's lines "One writes out of one thing only—one's own experience. . . . Everything depends on how relentlessly one forces from this experience the last drop, sweet or bitter, it can possibly give." Ask the students to identify the bitterness that Baldwin tastes, as well as how he reacted to it and tried to control his emotions.

Discussion Questions

1. What didn't Baldwin get along well with his father?
2. Why did Baldwin's father have ambivalent feelings about the white schoolteacher who came into their house?
3. How does Baldwin's essay echo the sentiments of Douglass and Washington? How does his essay differ?

4. What action does Baldwin take toward the waitress? (See paragraph 21.)
5. Why does Baldwin say that his life was in "*real* danger"? (See paragraph 22.)
6. What incident sparked the riot that spread across Harlem? (See paragraph 42.)
7. What resolution does Baldwin finally reach in paragraph 46?

Writing Assignments

1. In the manner of Baldwin, write a personal narration recounting an event or two from your past. Explain why the event(s) affected your personality.
2. Write a personal narration recounting your relationship with a special person from your past. Explain how that person has affected your character.
3. Write a personal essay of protest describing your reaction to and your accommodation of incidences of prejudice.

Marrying Absurd

JOAN DIDION

This essay enables you to discuss with your students the role of social satire as used with the essay format. Didion's columns on social issues for *The Saturday Evening Post* established her reputation for penetrating the mores and behavior of the American public. Ask your students to respond to her examination of the quick marriage, which she says symbolizes the decadence of the city. Discuss also the idea of "immediate gratification" that Americans seek so often. If you have already read the Camus essay, ask students to connect the story of Sisyphus with the setting of Las Vegas and to discuss the *absurd* in all its ramifications. Point out the paradox of the essay; that is, we laugh with Didion at the foolish behavior of some people, yet we weep with her at the many instances of exploitation. Finally, you might want to develop the connection between Yeats's poem "The Second Coming" and Didion's view of contemporary society.

Discussion Questions

1. What does Didion wish to criticize? Is her criticism justified?
2. What activities or situations other than marriage could Didion have used to show the absurd side of life in Las Vegas?
3. What is *irony of situation*? How does Didion use it to convey her message?
4. The language of irony, while straight-faced, has a biting edge. Cite examples of Didion's ironic voice.
5. What is meant by the reference "the ritual jokes about the wedding night had a certain Panglossian character"? What does "Panglossian" mean?
6. Didion provides several descriptions of weddings. Do the wedding scenes serve a special symbolic purpose?

Writing Assignments

1. Write a paragraph establishing a scene for ironic commentary, such as a group of professors gathering for morning coffee, a line of students waiting to enroll for classes, or a cluster of loud and obnoxious fans at a football game.
2. Write an essay in the manner of Didion by developing the topic from assignment 1, this time using exaggeration to achieve an ironic tone.

The Nuclear Winter

CARL SAGAN

This essay, like those by Petrunkevitch and Eiseley, gives you another chance to discuss the scientific essay. Writers like Sagan have the ability to explain complex issues to the non-scientific community. Mention to your students that Sagan published this essay in *Parade Magazine* in order to reach the general public. Discuss with the students the persuasive nature of the essay as well as its scientific analysis.

Discussion Questions

1. How does Sagan's technical and scientific analysis serve his persuasive purpose?
2. What was his purpose in publishing this essay in *Parade Magazine*?
3. What is the point of the essay? What does Sagan hope to accomplish?
4. Would the initial nuclear war, as described by Sagan, destroy life on earth? What would cause total loss of life?

Writing Assignments

1. Write an essay elaborating on Sagan's sentence "Fools and madmen do exist, and sometimes rise to power."
2. Write an essay exploring the question: Since 1983, when Sagan published this essay, have we made any progress in gaining control of nuclear weapons?
3. Write an essay using the same basic paradigm as Sagan uses in order to explore a catastrophe, such as overpopulation, AIDS, moral bankruptcy, and so forth.